PRAISE FOR *GOD THE LEADER*

"This book is a delight to read. Masking profound scholarship, Kathleen Rochester journeys through the Old Testament with a light touch. I wondered whether the lens of 'God the leader' would be sufficient to encompass the story. But it was. I'm amazed at the range of issues introduced, whilst firmly tracking the main message. It has much to teach both leaders and followers, whether familiar or unfamiliar with the OT."

—DEREK TIDBALL, author of *Lead Like Joshua*

"Jesus said less about sex than about money and less about money than about power. How does God use his power and how does he want us to use ours? That is the all-important subject of this engaging book, written *con brio*. I recommend it very warmly."

—STEPHEN ORTIGER, OSB, Emeritus Abbot of Worth Abbey, England

"Kathleen Rochester has crafted an extraordinary book. She takes us through the entire Old Testament hunting for a critical truth: how does God give leadership to his people? Reading this fine book will provide a way of relating to people, organizations, churches, and businesses that is truly life-giving. It would make a fascinating Bible study for people in small groups. I commend it heartily."

—R. PAUL STEVENS, Professor Emeritus, Marketplace Theology, Regent College

"You won't find in this book any fancy leadership concepts or theories. Dr. Kathleen Rochester expertly and chronologically goes through the OT and discusses this important theme in very practical terms. Each chapter is further enhanced by practical questions for reflection and discussion. I commend this book for a serious study. You will enjoy it!"

—VITALI PETRENKO, Director, Latvian Biblical Center, Riga, Latvia

"Using a mixture of Bible exposition and insightful accounts of human leadership, Kathleen Rochester pinpoints what to emulate and what to avoid. The Bible interpretation is presented in easy, lively language, though with a depth nuanced by years of academic study. The anecdotes are apt and without extraneous details. A useful mix that prompts many fruitful reflections on leadership."

—DAVID INSTONE-BREWER, Senior Research Fellow in Rabbinics and the New Testament, Tyndale House

God the Leader

God the Leader

A Journey through the Old Testament

KATHLEEN M. ROCHESTER
foreword by R. W. L. Moberly

WIPF & STOCK · Eugene, Oregon

GOD THE LEADER
A Journey through the Old Testament

Copyright © 2020 Kathleen M. Rochester. All rights reserved. Except for brief quotations in critical publications or reviews, no part of this book may be reproduced in any manner without prior written permission from the publisher. Write: Permissions, Wipf and Stock Publishers, 199 W. 8th Ave., Suite 3, Eugene, OR 97401.

Wipf & Stock
An Imprint of Wipf and Stock Publishers
199 W. 8th Ave., Suite 3
Eugene, OR 97401

www.wipfandstock.com

PAPERBACK ISBN: 978-1-4982-3980-6
HARDCOVER ISBN: 978-1-4982-3982-0
EBOOK ISBN: 978-1-4982-3981-3

Manufactured in the U.S.A. 05/29/20

Contents

Foreword by R. W. L. Moberly   ix
Acknowledgments   xi
Introduction   1

PART 1: GETTING TO KNOW GOD AS LEADER

Chapter 1	Beginnings	7
Chapter 2	A New Start	15
Chapter 3	Care for the Overlooked	22
Chapter 4	God is not like Pharaoh!	30
Chapter 5	Under New Leadership	39

PART 2: THE TEN WORDS OF THE LEADER

Chapter 6	Worship	51
Chapter 7	Blasphemy	61
Chapter 8	Sabbath Rest and Work	66
Chapter 9	Respect for Parents, Life and Marriage	74
Chapter 10	Boundaries and Punishments	81

PART 3: ETHICAL ISSUES IN LEADERSHIP

Chapter 11	Ethnicity	91
Chapter 12	A Place to Settle	100
Chapter 13	War	109

PART 4: IMAGES OF GOD AS LEADER

Chapter 14	God the King	119
Chapter 15	God the Shepherd	128
Chapter 16	God the Father, Mother, and Husband	136
Chapter 17	God as Wise Guide, Host, Helper, Rock	145

PART 5: GOD'S LEADERSHIP IN UNCERTAIN TIMES

Chapter 18	God and His Prophets	155
Chapter 19	Prophets of the Northern Kingdom	160
Chapter 20	Prophets of the Southern Kingdom and the Exile	166

PART 6: GOD THE HIDDEN LEADER

Chapter 21	Keeping Order	177
Chapter 22	Behind the Scenes Leadership	184
Chapter 23	When God Hides His Face	193

PART 7: NEW HOPE

Chapter 24	Rebuilding	203
Chapter 25	Expansion: God's Mission Beyond Israel	214
Chapter 26	God the Leader	221
Bibliography		225

Foreword

Some years ago, Kathleen Rochester worked with me in Durham for a PhD on the prophetic ministries of Jeremiah and Ezekiel. It has been published as *Prophetic Ministry in Jeremiah and Ezekiel* (Peeters, 2012). This work well exemplifies Kathleen's desire to combine good scholarship with the concerns of contemporary Christian faith. Since then she has been a theological educator in the two-thirds world. Her particular concern is to show how the Old Testament can be a living resource for Christian thought and life today.

This new book, *God the Leader*, is a fine example of how the Old Testament can be accessible and meaningful for ordinary Christians, who want to learn but without becoming scholars as such. Kathleen is aware of scholarly issues and concerns, but wears her learning with a light touch, and is happy to skirt around technical issues where exposition can get bogged down. Her focus on God as leader offers a fresh angle of vision that is not otherwise found in discussions of the Old Testament. She reads the Old Testament with a full imaginative seriousness that brings its subject matter to life and relates it to today. Those who are looking for a scholarly monograph on the nature and purpose of the biblical documents in their ancient context of origin will not find that here. But those who are looking for a thoughtful and informed handling of the biblical documents as Christian Scripture, that is entirely accessible, will find themselves well served.

I commend *God the Leader* to Christian ministers and congregations as a rich resource for their life and service in today's world.

WALTER MOBERLY
Abbey House
Palace Green
Durham, UK

Acknowledgments

Many, many thanks to the many leaders I have known who have modeled leadership well, in all kinds of contexts. I do remember you and appreciate all that you taught me, even though most of you are not represented in this book. Although I felt quite uncomfortable, and sometimes greatly distressed, under poor leaders, especially under narcissistic leaders, I can also be grateful for what they taught me, even if it was *not* to lead in the same way. For we cannot see and appreciate what is good unless we experience and question the shadow side.

I would like to pay a particular tribute to Dr Eugene Peterson (author of *The Message*), who long ago supervised my Master's degree thesis. I am grateful for his warm smile, his attentive listening, and his fatherly challenges that were given with grace-filled hope. It was he who strongly encouraged me to write, despite my severe doubts and procrastinations, and who many years ago promised to write the Foreword to my next book. However, I was too slow. In recent years he became unwell and passed from this life to the next before I was able to complete it.

Many thanks to Dr Walter Moberly, who supervised and supported my PhD project with personal warmth and grace, combined with incisive insight and helpful corrections. He unites academic precision with an everyday life of humility, prayer and faith. He has been an important and influential model of wholesome leadership for me and for many others. Even though the genre of this book lies outside his more usual academic sphere, I am very grateful that he readily agreed to read this book, to give some helpful feedback, and to write the Foreword. Of course, that does not mean that he necessarily agrees with every detail I have written!

Thanks to the following people who very kindly read a chapter or so each, and gave me valuable critical feedback along the way: Fred Baily, Anne Beness, Lorne Brandt, Greg Foot, Simon Hattrell, Monika Hildebrandt, Sue Hume, Tim Kuepfer, George Martin, Dan Mendis, Walter Moberly, Fr

Stephen Ortiger, Dennis and Elizabeth Sadler, Rona Seager, Angus Stuart, and Kate Young. From three countries and different theological backgrounds, these people have all raised very helpful questions that have helped me to sharpen my writing.

My husband Stuart, who teaches New Testament, has spent countless hours in reading and then proofreading, not to mention conversations about content and support in many other ways. Thank you so much, Stuart!

I have learnt much, but still have much more to learn. Any weaknesses and errors in this book remain mine.

Introduction

What kind of a leader is God? Is he a benevolent Santa Claus? Or is he really a narcissist? Is his leadership centered on law enforcement? Or is his priority focused on relationships? Is his interest in nations and systems? Or is he personally alongside the mistreated and oppressed? Is he a leader of armies? Or is he a leader of peace? These and many other questions about God's character and leadership are in the back, if not the front, of many people's minds—questions especially about the God of the Old Testament, who is often painted very differently from the God of the New Testament.

There are plenty of books on the topic of human leadership, but I am convinced that our ideas about God's leadership subconsciously shape our own ideals and priorities in leadership. We can look at many human models of leadership to our profit, but this book takes a different approach. Here we seek to learn more about the model of leadership displayed by God himself. It is about God as Leader. Not as a list of his leadership qualities, but as a journey of discovery, observing how he leads in many very different situations through the Old Testament.

I have seen people learn all kinds of theories about leadership. Yet, when they are placed into a leadership position, they often flip back to their default mode, unconsciously following the patterns of leadership which they imbibed from a leader they knew well. That could be a parent, a teacher, a community leader, a boss or a pastor. We unconsciously study and learn leadership from real people. But when our model turns out to be less than effective, we need to understand what went wrong and relearn how to do leadership. One of the most effective ways is through closely observing and experiencing another person who demonstrates a better model of leadership. I suggest that by more closely observing God's model of leadership we can reassess our own understanding and practice of leadership.

My doctoral level training in Old Testament and my life experience through many years of parenting, teaching, pastoring and leading organizations are both rich and relevant. I am still trying to observe and learn as I function in some situations as a leader, while in others I work under other leaders. While I write as a Christian, I am deeply grateful to insights by Jewish authors. It is my hope that this book might be useful to Jews and Christians alike. After all, we share the same Hebrew Bible/Old Testament.

Considering God as Leader has not, to my knowledge, been done with any degree of thoroughness. Many attributes of God are helpfully covered in depth in systematic theologies. Many images of God as Leader have also been explored, to varying degrees, to our benefit. These include King, Shepherd, Father and, perhaps, Wisdom. But there are others as well. Some of God's attributes are said to be communicable, because we humans have the capacity to imitate them. These include aspects like thinking, loving, and acting justly. These, of course, need to be integral components of our leadership. That is not to say that we imitate them perfectly. There are other incommunicable attributes of God which are totally out of reach for us humans to imitate, like having all power (omnipotence), being everywhere at once (omnipresence) and knowing everything (omniscience). These are aspects that we should not attempt to imitate.

The word "leader" is rarely used of God in English Bibles, but his leadership function in relation to his people is recognizable everywhere. God is called "leader" in some translations of 2 Chronicles 13:12, translating the Hebrew word for "head," and is said to have led the people in Exodus 13:17-21. His leadership is wider than what the images of king, shepherd and father can convey. It is broader than the function of a guide. It seems to me that the more general category of "leader" enables us to notice more of who God is in relation to people, in relation to us. In this era of thinking more about our human leadership, surely we can relearn and replace some of the bad models of leadership we have imbibed by looking more carefully at the leadership of the person of God.

Perhaps it is obvious that this book is not primarily about management techniques, financial expertise or institutional systems. Its focus is rather on relational leadership, character and principles. These can, of course, be applied to leadership in politics, government and business. However, there is also wider application in schools, churches, synagogues, workplaces and clubs, families and friendships. Some form of leadership falls to most of us, whether male or female, within the space of our lifetimes. I hope there is something here for everyone that can be applied in quite varied leadership contexts and cultures.

This book will traverse much of the terrain of the Old Testament. For those who would like to have a clearer grasp of the bigger picture of the

Old Testament story and literature, I hope that this book gives some help. For those who already have a good grasp of the literature, I hope that my retelling of familiar stories might highlight some fresh considerations. This is certainly not an exhaustive study through the Old Testament, but it is, I hope, suggestive of how we might investigate God's leadership in other parts of the Bible that are not covered in this book.

This book is not written in an academic style. There are few references to secondary sources, mostly because my desire is to use the Old Testament itself as my primary source. I have tried to write in a more accessible style than is usually the case in academic writing. I make my own judgments where there are alternative possible interpretations, but I don't want to interrupt the flow of the book by inserting the reasons for my choices. I work from the final text that is widely accepted by both Jews and Christians.

I also bring some imaginative license to this writing, sometimes going a little beyond what we can read on the surface and making connections that are not explicit. But I don't let my imagination run wild. Others may, of course, disagree with any of my imaginative suggestions. However, I include these in the hope that all of us might engage with these biblical writings in ways that traverse the distances of time and space and connect with our own experiences.

Woven into the fabric of this book are many examples of human leadership from my own experience. Some come to mind because of a point of similarity to what we have just read of God's leadership, and others because of a point of contrast. It is my hope that by sharing some personal examples others might be stimulated to make their own connections and assessments. I have made some small changes in the telling of many of my stories to protect the identities of people involved, but the essential elements are all true.

Each chapter will touch on issues that may be covered much more thoroughly in other books. I hope the reader may decide to follow up topics of interest elsewhere. However, this book deliberately takes a broad-sweep approach, in the hope that we might catch a more holistic vision of God as a multifaceted leader. While God's leadership adapts and changes from time to time, it is my conviction that the central divine character does not.

God's leadership shows some qualities that we typically call more masculine as well as some that we may call more feminine. Leadership is expressed humanly by both genders, whether in the family, at work or in other situations. We are told in the creation accounts that humans of both genders are made in the image of God. We might find, if we pay more attention to the ways in which God leads, that we are each better able to imbibe and emulate more of the model which he gives us in our own limited areas of leadership.

I have added at the end of each chapter some questions that might stimulate individual reflections or be used for group discussion. These questions attempt to draw out in a more pointed way some of the implications of the presentation of God's leadership for our own roles as leaders today. But readers may devise other questions that are more relevant to their own thinking and needs.

I hope that your journey with *God the Leader* brings discoveries that are personally enriching and applicable in your own contexts.

PART 1

Getting to Know God as Leader

Chapter 1

Beginnings

LEADERSHIP IN CREATION

The very first chapter of the Bible, Genesis 1, presents God's leadership vision and implementation at its most spectacular. In the mysterious epoch of beginnings, God speaks everything into existence. Yet this is not without preparation. The Spirit of God has been hovering, considering, observing (v.2). The void, the darkness, and the chaos do not need to remain like this. A grand plan emerges—a plan with distinct order and balance, a plan with careful steps of progression, a plan with complex interdependence between all of its component parts.

The first three steps, in three days, create contexts—light and darkness, water and sky, seas and land. Without suitable environments and means of nourishment it will be impossible for the creatures God has in mind to function and have their needs met. Even the specific bodies of lights in the sky cannot serve their purposes (vv.16-18) without the prepared resources. So, water and air are now each filled with creatures which can move easily in their own medium, but not in the other. The fit, for each one, is good!

Land creatures come in a range of kinds, each with its own style and speed of movement, its own colors and textures, its own limitations. Yet all are able to be embraced and welcomed by the one who is the Leader.

Not all of the creatures are of equal capacity. A choice is made for one species to be given a stronger likeness to God, including the capacity to lead. This species will be given responsibility that is commensurate with this capacity. So the human pair, both male and female, are together blessed and released to exercise the leadership gifts they have received over the rest of creation. However, they go in the knowledge that their own needs for sustenance will be provided, and that they will not be asked to lead in areas which for them would be impossible, like providing food for these other creatures.

And so it is time for the one who has envisioned and created all of this to rest. A pattern emerges in this initial great work of leadership. First, there is a vision. Then there is preparation. After this is the orderly and stepwise execution of the plan. Next is clear communication with appointed leaders under him. Then there is rest.

I marvel at the vastness of God's creativity. The explosive majesty and the quiet, hidden details are, at both extremes, beyond me. Yet we as humans are made in his image. There are certainly lesser ways in which we reflect God's capacity to create. We cannot bring anything out of entire nothingness, but we are intended to form new things out of materials that don't look anything like the end product, and out of conversations that could otherwise lead nowhere. Leaders are called to create and to foster creativity in others.

PLANNING AND DELEGATING

Thinking ahead is crucial for a leader. I find it particularly encouraging that God plans ahead. I once worked for a boss who called a meeting to plan for the year ahead but changed the date of the meeting at the last minute. Then he insisted that one man attend his meeting despite having given him permission, six months before, to speak at a conference on the same day a great distance away. So there was an immediate loss to the conference, and he himself was discouraged because of the loss of this opportunity to use his special gifts—the very gifts that his boss had asked him to use. Consequently, there was lessened trust in the word of the boss who went against the permission he himself had remembered granting. When we gathered for the meeting, the boss asked the team to work out a vision for staff increases in the new year. Yet it quickly became obvious that he had done no homework. We asked him for his vision, maybe some statistics, to ascertain needs and resources and anticipated areas of growth. He had none. We asked where extra staff might work, in what departments and in what office space. He had no idea. He simply demanded loudly that we give him a number—a number plucked from nowhere, a number without any planning, a number that could be guessed by an ignorant child. This number he would give to his superior, and it would look as if his leadership was strong. In this meeting none of us could contribute usefully. It would have been wiser to let the conference speaker go and speak. No wonder there was chaos when the new year started.

I struggle, whenever I am a leader, to avoid being swamped by urgent matters instead of giving enough time and attention to envisioning future steps. When we are bogged down and can't see the wood for the trees, we become depleted of energy. Vision revives us. There is purpose. We are going somewhere. We are going with God, and we are going with and for others. Creative, preparatory, visionary work is a key gift and service to the people under the care of the leader.

I love the formation of contexts in Genesis 1, before the creatures who will inhabit them: light and darkness, water and sky, sea and land. Leadership is often about making hospitable spaces where people are able not only to live and move, but thrive. It considers the particular needs of each kind, and makes a suitable place for each to work. It avoids placing a square peg in a round hole.

Amazingly, God gives some of his leadership power away to others. He recognizes potential in the human pair and refuses to micro-manage them. They are given sufficient freedom to learn and grow in leadership, together with resources to keep them going, but they are not given unrealistic expectations. God is not abandoning them but releasing them into their new roles with his blessing. And, as we find out later, they will go with his continuing companionship and resources.

Rest. Satisfying after all this work. But it is not prolonged, just one day in seven. Our tendencies towards workaholism or laziness are not exhibited by God the Leader.

A UNIQUE CREATOR

God as creator is obviously a unique and, in many ways, incomparable leader. He lays a foundation on which everything else is built. He does not reveal all of his secrets to those who follow him. His ways are beyond our grasp. His role, power and actions evoke awe and wonder. His ongoing presence provides security for those who trust him and fear for those who cross him. Beginnings and endings are in his hand. His big-picture vision extends beyond our imagining and yet his penetrating sight observes minute details that many would want to hide. As the Psalmist discovers, there is nowhere that is out of God's reach, and not even darkness will reduce his ability to see (Ps 139). In his wisdom, he sets limits for winds, rain and seas, and not even the forces of evil and death have the depth of understanding that he has (Job 28). He is not a leader who boasts of having greater capacity than he actually has.

We know that we humans are not God. Yet sometimes we forget. Leadership power goes to our heads and we are happy for people to display awe, adulation and higher levels of trust than we can live up to. This can lead us into narcissism. Some human leaders are satisfied if their presence evokes petrifying fear, and they play games of intimidation to trick others into staying underneath. But no matter how responsible our positions of leadership are, we are not God the creator. We are reminded that no object or person is to be put in place of God to be worshiped instead of him (Exod 20:3-4). We do not do well when we are put on a pedestal. Inevitably, we fall off. And using threatening behavior only turns us into bullies, stripping us of any genuine leadership credibility.

Yet God the creator is genuinely worthy of the utmost respect. There simply is no other like him. Even though we do not have his capacities, wisdom or power to create or to destroy, the more we understand his ways of leadership the more we can learn of how we humans might lead in our much more narrower spheres. Human leadership is also to be respected, but in a much more limited way, commensurate with our much more limited responsibility and capacity.

LEADERSHIP IN COMMUNITY

The unexpected plurality used in Genesis 1:26 ("Let us make humankind in our image") suggests that, from time immemorial, executive leadership decisions were made within a divine community. Admittedly, the details are not made explicit. Then, in Genesis 2 and 3, God makes a move to establish community with and between the humans in his creation.

God's creative leadership in the formation of humans is careful, deliberate and intimate. As a potter's fingers sensitively feel and mold the clay, God's hands work the soil and tenderly touch and shape the focus of his love, a humble man. Then he stoops to put his mouth next to the man's mouth. The breath of life is transferred through an intimate act.

The context for the man has been prepared: a garden with attractive and edible food, rivers to water the land, and purposeful work for the man to do. God gives simple and clear instructions without controlling human choice. The man has an abundance of options which can be productive, but warning is given about the one option which would lead to harm. God will continue to come alongside this man in his daily life, to provide a shared experience of continuing divine-human community (Gen 3:8).

Now the man is also to have community with his own kind—with one who can give him help in his areas of need, one who can share his delegated leadership, a woman who is truly on his own level. In this human community, there is great delight and profound intimacy as with no other! And between the members of this human team there is no pretense and no barrier in their relationship.

For us, there is certainly a kind of loneliness in leadership. Many have commented on it, and I have felt it at times. But we can exacerbate the loneliness in a direction that not only becomes unhealthy for us, but also for the people we are leading. We can become aloof. That can degenerate further into stubborn arrogance or brittle anxiety; it can lead to disconnected harshness, or to incompetent mismanagement.

I have conducted and directed many Christian musicals and can remember several times when a crisis occurred that threatened to disrupt our functioning. I did not know the way ahead, because the disruptions were completely beyond anything I anticipated. I knew that I could not find the way forward alone. I met with others, sometimes a leadership group, sometimes the whole group. We talked and prayed, and the way forward quickly became apparent. It was different than any of us could have imagined alone. And it worked.

CHALLENGES TO LEADERSHIP

God's leadership does not go unchallenged! It is quietly reinterpreted and questioned from a hidden corner, as a sneaky, base creature purports to offer further truth (Gen 3:1-5). Succumbing to his divisive strategies, the humans feel the experience of shame. No longer able to face each other openly, they instinctively run to hide from their Creator-Leader. Fear interferes with their ongoing conversations, and the blame of each other dominates their defensive reactions.

From now on, the story of this world will be imbued with suffering. Human leadership over the other creatures will now be infected by mutual enmity in some quarters; the balanced and delicate teamwork between the man and the woman will now be distorted by the dominance of one over the other; work (whether male out in the fields or female in childbearing) will now be thwarted by pain and frustration. Decay and death will return mankind to dust.

Yet, God is still in charge and assesses the new needs of the humans in this altered condition. He personally provides suitable and long-lasting clothing, assesses the new dangers and devises a way forward.

A leadership challenge has been asserted, right where the Leader has provided idyllic conditions. We now know that leadership challenges are a recurring theme in any context. We sometimes think, "If only the leader had done . . . (fill in the blank), a challenge would not have occurred." But even God was, is, and will be challenged. That is not to say that the challenger will win. But, in the meantime, something is spoilt. Trust is broken and community is infected.

Challengers may think of leadership primarily in terms of status instead of responsibility and service. They may be envious and lust for a raise in their sense of self-importance. Or they may want to satisfy any one of their other passions. Those who join in this game against their rightful leader lose far more in the process than they gain.

God the Leader is swift to sort out the mess and to confront the challengers. He knows what has been said and done in hidden corners and he knows that the offenders have now retreated into other hidden corners. But no one is beyond his reach. He calls and, as rightful Leader, invites them out into the open to talk with him (Gen 3:9). He is not put off by their avoidance tactics. He addresses each person involved, hears each version of the story, and states the consequence that each has brought upon him/herself. The challenge is not allowed to fester and must be stopped. Yet God takes the risk of giving them another chance to start again.

STRUGGLES

From this point on, the peaceful and productive community established by the divine leader begins to struggle. A jealous envy squeezes out brotherly care (Gen 4), and people compete for favor with God and others. Some even boast of destroying others who get in their way. Infected, evil thinking is bent on destruction of community, and wicked acts ensue. God's heart is pained; he cannot simply stand and watch the violence multiply. So, he decides to bring an end to such hopeless disorder and chaos.

However, from time to time, some individuals have dared to go against the crowd and have shown that it is possible for humans to continue to take their instructions from God and live uprightly, even in the midst of a wicked community. An outstanding example is Noah, a man said to be in a right relationship with both God and other humans (Gen 6:9). So, God devises a plan, explains it carefully to Noah, and executes it so that Noah and his family—and anyone else who cares to listen—are safe. Then, once again, a nucleus of humanity is sent out to multiply, to fill the earth, and to rule over the rest of creation. They go with clear instructions and warnings. They also receive a fresh promise of divine help which, this time, is accompanied by a reminder of what they have heard in the form of a recurring visual spectacle—the rainbow.

Soon after this, new struggles appear. One of Noah's sons seriously disturbs family relationships by exploiting and shaming someone in a weakened condition. This act is made worse by the fact that it is against his own father (Gen 9). Generations later, other struggles disturb whole communities. The constructive work of city-building becomes severely tainted with arrogance, fear and insecurity. The work is no longer primarily for the establishment of communities, but for some to make a name for themselves. It is no longer for the establishment of bases from which some may freely go further to fill the earth. It issues from a sick attitude of control that is afraid of letting anyone go out of sight of these small-minded puffed-up leaders (Gen 11:4). God's leadership is once again tested. He acts decisively to curb the folly of such misguided human leadership and scatters the people so that they might think again

God the Leader is grieved (Gen 6:6). Leaders who feel no grief when their communities are disrupted and show signs of decay don't care. There has to be disappointment, there has to be frustration, there has to be love. Perhaps this is the most difficult aspect of leadership. Their vision for good is threatened, if not undone. Before the people can envisage the impact of their own disruptions on their future, the leader knows and weeps. Again, something must be done. In this story, again and again a leadership intervention is required and taken.

Parents, as leaders of their children, know this. It is not that long from the time when innocence and glorious potential are celebrated until the time of the first challenge and the need for intervention. And then parents become alert to the need for further interventions along the way. Parents see, in full technicolor horror, what the consequences of certain childish courses of action, if continued, are likely to be. The vision clashes with their fondest dreams for their child. And so they act. The cries of hurt feelings and the threats from angered children are suffered because they do not compare with the horrifying ramifications the parents have seen in their imaginations. They will not be content to allow their children to slip into that kind of future.

QUESTIONS FOR REFLECTION OR DISCUSSION

1. What aspect of God's leadership is most striking?
2. Is there anything surprising or anything that raises questions about God as Leader?
3. What does the Creation story tell us about the purpose of leadership?
4. How can leaders take appropriate rest, without becoming workaholic or lazy?
5. How might we handle challenges to leadership?
6. Setting limits to chaotic and destructive behavior is difficult. What might we learn?

Chapter 2

A New Start

A MOMENTOUS JOURNEY

God the Leader observes each person who lives on the earth and his attention rests on one couple who have already started on a journey but think they have gone far enough (Gen 11:27–32). God initiates a conversation with the man, Abram (Gen 12). Abram shows that he is attuned to discerning the divine voice, as Noah had been.

There is an instruction to leave what is known and travel to what is unknown; the divine Leader will show the way. There are also mysterious promises of greatness and blessing that will extend beyond Abram's natural family, even to all the other peoples on earth (Gen 12:1–3). At seventy-five years old, with little understanding of the big picture but with seasoned humility and grace, Abram leads his people to follow the divine Leader. Periodically God encourages Abram through further words and personal appearances, and Abram reciprocates by offering worship to the one he is following.

Along the way, Abram shows moments of unselfish generosity. He allows his nephew to take his first choice of the land. This pleases God. Yet there are other moments when feelings of insecurity arise, perhaps on account of being moved from his known stamping ground. Abram then allows fear and self-interest to drive him to deceit: he places his wife in the traumatic position of being taken into another man's harem so that his own life will be spared (Gen 12:10–20).

The journey is not simple or straightforward. It both tests and expands Abram's commitment to following God as leader, as well as testing and expanding his own ability to be an effective leader of his own people.

Three incidents make it clear that God's kind of leadership invites reciprocity in his relationship with Abram. The first concerns a specific divine promise of a son and heir. After considerable time has elapsed without any evidence of its fulfillment, Abram is understandably disappointed and candidly questions God about it (Gen 15). He hears the reiteration of the promise and sees the display of stars above as a visual representation of his future descendants. As he does so, a significant shift takes place within himself, and he comes to a deeper trust in the One who is speaking (Gen 15:6). So, in this incident, questioning, listening and trusting together characterize an acceptable and active human response.

The second incident is the formation of a covenant between God and Abram (Gen 17). God initiates it and gives both instructions and promises. Abram (now to be named Abraham) is called to "keep the covenant." He is given the responsibility to pass the instructions on to future generations and to enact circumcision as an outward sign of participation in the partnership.

The third incident concerns God's displeasure over the people of the villages Sodom and Gomorrah (Gen 18) and his intention to bring destruction. Abraham engages in vigorous debate with God over what, to him, is a matter of justice. Will God destroy these people if there are fifty upright people among them? God says no. Eventually Abraham brings the number of upright people down to ten. No, not even then.

This permission, and, indeed, invitation into a relationship that invites this level of reciprocity is somewhat unexpected, given that we have just read of God the Leader's unparalleled power and glory as creator and the human penchant for distorting the power we are given. And yet many other human leaders, who are clearly not so genuinely gifted, require unquestioning and silent subjection, and sometimes especially from intelligent, upright people who just might be able to help them.

As a child, I was fascinated by the story of Abraham. What particularly caught my attention was his relationship with God. It seemed like a friendship to me. I had heard of people praying and speaking *to* God. But I had never before heard of anyone capable of hearing *from* God. My Sunday School teacher thought I should be impressed by the fact that when God told Abraham to move he did. He obeyed. What I was more impressed with was that he *heard*. That hearing was the basis for acting, speaking, further hearing, arguing, and trusting. The theme is picked up by Jesus when he says that his followers know his voice (John 10:4).

Abraham is not a perfect hero. Yet this relationship with God that includes repeated speaking and listening means that God the Leader walks close to this follower. God's call for Abraham to follow him is not empty. Through the various twists along the unseen path, God will continue to lead. And confirmations of his ongoing leadership provide security, direction and comfort along the way.

SEVERE TESTING

"Some time later God tested Abraham" (Gen 22:1). God the Leader plans this test and asks Abraham to do something that we can only perceive to be unthinkable and absolutely abhorrent—to sacrifice his promised son, Isaac. However, in some ancient cultures, fathers held the power of life and death over their children and wives. The Herod family of New Testament times saw nothing wrong with putting wives or sons to death if the ruler perceived them to be a threat to his power. The history of British and continental European royalty is replete with examples of family murder because of rivalry in power. Tribes in Fiji, only a hundred and fifty years ago, would often sacrifice a son in the building of important new houses and bury their remains under the corner post. But does God, as leader, condone any of that kind of behavior?

We discover, eventually, that this is a test of Abraham's leadership, rather than of God's leadership. It turns out that God does not condone family sacrifice and provides a ram to be sacrificed instead of Isaac. To some ancients that conclusion may well have been startling. Much later in the biblical story we discover that the "leadership" of other gods is different—they *do* require the sacrifice of children.

Abraham, as a follower of God and the leader of his family, is caught between loyalties. But he most likely doesn't know it. After the desire and struggle and years of waiting before receiving this promised son, he naturally treasures this miraculous gift. His affections and dreams focus on Isaac.

He had had another son, Ishmael, with his wife's maid. But that son was not the promised child. He was born through the frustrations of Abraham and Sarah when the wait seemed too long. But now that Isaac, the promised son, has miraculously arrived well past natural childbearing years, there is sibling rivalry in the household (Gen 21). Abraham is father to them both, so is distressed when his wife Sarah asks him to get rid of the maid and her son. He reluctantly agrees, at God's command. Isaac is now the only son who is left with him.

It is very easy for a parent to have so much emotional attachment to a child, especially a longed-for child, that they lose the capacity to lead that child and instead end up following that child. Through no fault of its own and entirely unintentionally, the child can become a rival to the parent's leadership or to God's leadership.

God spots the danger and knows that if this distortion is not remedied, the lives of both Abraham and Isaac, together with the future wellbeing of this people of promise, will be set in a destructive direction. So, he creates the test. Abraham is pulled back to his senses and realigns his position as follower of God, not of Isaac. In this intervention there is no actual destruction, just the threat of it. Because Abraham is not a stubbornly hard-hearted man, a threat is enough.

We read of Isaac's very natural question along the way, and Abraham's ambiguous answer (Gen 22:7–8). Yet the writer tells us nothing of the emotional upheavals for Isaac, just as he tells us nothing about Sarah's emotions when she is taken into harems. We may speculate, but in the end, we know nothing apart from the record of Abraham's obvious love and respect for his wife Sarah when she dies, and Isaac's faithfulness in marrying the girl of his father's choice (Gen 24) and in leading his family to follow the same God his father followed.

Later, God's leadership of his people through the wilderness is also described as testing the people (Deut 8:2, 3). None of us likes to have a leader who plays cruel, manipulative games with us. We resent tests that smack of games. But this narrative is not an example of that kind of thing. I am very grateful for some leaders along the way, some teachers, some pastors, some mature friends, who saw that I had potential for something better and tested me by giving me challenges that I thought were impossible for me to meet. They all involved some realignment in my own heart—adjustment of my self-image, recognition of emotional addictions, challenges to my will. I did rise to some, but I don't think I passed them all. I am, however, grateful now that they tried. And those challenges which I eventually discovered that I passed (even if I was angry in the middle) have helped me to take the larger leaps that I could not take otherwise.

In some quarters, the very presence of tests in school evokes protests from certain parents in Western countries. They say tests are stressful and stress is bad—surely our children will only be able to flourish in an environment of continuous appreciation and encouragement. In certain places even the red pens of teachers are banned—we don't want children to be told that something is wrong or should be rewritten. However, it is interesting to me that in countries where poverty is normal and children know the daily tests of trying to find food, water and other essentials, the tests in school are more readily embraced, even welcomed. Students are taught to say (and mean) that this is an opportunity to learn, a gift to be received, so that their future lives will be better. Parents know that there is no way for their children to grow to be responsible citizens without challenges along the way. As a teacher, I have also seen the huge encouragement that children feel when they perform well in an exam, a sports event, a competition or a performance, so long as the goal set is not beyond their abilities, and sufficient help is given for them to achieve an appropriate goal. So setting tests that are within realistic and safe boundaries, and for a good and necessary goal, is within the remit of leadership that God models.

Abraham needed his character to be developed in order to grow into being the faithful human leader that God as the higher Leader envisaged. His long years of waiting and the challenges along the way were no accident but were tests that bore fruit.

WRESTLING A DECEIVER

Jacob, son of Isaac and grandson of Abraham, is born as the second twin but comes out grabbing his brother's heel (Gen 25). His name reflects this origin and characterizes him as a deceiver. He lives up to his name, using a range of deceptive tricks, in order to get ahead in life at anyone else's expense. Yet, despite a clearly unacceptable repeating pattern, he is seen by God the Leader to have potential. His brother Esau is prone to taking unthinking short cuts, so rules himself out of a place of leadership for the next generation. Yet Jacob does not appear to be a good alternative.

The story of Jacob is punctuated by flashes of insight, received by Jacob through God's unexpected presence at strategic points of his life. A dream (Gen 28) shows him that his way ahead will not simply be won by his own cunning; God has a purpose for him and his offspring. What is more, God says that he will accompany Jacob. Perhaps Jacob had not realized that the blessing he so much craved from his father would require him to be a follower of God rather than simply give him a privileged position.

After time away from his family of origin, Jacob returns, and faces the source of his greatest fear: his twin brother Esau. He has good reason to expect murderous anger. So, in desperation, he prays (Gen 32:9-12). It is not clear, on first reading, whether the prayer is yet another self-centered attempt by Jacob to worm his way out of difficulties and to hold God to account to help him. But his fear at least prods him to remember and show gratitude for the kindness and faithfulness which God has already shown him. He is still wary. Perhaps Esau's anger might be appeased if he sends gifts ahead of him.

Eventually the whole of Jacob's party, together with a costly number of animals as gifts, has gone before him. Jacob is alone. Then the text simply says, "a man wrestled with him till daybreak" (Gen 32:24). By the end of the wrestling match it becomes clear that this is a kind of prayer-wrestle; the "man" is referred to as "God." Perhaps God is testing Jacob to see how serious he is about addressing him. Jacob will no longer be able to speak to God from the side of his mouth. God must be faced directly. Jacob rises to the occasion and realizes that the favor he has connived to gain from human leaders—his father and his uncle—is not enough. What he really needs must come from God. So neither he nor this God-representative will give up until his name is changed and a divine blessing is given. The concern about Esau is dissipated, and the price of an ongoing limp is worth it. Jacob the deceiver has gone and he takes his place as the leader of Israel.

God the Leader does not immediately take a person of potential and make him a patriarch. He is persistent in watching and waiting for the right time in the person's journey. Character flaws must be faced and dealt with. But many flaws become ingrained as a defense system, so it is difficult for anyone else to get really close to them. But a moment of weakness may become a moment of truth—a turning point for better and greater things. The way up may first need to be a way down. God sees the moment of openness and responds. He enables the potential he sees to become reality. He is a strategic leader in the lives of his followers.

Too many young ministers, who begin with enthusiasm and a sense of call, flounder. No one told them about the ugly side of humanity. Their own character flaws have not been sufficiently dealt with for them to be able to cope with some difficult emotions. Yet in the moment of floundering there is hope. There are others who appear to have charmed lives and expect to be always in favored positions, confident that they can talk themselves into or out of anything they want. But it may be when the crash comes, that they, too, have an opportunity for hope. Yet these opportunities that involve God can also involve wise human leadership—leaders who will gently or strongly confront them at productive levels, and, even if it takes some time, will show them firmer paths.

QUESTIONS FOR REFLECTION OR DISCUSSION

1. Have you ever been given a new start?
2. How does God as Leader enable people to change for the better?
3. Have any tests along your way become opportunities for a better relationship with God? Or for significant growth?
4. Under what conditions could a manager offer a second chance to an uncooperative employee?
5. How might we help a child to develop greater responsibility?
6. What do we understand about God's attitude towards us while we are still "a work in progress?"

Chapter 3

Care for the Overlooked

The main story line of Genesis follows the men who are heads of families. But God's leadership is noteworthy regarding the minor characters in the story. Each one is of interest to God the Leader. In this chapter we will consider God's dealings with those who are not the major players: Eve, Hagar, Sarah, Lot, Abraham's servant and Rebekah. Then we will examine the larger story concerning Joseph, who was, for many years, hidden away in Egypt, unjustly betrayed and imprisoned, before he unexpectedly became a major character in the story.

EVE

Eve is tempted, not only by the serpent but through the sensual attractiveness of the fruit and her own thirst for gaining wisdom. Fruit and wisdom are gifts to be enjoyed, but to be accessed and used within given boundaries. In the Genesis 3 story, it is both the man and the woman who transgress clear boundaries. When God confronts both the man and the woman, each for their own part, Eve, like Adam, is held accountable only for her own actions. While the man and woman are each given comparable consequences for their similar actions, there is an additional mysterious promise given to the woman. God motivates her for her future offspring-bearing role. One day her offspring, or one of them, will win the battle against the evil that is represented in the snake. God the Leader has stated the sad consequence of her error yet brings a promise of hope. This will not be the end of his concern and care.

HAGAR AND SARAH

Hagar, Sarah's Egyptian maid, has no say in being given to Abraham by her mistress (Gen 16). She is a servant with few rights. Pregnancy changes the dynamics of the household. She soon despises her mistress for putting her in this position and is subsequently mistreated. She becomes the pawn of both master and mistress. She is lonely and distressed, without any power to speak or act. She runs away to the desert but does not have the means to take care of herself and the coming child. God sees her there and comes to her in the form of an angel. He gives her an opportunity to speak, sends her back for nourishment and protection, and adds a promise. He sees ahead to what this child will become. Even if this child is not the child of the promise given to Abraham, God still has a purpose for him.

God's messengers appear to Abraham and a table is spread (Gen 18). In line with the custom of the day, men speak and eat with men while women remain hidden and eat with the women. But this time the messengers are instructed by God to give a message to the wife, Sarah. The content of the message is also unexpected: she will have a son. How can a woman well past childbearing years have a son? She has already made one mistake, that of following common custom to give her husband Abraham a child by her maid. However, something new is envisaged here, so she, not only her husband, needs to know. Care is taken that God's message comes to her ears. She laughs to herself at the ludicrousness of the proposal, but God's messenger picks up her laughter even though there is no outward sign of it. She cannot be seen and she utters no sound. His subsequent rebuke may sound harsh to our ears, but it actually serves as a reassuring sign to her that the message does, indeed, come from God the Leader. And so, in due time, it is fulfilled.

Later, when rivalry arises between Hagar's son and Sarah's son (Gen 21), Sarah requests that Hagar and her son be sent away. The concerns are around inheritance. God as leader guides Abraham to do as Sarah is asking. However, he also guides Hagar to find water in the desert so that she and her son can live and so that God's promise of building his offspring into a great nation can be fulfilled. God acts to manage and reduce the conflict that is set to become destructive to parents and children. He judges that the weaker members can now live independently with some divine help. He enables the specific lineage of promise to be maintained, and leaves none of the people involved without adequate support.

LOT AND HIS FAMILY

The people among whom Abraham's nephew Lot settles, prove to be so thoroughly entrenched in wickedness that a line must be drawn. When two of God's messengers visit Lot, the men of Sodom demand sex with these visitors (Gen 19). They will not heed Lot's pleading to stop such a disgraceful proposition, even though his offer of sex with his virgin daughters instead of with the more desirable male guests is totally despicable. Clearly, Lot is not on the moral high ground here! The laws, which will come later, judge both homosexual rape and the raping of women to be extremely serious crimes. However, we see just a faint remnant of more decent values in Lot, shown in his hospitality and in his protection of strangers. Perhaps this suggests that he is not quite in the same position of fully entrenched wickedness that the townspeople are in. There is, for him, a glimmer of hope. God sees that glimmer and offers him and his family, including the young men engaged to his daughters, the opportunity to be spared from the coming destruction.

There are clear instructions and a clear warning; both are to be heeded exactly to ensure the safety of this family. If they fail to flee quickly enough they will lose their lives. If they turn back, valuable time will be lost and they will miss God's protection.

The young men engaged to Lot's daughters treat the warning as a joke and won't go. Lot's wife begins the journey but disobeys the condition of protection. She stops, and lingers long enough to look at the spectacle, perhaps becoming absorbed in its drama, and then falls victim to the burning sulphur and its products. None of these people are treated unfairly, for they have been given the clear and compassionate means to live, but their deaths are, very sadly, the result of not taking the directions of God's messengers seriously.

The story ends with an ironic twist. Lot was willing to give his daughters to be sexual slaves to wicked men. Now he becomes a sexual slave to his daughters (Gen 19:30–38). Now that they have no prospects of marriage and Lot has no wife, they make him drunk in order to produce offspring by his own daughters. Clearly, the family has been desensitized to the evils of the community in which they lived. Lot disappears from the story, and many conflicts ensue, yet God the Leader does not give up on all of the descendants of those illegitimate unions. Ruth, a descendant of the elder daughter, will one day join the family of Abraham, worship his God, live righteously, and bear a child who will be in the family line of both King David and Jesus the Messiah.

ABRAHAM'S SERVANT AND REBEKAH

When Abraham is old he sends his servant out on a mission to find a wife for his son Isaac. God the Leader acts as guide to the servant and confirms God's choice of the young woman Rebekah. It is a delightful story (Gen 24). The servant prays to the God of his master Abraham, requests a specific sign and is answered with remarkable speed and accuracy. He verbalizes his recognition of God's leadership. Rebekah is hospitable and generous. She is able to accept God's leadership and readily agrees to marriage. Later, she has difficulty conceiving a child, so Isaac prays. During her pregnancy she asks God about the jostling in her womb, and God answers, speaking to her about the future of each of her twins. Although she, like Sarah had done earlier, tries to fulfill a promise by manipulative and unacceptable methods, in this case concerning Jacob the younger twin (Gen 27), she turns out to be right in her expectation that it will be fulfilled.

PERSONAL LEADERSHIP OF ORDINARY PEOPLE

These more intimate stories of attention given to ordinary people set God's leadership apart from that of many modern corporate leaders. Our human capacity is limited, so we tend to focus on what we consider the most strategic and productive aspects of our leadership task. This means that we cannot give significant attention to those who do not seem to fit our leadership purposes. Perhaps we delegate the leadership of less strategic people to others whom we consider to be much lower down our leadership ladders. Yet these examples of the great and mighty God showing interest and involvement in the lives of people whom some of us might dismiss may challenge our perception of leadership priorities.

I can think of one church where the leaders were all men who assumed that women's needs were not of their concern and would presumably be met within the women's groups. A married woman temporarily moved away from her home to care for her dying mother, as she was the only child and the mother was unable to travel to her home. The woman's husband became very angry because he thought his wife should be prioritizing his own needs over her mother's needs. The leaders took his side and did not seek to hear from the woman or recognize her dilemma. They did not make any attempts to help the couple towards a solution that would consider the needs of the husband, the wife and the mother. Instead, they chose to publicly condemn and disgrace the wife. Although this example is extreme and hopefully uncommon, it does illustrate how far our view of leadership can stray from what we see of God's leadership in these simple stories, where every person, male or female, family head or servant, ethnic insider or outsider, is heard, seen, helped and directed to be able to move forward if they choose to cooperate. Leadership in personal, and sometimes complicated and hidden situations is, to God, important.

Throughout these stories we also see negative consequences of human behavior that ignores the advice and warnings given by God. Those who follow his leadership discover that his words turn out to be wise and reliable for safety and peace. He does not quickly dismiss people who make mistakes, even serious mistakes. But in giving the same freedom to make moral decisions to both the central and peripheral characters he also allows each person to experience the discipline of consequences.

THE MAKING OF A HUMAN LEADER

In the musical *Joseph and the Amazing Technicolor Dreamcoat*,[1] Joseph is portrayed, in his early days, as a spoilt brat. Whether his disclosure of certain dreams to his brothers arises from a sense of superiority and entitlement (a result of his favored position in his father's eyes) or whether it simply demonstrates his youthful naivete in telling what he saw (at least as likely) is initially unclear in the text (Gen 37). However, we soon discover that these dreams turn out to be of divine origin, and the story line moves steadily towards their fulfillment under the guiding hand of God the Leader.

The barriers to their fulfillment appear insurmountable—Joseph being abandoned in a pit by his brothers and left for dead, being falsely accused and imprisoned, forgotten by someone he helped, and left languishing in a hidden corner unseen by anyone of importance. However, this story is full of tension and drama because there are people in it who need to undergo personal change, in order to be able to fulfill their part in this story.

Whatever sense of privilege Joseph might feel in his youth seems to be relentlessly squeezed out of him through his many long and severe setbacks. There are glimpses of hope, as he is periodically raised to positions of responsibility only to have them dramatically ripped from him. In the middle of the story, questions about what God might be doing inevitably arise, especially when we remember those dreams that seemed to promise that one day Joseph would be raised to a position of authority. There is certainly reason to be angry about the injustice of it all. We know nothing of Joseph's prayers or personal reactions yet. It is only at the end of the story that we can make any sense of such a tale of repeated oppression.

---

1. Lyrics by Tim Rice, music by Andrew Lloyd Webber.

At the end of the story Joseph emerges as a man of integrity who is ready to assume leadership in the powerful nation of Egypt. It is his position, combined with his now more mature character, which opens the way for his whole family to leave famine behind and flourish in Egypt. However, Joseph is not the only person who has been changed for the better over the years.

Near the end we discover that Joseph's greatest pain has been from his brothers' betrayal and abandonment. Joseph is human. When they appear in Egypt requesting food, his emotional pain is overwhelming. Yet he longs to help them, and his decision to forgive is apparent. But can he trust them now, after what they have done? He needs to know if they have changed—a very reasonable need in the circumstances. He has lived as an outsider in this foreign land, belonging to no one, for a long time. Might he dare to hope that his own kith and kin might give him back his place of belonging? Or is it he who will have to invite them to belong to him in his new world?

The brothers have grown up, and so has his father Jacob. Perhaps Joseph's displacement has given Jacob the opportunity to better know and embrace his other sons. The dynamics are no longer the same. The brothers are willing to act sacrificially in order to save their youngest brother Benjamin. And they are ready to ask for forgiveness from Joseph.

Eventually Joseph is assured of their contrition, and reconciliation between himself, his brothers and father can be made. Truth is faced and told and there is a satisfyingly happy ending. Yet all of what has happened is reinterpreted as part of the bigger story, the story that is under God's leadership. Joseph famously says to his brothers, "Don't be afraid. Am I in the place of God? You intended to harm me, but God intended it for good to accomplish what is now being done, the saving of many lives" (Gen 50:19-20).

Could God the Leader use oppression, near-murder and slavery as a means to an exalted end? The text never states that God forces, encourages or even condones bad, let alone evil behavior—that is attributed to humans. Joseph makes a distinct separation between the motive of malice on the part of his brothers and the motive of salvation on the part of God. So it is inaccurate, if we pay close attention to the text, to suggest that God plays any active role in leading people to oppress, betray, abandon, falsely accuse or mistreat others. Yet God clearly has a leadership role in giving a promise through a divine dream and seeing it fulfilled at the end of the story. And, in knowing the hearts of Joseph's brothers and others who perpetrate evil, God works to prepare and change Joseph.

Many years ago, we were in a small group praying for the church and the community. Then the praying stopped, very unusually, as someone spoke our names. A man said that a vivid picture that concerned us came into his mind. He felt that it probably came from God so he shared it. Two women also said that they also had been given something for us—another picture and a Bible verse (Isa 43:19). None of this made any sense to us at the time so we paused and wondered. Just a week later we both lost our jobs through no fault of ours. Then my mother-in-law unexpectedly died, and we had to leave our rented home and fly home across the world. There my husband was found to need urgent bypass heart surgery and our PhD studies were put on hold. We were homeless, without income, my husband facing surgery and recovery, losing a parent and also facing a couple of other secondary crises. I felt like our lives were coming to a dark end but I remembered the pictures and words we had been given. They gave hope that God our Leader had some new purpose ahead. And it turned out to be so. God was not responsible for the unjust terminations of our jobs or my husband's heart attack. But his leadership was already actively preparing us and the way ahead for good purposes to come, even through this trying time.

In the Genesis story, Joseph is the key person led by God. We are not able to account for the choices of others, and I suggest that we are not meant to. There is a clear thread between the dreams, the shaping of character through suffering and the fulfillment of the dreams at the end. It seems that God saw more than Joseph and his brothers saw. He saw potential for leadership, though Joseph was not ready for it. He also saw that difficult circumstances could make him ready for it.

Joseph's family, too, is being led by God, perhaps both despite and through their distorted values and actions. Joseph's father sets him up for sibling rivalry by making Joseph his clear favorite. As a result, he temporarily loses Joseph. Joseph's brothers despise him, treat him like dirt, and leave him for dead. As a result, they find themselves bowing down to him in his exalted position and begging to be allowed to live. God's leadership rights wrongs caused by these people. The upside-down nature of the ending meets our need for justice and shows that God as Leader works persistently for it.

GOD'S SHAPING OF HUMAN LEADERS

God is a leader who trains people to be leaders and takes that training seriously. I have often been asked by eager young students who aspire to be leaders, "What do I need to do to become a leader?" I reply with a question, "Are you willing to suffer?" That is not the answer they expect or desire. Of course, there are plenty of leadership courses and manuals which can be useful for many aspects of leadership. But leadership is too often assumed to be nothing more than a set of skills that are added into a person's tool kit.

God's training of leaders goes deeper. God is most interested in shaping the character of the leader. In fact, if someone has acquired a toolkit of the latest leadership skills, he or she may be well-equipped to abuse power if he or she has not been readied in their own person. Suffering, which no one likes and so often seems to thwart productivity or forward movement, can be used under God's leadership to be his most fruitful means of training leaders.

QUESTIONS FOR REFLECTION OR DISCUSSION

1. How have these stories in Genesis enlarged your view of God's leadership?
2. Is God's care for people who seem to be "on the side" comforting or challenging?
3. How does God relate to the women in these stories?
4. Is it a leadership role to find potential in unlikely candidates?
5. What place does speaking to and hearing from God have in human leadership?
6. God is never said to be responsible for the evil deeds that humans do to each other. How can he, as ultimate Leader, use difficult, even terrible, circumstances for good?

Chapter 4

God is not like Pharaoh!

Many years ago, a leader began a rather uncomfortable meeting with an unusual confession. He claimed that God had spoken to him and rebuked him for treating me too harshly. What a relief to me to hear that the light had finally dawned! But the dawning lasted no more than five minutes, or at the most ten. What followed was a clear demonstration of unmitigated harshness, all, supposedly, in the name of the God of the Bible.

Somewhere in the back of our minds we may hold a sneaking suspicion that, even though Jesus seemed mostly to be meek and mild (not mentioning the uncomfortable overturning of tables in the temple area), God, if we probe him too deeply, may turn out to have harshness at his center. After all, there must be good reason to fear him.

The dramatic rescue narrative in the biblical book of Exodus provides us with much more than some kind of historical foundation for the Israelite people and their Law. Fundamentally it exposes, in stunning relief, the character of God's leadership of a unique group of people through a transition from slavery to freedom. In particular, God's leadership is played out in opposition to the leadership of Pharaoh. We can take the whole narrative as a case study of two very different leaders, God and Pharaoh.

IMAGINED THREATS

The new Pharaoh is concerned that the thriving minority group of Israelites within his territory may one day pose a threat to his control over them, not that there are any signs of animosity or even discontent right now. He decides to show them who is boss and turns them into his slave labor force. Their work will be to bring glory to Pharaoh, by forced oppression, in the building of his own iconic cities. Yet his plan to curtail the multiplication of their population fails, and instead of losing their fertility they become more abundant.

So he resorts to Plan B. This time he will use women, perhaps assuming that they will be more easily intimidated than men. He commands Hebrew midwives to kill every baby boy that they deliver. This plan also fails because these women are courageous and conscientious enough to quietly disobey. They know that their God would never support such an evil scheme. The narrator inserts a small comment about where God seems to fit into this scenario. He is *kind*, apparently not like Pharaoh, kind to the midwives (Exod 1:20). Even though the midwives have skirted around the truth in answering Pharaoh and acted against the unambiguous command of their overlord, God seems to be much more interested in their adamant desire to foster life and keep true to what they think is right and kind in the sight of God. Any requirements about their submission to authority figures is, in his view, secondary. This life-care seems to be equated then with fearing God (Exod 1:21). God responds by multiplying life even further. So Pharaoh turns to inciting all of his people to murder by throwing every baby boy into the Nile. But little does he know the ironic twist that is around the corner.

Women, once again—Moses' mother, his sister and even Pharaoh's daughter—are the instruments of rescue for the baby. Even though this child is put into the Nile as Pharaoh commanded, the way in which it is done is subversive. This mother creatively adds to the command by placing her child in a protective basket, thus thwarting the cruel intent of her overlord for full-scale infanticide. The outcome is that the child becomes Pharaoh's adopted grandson, no doubt growing up right under his nose in his own palatial precincts!

I notice that this story discounts the idea that God requires full and unquestioning obedience to every authorized human leader on every occasion. Not that there is any suggestion that anarchy is an acceptable alternative. In this case a clear line is drawn at a command to kill the innocent for no good cause. They are not even children of a rebellious group. Neither they nor their clans are plotting an overthrow. The idea of their being a threat is a fantasy in the mind of the Pharaoh, who assumes an animosity that is not there. However, his subsequent actions are highly likely to provoke the animosity he is looking for.

SLAVE-DRIVING

The rescued child, now the man Moses, ultimately chooses to place himself under the leadership of God in preference to the leadership of Pharaoh and finds himself right at the point of friction between these two leaders. In his newly appointed position as primary leader under God of the Israelite people, he speaks on their behalf to Pharaoh, requesting that they be given a temporary absence from their unreasonably demanding work (Exod 5). Pharaoh is not moved. He is still obsessed about numbers—the Hebrews are thriving! Any sign of their doing well is anathema to Pharaoh.

Work conditions deteriorate further. The equipment needed to work effectively is denied and unreasonable workloads are demanded (Exod 5). This is compounded by false accusations of laziness and deceit. The Israelite foremen speak on behalf of their people to make their unreasonable conditions known to Pharaoh and to ask why he has treated them like this. Surely, he will listen to their genuine complaints and recognize what is right and just! Their hopes in Pharaoh are shattered and they are rebuked for daring to request improvements in their working conditions. But the Israelite foremen turn around and, in their exasperated distress, blame Moses. His request for some compassionate leave has only further provoked Pharaoh's anger. Now they, not just their infants, are at risk of being killed!

As the foremen have gone to their leader Moses, Moses goes to his leader God. He faces God with his questions (Exod 5:22). To Moses this does not seem like the rescue mission he anticipated, but rather a compounding of his people's misery. The divine response indicates that God can and will exert more power over Pharaoh. The only way for the Israelites to survive and thrive now is to leave.

I am a creature of hope, hope that even stubborn narcissists might see sense if faced with the facts. Surely Pharaoh can be helped to understand that thriving, in and of itself, does not constitute a threat? Perhaps if the Israelites adopt a more subservient approach, Pharaoh will show them some kindness? Is there some specific way in which the Israelites are provoking this animosity? The storyteller does not refer to any provocation on the part of the Israelites, aside from their proliferation.

It is difficult to absorb, but my experience of conflict with the occasional Pharaohs in my life tells me that naively assuming equal blame on both parties, or worse assuming that blame must lie with the person of lower rank may, at times, not only be totally inaccurate but may obscure the true location of the provocative aggression. Peacemaking studies have contributed enormously to conflict resolution in many situations, and I strongly applaud them. But, in dealing with Pharaoh personalities, we may comply with their requests as much as possible and try every avenue that we know to promote peace, yet nothing more than a very temporary civility, at best, will ensue. If the problem still exists, ready to erupt from beneath the surface without notice, it won't be solved. Unfortunately, there are some leaders who seem incapable of anything apart from hostile rage and perpetual cruelty.

A hard, harsh heart towards subordinates can sometimes be expressed in unabated, ruthless mistreatment, driven by a distorted, crazed fear. This is worse if the leader is a narcissist who is merely reacting against an entirely imagined threat. There are others who express their unjustified harshness and control in more hidden but equally damaging ways, quietly moving things relentlessly against people who do not deserve such mistreatment. Yet any of these Pharaoh figures may know how to be charming and delightful to others, when their reputation and influence are at stake![1] And all may prove totally unyielding in the face of negotiations, persuasions, challenges—and even kindness. In their hardened narcissism they are beyond feeling empathy for anyone affected.

ENOUGH IS ENOUGH!

God the Leader listens to the groaning of the Israelites (Exod 6:5). He is moved by the compassion of relationship and does not speak with the detachment of distance. He promises to bring them out from under the yoke of the Egyptians. This happens to fit with the promise he had expressed years ago, to take them back to their ancestral homeland Canaan and give them their own space. Up until recent years Egypt has been a pleasant place to herd their animals and call home. It was once a generous gift to them in a time of need, from a previous, more kindly-disposed Pharaoh, when their ancestor Joseph was second in charge in the land.

Now they have been through enough. Need and promise coincide, and God says he will do more than they can imagine. He will release them from slave labor, from Pharaoh, and from Egypt. But the Israelites cannot hear it. This kind of promise seems too far-fetched. It is not just their physical bodies that have suffered; their emotions have been severely battered. Their hope has been diminished, and they are locked into despair.

They need someone who will stand on their behalf and God's, someone who is not quite so damaged, someone who will speak to Pharaoh boldly and tell him to let these people go. Moses is not sure that he can do it. He is not an eloquent speaker. He can't even convince the Israelites to listen

---

1. See Rom 16:17–19 for a New Testament description of similar people, with a warning to avoid them.

to him. Any credibility he once had in the Egyptian court has been eroded by many years away in the desert and an unfortunate incident in the past, with a slim chance that an old murder charge could be laid against him. Yet God persists. It is Moses, helped by his brother Aaron, who must do this. However, it won't be straightforward.

There are certainly times when the repeated, unbending harshness of a leader can so demoralize us that we feel paralyzed. I remember making an appointment to speak with the leader of a supposedly Christian organization years ago. I was troubled by his overly severe treatment of certain people within his group and by the harshness of some of his stated policies. They did not seem to be consistent with what I understood as biblical, but I thought, since I was much younger than he, that I might be mistaken. So I gave him my questions in advance, so that he would have time to consider his answers. I was open to being corrected, but I was not prepared for a solid two-hour tirade at *fortissimo* volume in which I was never permitted to speak and, in fact, felt totally unable to speak. In contrast, in a very different context, another conversation with a leader about the way in which he was excluding certain people resulted in his thanking me for helping him to see what he had been blind to, and for clarifying what was happening. He speedily apologized and corrected the problem.

We may have attempted to speak, to try to sort things out, to clear the air of any possible misunderstandings, to apologize for any known mistakes, to appeal to their softer side, to defend our intentions and actions and perhaps even to make a joke of it. But at some point, we can be so confounded by unrelenting obduracy that our internal resources dry up. The power difference between us only confirms that there is no point in trying anything more. We long for a mediator, someone who *will* listen to us, and who has greater power to act than we have. But if one attempt to mediate fails (like the Israelite foremen in the Exodus story) it may be difficult for us to put our hope in another.

God knows the kind of leader that this Pharaoh is. He knows there is no chance of him relenting and showing kindness to his slaves, for he has already objectified them as potential threats. So the issue needs to be brought to a head. Pharaoh's harsh heart will be hardened by God to show it for what it is (Exod 7:3). This is not a matter of God making a soft or a neutral heart hard. Pharaoh's heart has been shown by his behavior to be consistently hard. But now God will use his powers to expose the degree of this hardness. It will become abundantly clear that Pharaoh will never really listen to Moses or consider the needs of anyone apart from himself. God will show that his power is greater than that of this god-king Pharaoh.

Eventually everyone—both Israelites and Egyptians—will see who the real Lord is. And God will see to it that the Israelites are released, and Pharaoh is judged.

FINDING A WAY OUT

Ten temporary plagues, brought on by God, demonstrate that God's power is greater than that of the Egyptian gods. But they are more than a point-for-point display of superior power. They also provide an opportunity for Pharaoh to think, reflect, even turn away from his stubborn harshness. After all, we do hear of others who change and, even though there don't seem to be any signs of hope, he is, even at this point, given several chances.

After the plague of frogs (Exod 8:19) Pharaoh is sufficiently concerned to ask Moses and Aaron to pray that the Lord might take the frogs away from him and his people. He even promises to let the people go, and God answers the prayer. This is the first ray of hope. But then his relief reverts to his hard-hearted position against the Israelites, and the hope is dashed. The same pattern repeats itself after the plague of flies. Then twice (after hailstones and locusts) Pharaoh appears to relent. Perhaps the patience exercised by Moses and God have paid off. He even acknowledges that he was in the wrong. Moses prays again and the prayers are answered. Surely now Pharaoh will climb down from his pedestal of arrogance. However, he returns to his hard-hearted position yet again. He even goes so far as to command Moses never to appear before him again. If he does, he will die. This is now the last straw.

What else might God do to allow the Israelites to be released? With what appears to be great reluctance, the decision to give Pharaoh some of his own medicine is made. The one who had killed Israelite baby boys will experience the same loss among his own people. This principle came to be known as "an eye for an eye, a tooth for a tooth." It is horrifying to read that God used his leadership position to kill—and to kill innocent babies. Yet it is a carefully constructed last-resort punishment that will not exceed what the Pharaoh has done to others. What is more, it comes not as a first point of retaliation but only after other attempts have been tried and opportunities have been given for Pharaoh to relent. Even with this final, horrifying plague, there is a way to avoid it.

The way is costly. God asks them to give an innocent lamb (Exod 12). It won't be just any lamb, but one that they know. Each family is to choose the best lamb from their own flocks, and have it live with them for four days. I imagine the children giving it a name, feeding it and patting it, playing games with it, delighting in it. Then, on the fourth day, they are to kill it! They must eat it quickly and put some of its blood around their doorways. Then escape! The angel of death will kill all firstborn sons except those of the houses with this blood.

We discover later in the biblical story that some Egyptians become part of the Israelite group. I wonder if they also might have killed a lamb and placed some of its blood around their doors. It seems that some do respect the God of the Israelites enough to escape with them. There may also be some Israelites who think this whole threat of an angel of death is rather ludicrous and suffer the consequences. So, it is not a matter of drawing clean, racial lines here—there is choice. Presumably, even Pharaoh can choose to sprinkle the blood of one of his lambs around his doors. But he does not. Obedience to this command for a blood sacrifice will mark a difference between those who follow the God who is speaking and those who follow the gods of Egypt. This event marks both death and deliverance.

I wish that deliverance could always be bloodless and without any form of violence. But in order to save innocent victims in the clutches of hardened terrorists, it is, unfortunately, not always possible. Salvation and judgment can appear as two sides of the same coin. Salvation in times of war may involve the killing of enemy captors. Even leaving a job under a hardened narcissistic boss will have its costs—perhaps loss of income, perhaps loss of aspirations, perhaps loss of friendships, perhaps a smear campaign. Getting free involves loss in order to discover new gains.

THREAT DEFEATED!

God is now the recognized leader of the Israelite people. He does not lead them by the shortest route because, if they face war, they may change their minds and return to Egypt (Exod 13:17). He considers the vulnerability of the people and protects them from their own weakness. He also gives them symbols of his leadership: a pillar of cloud going before them during the day and a pillar of fire at night. The people are in unfamiliar territory so they need a guide. However, they are initially led on what appears to be a wild goose chase, apparently to confuse Pharaoh.

Signaling that their difficulties are not yet over, God warns Moses that Pharaoh will pursue them. Here again we find the strange expression that God will harden Pharaoh's heart. The effect is to make his relentless rebellion more obvious. The result will be to bring about a showdown between the forces of God and the forces of God's opponent.

The people with Moses are understandably terrified. With a sea in front and a ferocious army behind them there is nowhere for them to go. They begin to complain to Moses, accusing him of bringing them out into the wilderness to die. Moses addresses their fears: "Do not be afraid. Stand firm and you will see the deliverance the Lord will bring you today. . . The Lord will fight for you; you need only to be still" (Exod 14:13). There is no time to lose, and Moses has a strange action to perform. He can't save them, but he must cooperate with the one who can save them. In an act of obedience to his Leader's command, he stretches out his hand over the sea and the people must stand and wait. Then God acts: he brings a strong wind to turn the sea bed into dry land.

The Israelites cross in safety, but as the sea returns the Egyptians who pursue them are plunged into confusion, disablement and death by drowning. Yet at least some, in the process, recognize that God is fighting for the Israelites against Egypt and they even suggest that they stop their pursuit (Exod 14:25). Even now they can withdraw. But they don't—and they lose their lives as a consequence.

I suspect that only those who have experienced some kind of dramatic liberation from the fear of death can understand the depth of the relief expressed in the jubilant song of Exodus 15. I remember talking to a man who, as a child in a time of war, was left fatherless, without food, and at a very high risk of being killed by the enemy. All he could do was to pray. I felt his palpable, huge relief as he spoke of a military truck coming out of the blue, without being told of his plight, and driving him to safety.

Up until now, in our Exodus story, the enemy, represented chiefly by Pharaoh, has appeared to have ultimate power over the lives of the Israelites. But now that power is broken. Seeing the enemy armies drown in front of them does not evoke some kind of sadistic pleasure in the distress and demise of others. It is simply astonishment that their God is so powerful that he can totally vanquish all of that harsh and evil power, and amazement that they have escaped from it. There is, in this transaction, a sudden removal of the most dominant leader in their experience to date, and a claim to leadership being asserted by the one who has acted on their behalf: God.

GOD IS NOT A NARCISSIST!

The contrast between the harsh, narcissistic and even sadistic leadership of Pharaoh and the leadership of God is made clear, and we need to allow our hearts and minds to absorb the difference. We have too many examples of human leadership that have a little or a lot in common with Pharaoh. Some of these are even inside our churches and synagogues. Unfortunately, we can unconsciously transfer images of harsh human leadership onto our image of God's leadership and become confused about God's character. Once we separate these two contrasting types of leadership, we will be wise to look intentionally towards the one who is NOT a narcissist, but who stands against narcissistic cruelty—the one who listens and who liberates. That one is God the Leader.

QUESTIONS FOR REFLECTION OR DISCUSSION

1. What contrasts between the leadership of God and the leadership of Pharaoh stand out to you?
2. Have you ever experienced harsh leadership?
3. When is it appropriate to withhold obedience to an authorized leader? When is it not?
4. How might we approach a leader who is overbearing?
5. To what extent has your concept of leadership been (mis)shaped by poor leaders?
6. "Getting free from oppression may involve loss in order to discover new gains." Do you have any experience of this, or know someone who has this kind of experience?

Chapter 5

Under New Leadership

Although the Israelites now have some experience of God's dramatic rescue from a cruel overlord, it will take some time for them to learn how to live under God's very different kind of leadership. Moses is the dominant human leader but he stands under God, is appointed by God, and must only speak and do as God commands. He is permitted and encouraged to express to God his thoughts and feelings, but he is not the ultimate leader.

When we begin to work under a new boss, we may know something about him or her, but it will take time to understand and adjust to their style and expectations. We initially bring our hopes and our fears from our previous experience, and soon find that they may not fit under a new leader. We begin our journey with God with some knowledge of God's character, but it takes a lifetime to discover how his kind of leadership differs from that which we know from other sources. Along the way our assumptions about leaders can be unwittingly misapplied to God as he turns out not to be quite like any other human leader we have known.

Perhaps those who have been brought out from powers of terrorism or addiction or abandonment understand this process the best. I remember that, when I was teaching in a prison, one young woman interrupted the class because she felt compelled to tell me her story before the whole group. She spoke of a God-encounter at the moment before she was about to commit suicide, several years earlier, while serving a long sentence in prison. She was saved from death but had no idea how to live. Who was this God who intervened? She began to learn. As one who had been in bondage to drugs and crime she needed a lot of help. She saw the miraculous power of

God heal her arm. She felt God's power in radically changing her focus from being self-centered to being God-centered and concerned for others. In her deliverance from severe self-absorption, she became an effective and much-loved counselor of other prisoners. The other women in the class confirmed the positive changes they had seen in her. Even the prison authorities recognized the profundity of her transformation and released her early.

The people in our Exodus story move from being under one very powerful leader to another even more powerful leader. But this time they begin to see that the power is used *for* them instead of *against* them. Pharaoh used his power to meet his own perceived needs, but now God's power is used to meet the real needs of the people.

God as Leader in this biblical Exodus is not averse to displaying his unusual and sometimes spectacular power, like parting the sea, eliminating the aggressors, appearing as fire in a bush that remains unaffected by it, putting on a fireworks display on top of Mt Sinai, providing miraculous nourishment from empty places, and preserving clothing and footwear long past their use-by date. Throughout the journey his presence remains obvious in the cloud and the fire. He is an ever-present, upfront leader. His words, delivered through Moses, command attention.

These people are in a crisis of upheaval of tremendous proportions and are absolutely reliant on leadership that must show them and tell them, in no uncertain terms, where they must go. It bears some analogy to sailors in earlier days, before modern communication systems, being utterly dependent on the captain for their lives, direction, and wellbeing. One of my nineteenth-century ancestors was such a captain. James Robinson's published reminiscences[1] provides fascinating insights into his leadership character, concerns and decisions over a long life at sea. In today's world of specializations, it is difficult to imagine having one generalist leader who skillfully navigates through unchartered waters in harsh, remote regions, repairs damage to any parts of the ship, sources and manages food supplies for all the people on board, makes all financial decisions, ensures the safekeeping of cargo, maintains hope in long periods of isolation from human contact, quells mutinies when crew risk their lives in rebellion, delivers babies in Antarctic regions (his wife and young children often came with him, and his children bore the names of the remote places of their births), serves as medic in all cases of sickness (even amputating body parts without anesthetic when need arose), and acts as chaplain, offering prayers onboard and services for those who have died.

---

1. Robinson, *Captain Robinson*.

God's leadership is generalist. We sometimes latch onto one aspect of God's character, turn it into an abstraction, then speculate how that might work. Our neatly theorized caricatures of God and his leadership risk becoming very wide of the mark and quite inaccurate. We need, rather, to journey with the Exodus people, who learnt through personal experience, not through abstractions. Captain Robinson's leadership could really be understood only by those who journeyed under him. The quality of one's leadership is tested most acutely when difficulties and needs arise. The character and capacity of the leader are of profound importance.

The Israelites have no means to know where to go and no means to provide for their needs. At other points in the bigger story of God's leadership of his people he seems hidden, perhaps silent, or at least perplexing. But God the Leader chooses the mode of leadership that is most needed for the people at a particular time. And right now, in this story, his mode of leadership is that of a commanding, powerful, and provisioning presence, just as Captain Robinson needed to be obviously upfront and in charge, in order to keep everyone on board safe.

SOME COMPARISONS BETWEEN PHARAOH AND GOD AS LEADERS

If we compare Pharaoh and God as leaders we find sharp differences in their concern to provide for people's needs, in their attitude to working conditions, and in the ways in which they express displeasure.

Provisions

The difference in attitude is striking. Pharaoh deliberately withholds provisions that are essential to the work he demands from the Israelites. God as Leader provides food and drink along the way and does not demand deprivation of the people in order to fulfill his requests. This point is obvious in the story. Yet its application to Christian leadership is not always so obvious. While any decent leader would not dream of committing the sort of outright cruelty that Pharaoh committed, more subtle neglect of provisions, when provisions are available, can easily drift towards the Pharaoh pattern of leadership.

I remember a non-musical church leader who moved the piano away from the light source and away from the other musicians. I was to play that piano in the evening service with a team of singers and other musicians. In the rehearsal I requested that the piano be put back as I could not read the music for the new songs in the dark and could not see the signals from the worship leader or hear the other musicians with whom I wanted to work as a team. He knew about my hearing loss. The church leader adamantly and angrily refused and gave a reason that had no real substance at all, apart from trying to demonstrate that he was in the position of power.

Perhaps he feared being too soft and pandering to people's unnecessary wants, without listening sufficiently to the expression of a legitimate need. Sometimes human leaders can falsely assume they are a little more like God in the power that they should wield and ironically become a little more like Pharaoh in their withholding of legitimate provisions.

Work

Both leaders, Pharaoh and God, engage the people in work. But there are distinct differences in how this work is to be carried out. Work demands under Pharaoh are harsh and relentless with inadequate provision of necessary tools; the productivity requirements are intentionally impossible to fulfill. God as leader, in contrast, provides a sabbath, one day in seven for rest and recuperation from their work duties. Work is not to occupy the whole of their lives. Manna is to be gathered on six days only, with God miraculously preserving the food on the sixth day so that it does not go bad and can be eaten on the seventh. Everyone—men, women and children—gets an opportunity to be refreshed. It seems that God even works with his people to ensure that their labor for food is made satisfying.

Both leaders call for building projects that require significant cost. Pharaoh wants to create store cities for himself, and so the Israelites are forced to do his bidding. The narrator implies that the Israelites are not in the running to receive any acknowledgement of their labor or any share in its provisions. These cities are to bring credit and usefulness to Pharaoh alone.

The building project in the desert is the tabernacle. Israelites are invited to bring offerings of materials, as much as each chooses to give (Exod 25:2-3). Most of these materials have already been donated by wealthy Egyptians (Exod 12:35-36), but still each family is given choice over what they will keep and what they give. Being given a choice is new! Work is needed to take the raw materials and craft them carefully into items of beauty and utility. The workers are graced with wisdom (Exod 28:3) and the Spirit (Exod 31:2-6; 35:35) from God himself. Their skills are valued and the workers are honored. The community is called to work together for something which will benefit the community.

Both God and Pharaoh may seem, at first glance, to desire glory for themselves. But closer reading makes the differences clear. Pharaoh seeks to obtain glory through oppression of others in order to exalt his own name, and his glory does not seek the wellbeing of his people. Even Moses defers to him and lets Pharaoh set times for Moses to pray for him (Exod 8:9). Pharaoh presupposes that his position of honor gives him the right to take choices away from others, and even to quash the needs of others. It requires nothing from him, in terms of character or integrity, and demands everything from his subjects. In fact, his glory is empty. There is nothing to be admired or emulated. He leaves the story drowned in the waters of anger and self-pity.

God's glory is demonstrated in works of provision and power for the wellbeing of the people (Exod 16:7, 10), in awe-inspiring revelation that invites the people to trust him (Exod 24:16), and in the consecration of a place for him to dwell in the midst of his people (Exod 29:43 and 40:34, 35). His glory is made known after he has listened to the cries and groans of his people. His glory is not predatory; it does not feed off the people as Pharaoh's does. Rather, it gives to the people. Moses' face shines after every encounter with some measure of God's glory. Aaron is to be given glory as he is made beautiful by the majestic robes of his undeserved priesthood (Exod 28:2, 40). An ordinary place is elevated to a special and holy place when God's glory inhabits it. God's glory attracts but also bestows something good wherever it touches.

Working for a leader can be satisfying or torturous. Although neither Pharaoh nor God regards laziness as an option, God's work is measured, bounded and attainable. Some people put themselves in an unnecessarily difficult position when they think that working themselves into a frenzy, supposedly for God, is what is required. This is a misperception. God, as a boss, does not operate in the same relentless way that Pharaoh did.

Anger

Both Pharaoh and God display anger. Both are displeased when the people below them rebel against their orders. So, is there any difference? Anger is often a symptom of a goal being thwarted. Pharaoh's primary goal is to diminish the Israelites; God's primary goal is to enable the Israelites to thrive. Pharaoh's anger over a request for time out for his workers may, in another context where it is simply a work avoidance tactic, be legitimate. But the people have already worked far more hours, and under totally unreasonable conditions, than could normally be expected. This is not an issue of work avoidance.

God's anger is aroused when the people grumble against him and against Moses. Yet each time that he is asked directly to provide for their needs, he obliges. This suggests that the anger relates to their grumbling in resentment rather than asking for their needs. Outright rebellion against Moses on account of envy leads to various punishments: temporary leprosy for Miriam (Num 12) and death for Korah and his followers (Num 16). It is noteworthy that differences in the severity of the punishment show careful discernment on God's part between those who would respond positively to milder but significant reprimands, those who needed firmer treatment, and those whose attitudes are fixed and incapable of change.

Perhaps the strongest display of anger from God the Leader occurs in the Golden Calf incident (Exod 32). Prior to this episode, the special relationship between God and his people is affirmed in Exodus 24. Then a select group, including Moses and Aaron, experience a wondrous sight. God himself appears, and this group eats and drinks in his presence. Moses goes further up the mountain and leaves Aaron and Hur in charge. While Moses is absent, the people and Aaron ostensibly abandon God as leader, on the pretext that Moses may have abandoned them. This clear rebellion against God's leadership leads to revelry, idolatry and lies. God's fierce anger is aroused because they have become "a stiff-necked people." They have become hard-hearted, harsh and arrogant, more like Pharaoh than God. Although he expresses enough anger to kill them, he shortly afterwards is ready to show forgiveness (Exod 34). God's anger emerges when his goal to bring them to a new life of freedom from slavery (Exod 20:2) is thwarted.

Anger is a delicate and difficult issue. Many of us have been taught that all anger is wrong, because we see too many harmful effects. It has now become more common to say that anger is an acceptable emotion so long as it is expressed in ways that bring no harm. There are also different attitudes regarding when and how a leader might express anger. Some accept any amount of unbridled anger from a leader but none from anyone else. I once met a leader who shouted very loudly while thumping the table, "I do *not* get angry!" The Bible does not cater to idealists who would like to deny the full range of human emotions, including the more difficult emotions. So, anger is attributed to God as leader, just as it is attributed to Pharaoh as leader. But the causes of the anger are not the same, primarily because the nature of the relationship between leader and people is not the same. Pharaoh's anger becomes sadistic and unremitting, while God's anger is controlled and limited.

COMMUNICATIONS WITH GOD

Throughout the long journey in which the people are led by God through the wilderness there emerges another distinctive difference. It is between the direct speech of Moses in his communication to God and the avoidance, by the people, of any direct confrontation with God.

Of the whole group wandering in the desert, there is only one man who has not experienced Pharaoh's leadership in Egypt from the perspective of being a slave. That person is Moses. The slaves discovered that it was pointless to go directly to Pharaoh, or even to his slave masters. They had no experience of Pharaoh being even remotely interested in their daily lives, their difficulties, or even their potential suggestions of helpful improvements for the people of Egypt. Their ability to speak had been frozen out of them. Although they are initially very grateful to God for taking them out of bondage, it is a much more difficult transition to work out how to relate to and communicate with this new leader. Throughout the long journey they never feel able to speak directly to him. Sometimes they have enough courage to ask Moses to speak for them, and when he does, God answers promptly. Mostly they merely grumble about God to each other. That is the most they could do under Pharaoh, and it is difficult to even begin to understand that this new leader accepts and even invites direct speech to himself.

Moses, on the other hand, has grown up free. I like to imagine that he may have even jumped up onto the lap of his adopted grandfather Pharaoh and asked for a story. He may have been granted the privilege of walking right past the guards when others needed to show good reason to be given access. He was at home in the world of pharaohs and courts and kings. Admittedly, he has been out of that world for quite some time and has lost confidence. But the memory of open conversation with people in leadership places him in an advantageous position in speaking with this powerful leader, God. And God never objects to his direct and even challenging conversation.

Recalling the candid exchanges at the Burning Bush (Exod 3) we see that God the Leader is willing to answer any reasonable questions from Moses. Moses doubts that he can fulfill the task of leading the Israelites, but God assures Moses that he will not go alone—he will go in partnership with God. Moses asks what he will say to the Israelites to convince them that he is appointed by God. God gives him some particular signs, involving miraculous power, that he can use. Moses protests that he cannot speak eloquently, but God says he will help him to speak. The one time when God displays anger is when Moses gives up and says he won't go (Exod 4:13).

However, God perceives the problem and offers to send his brother Aaron to speak for him.

Throughout the journey Moses builds on this foundation of candid speech and wrestles verbally with God frequently. He persuades God to change his mind (Exod 32:11–14); he asks for help when he reaches his limits (Exod 33:12—34:9); he asks why God has brought so much trouble on him through these difficult people (Num 11:10–15). There is no rebuke. God the Leader welcomes those working with him to engage in honest, even brutally frank, conversation with him. Now that is different from Pharaoh!

When I was in high school a new principal arrived. She was, to some people's minds, a little eccentric. She was certainly different from our previous principal. One of the striking features of her leadership was that she publicly invited any of us students to come to her with any ideas that could help to change the school for the better. I took her up on it, with some fear and trepidation, not quite knowing whether she was serious. Often a friend and I would go directly to her office with yet another bright idea. She repeatedly told us not to go to the secretary—the guardian of her office—as we would be stopped, but to go directly to her. When I recall how many stupid ideas she patiently and encouragingly listened to, I am somewhat embarrassed. I knew, deep down, that many of our ideas were immature and foolish. I never cared if she implemented them or not, because I knew that she had listened, and was fully committed to the wellbeing of all the students. I trusted her to sift out the gold from the junk. But occasionally we hit the jackpot with the seedling of a good idea. She was able to take those seedlings and transform them into projects that could benefit the school in a major way. I am thankful that she showed me a glimpse of how a human can emulate the leadership of God rather than the leadership of Pharaoh.

COVENANT

God takes the initiative to affirm the historical relationship between himself and the Israelite people by confirming a covenant (Exod 24). It was not the first covenant that God made with this people, but now there is a new generation and a fresh start in their relationship. This covenant reminds them (and us) of national treaties made between superior and subordinate nations, setting out obligations for both. But it also reminds them (and us) of a marriage covenant between a bridegroom and bride, a covenant where love and commitment are mutually given and received. God the Leader has already demonstrated his commitment to care for these people. He has already rescued them from Egypt, out of the land of slavery (Exod 20:2).

Pharaoh's grip of fear has gone. God's leadership is now firmly established through means that involves both parties. Under Pharaoh, the only person who ever expressed his view was Pharaoh. Under God, the covenant establishes reciprocity of relationship. Now obedience is not forced but voluntary. The kind of candid, reciprocal communication that we have seen between God and Moses is desirable between God and each of his people. The blood from animal sacrifices is shared between an altar (representing God) and the people (Exod 24:6–8). The members of this covenant are like blood brothers—they are family.

A large number of the elders of Israel see a vision of God, and they experience a scene of astounding beauty (Exod 24:9–11). God and his surroundings are enjoyed. Eating and drinking together in such amazing closeness to God reinforces the idea of family, the memory of fellowship offerings, the sheer delight of enjoying each other's company. Covenant with God looks more like an ideal relationship with an adored father. It looks like true friendship.

However, we see these ideals shattered when a false god, a golden calf, is erected and worshiped (Exod 32). But we discover that the justifiable anger of God is not the end of the story. A process of putting things right, restoring the relationship, and forgiveness (Exod 33 and 34) demonstrates that God, even in his anger, is not at all like the hard-hearted, narcissistic Pharaoh!

QUESTIONS FOR REFLECTION OR DISCUSSION

1. What aspects of God's leadership did you particularly notice in this chapter?
2. How is God not like common misconceptions of him?
3. Is it ever acceptable for a leader to show anger? What are the limits?
4. Have you ever experienced God's dramatic intervention on your behalf?
5. What degree of power do you have as a leader, and how do you use it?
6. Do you feel comfortable speaking to God as Moses did?

PART 2

The Ten Words of the Leader

Chapter 6

Worship

I was once called to mediate between two groups within the one community who were in heated debate about which rules they should follow. According to one group, the decision should be made according to the rules that a respected leader had laid down. According to the other group, the decision should be made according to the rules which a more recent national committee had made. The leaders which each group followed did not agree in this matter. The particular issue at stake was not one of the highest order, but it did demonstrate that both groups expected their leaders to set rules, and their duty was to keep those rules.

Rules are not the favorite topic of conversation or meditation for most people. Many try to wipe the slate clean and live without rules. I have seen this tactic tried in classrooms. Sooner or later chaos ensues. The aim of the teacher is to help the students to discover that rules are needed through their dissatisfaction with the alternative: chaos. So, the group discovers the need for one rule, and later another rule, and then two or three or more.

Some people like to boil the Christian message down to one Golden Rule: "Do unto others as you would have them do unto you." But what, exactly, does such a general statement mean when it is translated into everyday life? Sooner or later teachers and parents and governments and charitable organizations find that rules need to be added—not to go against the Golden Rule, but to spell out what it means in practice. This entails defining the boundaries sufficiently clearly to help people to understand what it does and does not mean in their context. If there are no defined boundaries, many people will almost inevitably be cheated, hurt, beaten, stolen from, abused and perhaps murdered.

Leaders are inevitably involved in setting some rules and in enforcing some rules. God does engage in making rules as part of his role as leader. So it is instructive to see what kinds of rules he makes, and to think about their purposes and applications.

Some misinformed people think that the Old Testament is mostly about rules, and archaic ones at that! Not so. The giving of rules occupies only a minor proportion of the big narrative. Later prophets seek to turn people back to the most essential rules, after people have got themselves into a mess. But the Old Testament has a rich variety of types of literature, at the core of which is a living, vital and dynamic relationship between God the Leader and his people. Laws are servants of this relationship, not masters.

The rules or laws in the Old Testament are given in summary form as what is popularly known as the Ten Commandments. In Hebrew, these are simply called the Ten Words. They are communications of great importance, principles that can easily be remembered on the fingers of two hands as guidance for life. However, each of these commandments is intended to remind people of any other instructions that relate to each of these ten areas.

We will look at each commandment, or, in the first case, a pair of commandments. Then we will look at some of the other laws that relate to and expand on different aspects of these ten. Many are case laws, where examples of specific violations and specific punishments are given in Exodus, Leviticus, Numbers and Deuteronomy. Reading these further cases in conjunction with Jesus' teaching in Matthew 5 shows us that the principles in the Ten Commandments are not to be confined by narrowly legalistic interpretations, but are to be taken as umbrella principles that include or refer to a wide range of related issues. While the Old Testament spells out regulations for outward behavior, Jesus later, in the New Testament, adds more stringent applications to the inner thought life.

We have seen that God the Leader acts for the salvation and liberation of his people, so that they may walk in freedom and away from slavery. He does not begin to give any rules until the people have experienced enough of God's character to be able to trust his intentions. Then they can place the rules in the context of their already established and covenanted relationship with him.

And so, before setting out his Ten Commandments, we are told, "God spoke all these words: I am the Lord your God, who brought you out of Egypt, out of the land of slavery" (Exod 20:1, 2). This statement and the rules must be read together: God is the one who has already gone to the trouble of liberating them from slavery. Because he understands human weaknesses, he is giving these particular rules to help the people to stay away from other potential forms of slavery. His purpose is that the people should stay free! It is in this context that the famous Ten Commandments are given.

COMMANDMENTS ONE AND TWO: WORSHIP GOD ALONE

The first two commandments (Exod 20:3-6) concern who or what the people allow to lead them.[1]

> 1. You shall have no other gods before me.
> 2. You shall not make for yourself an idol in the form of anything in heaven above or on the earth beneath or in the waters below. You shall not bow down to them or worship them, for I, the Lord your God, am a jealous God, punishing the children for the sin of the fathers to the third and fourth generation of those who hate me, but showing love to a thousand generations of those who love me and keep my commandments.

God the Leader first establishes the requirement that the people should not try to follow other gods instead of him. Is this because God feels very insecure about his own position and doesn't want to lose his control over these people? For some human leaders that would certainly be the case, as it was for Pharaoh. But God is not like Pharaoh! Rather, he knows that following other gods will inevitably lead the people into deception, which, in turn, brings various kinds of slavery.

The second commandment concerns following created things, whether they are natural or formed into a particular image by humans. Even over-reliance on good things that God has created, distorts wholesome order in the world. If we attribute leadership to any other supposed being in the heavenly realm, or to any entity or being in the created world, that leadership will inevitably fail us, because it does not have the capability of God the Creator. God is large enough, gracious enough, and generous enough to receive worship and enlarge the heart-space for freedom at the same time. Lesser beings cramp it.

No human leader or leadership group has the right to demand absolute obedience and absolute loyalty. Even if we have rescued some people from slavery, from abuse or from the risk of being killed, we may not presume to

---

[1]. I will follow the numbering normally used, based on the account in Ex 20:2-17, as there are minor differences in the account in Deut 5:6-21. The commandments are quoted from the account in Exodus.

take over the role of supreme leadership in their lives, as it belongs to God alone. If we do, we run the risk of placing ourselves in the position of "idol" for that person, and that can get in the way of their coming to a fuller freedom. It will stunt their growth, and give them a new, but false, dependence. This needs to be seriously considered for any of us in a helping profession or having a "rescuing" or even "caring" mindset. That is not to say that we prematurely send vulnerable people out on their own, but we do need to consider the appropriate boundary between helping and hindering.

Unfortunately, I have been in a church where the leaders did take too much authority on themselves. They thought they were the sole interpreters of what God thought and they presumed that it was their rightful position to direct people in details of their lives that had no reference to ethical or moral issues, including who they may and may not speak with, and where they may and may not live. The level of control that they exercised became extreme. Their dreams of creating a more perfect church crashed because they were ill-equipped to handle the load of their ill-conceived and pompous version of leadership. Along the way they excommunicated anyone who thought or did something unexpected—not wrong or bad, but unexpected. To their credit they ate humble pie many years later, apologized to their victims, and backed down from their arrogance.

Another important aspect of worshipping God is giving. This suggests that God delights in the gifts of his people, however imperfect they might be. I think of a mother I knew, a woman who must be obeyed. Whenever her young children made her gifts out of paper for birthdays and Christmas, she immediately ripped them apart, exclaiming loudly and repeatedly that they were worth nothing. As time went on, her children tried to buy small gifts that they really thought she would like. She found fault with every one of these gifts and demanded that they be taken back to the shop. Yet she also demanded that her children continue to give her gifts on these occasions—gifts that she never actually received. Sadly, she never saw the love in the hearts of her children. She never received their childish desires to please nor their adult attempts to show her kindness. I am so glad that God invites and receives our gifts. He sees our hearts and treasures our offerings. The call to worship is not a call that demands perfection.

The section about punishing children to the third and fourth generations worries many people. We have a tendency to be drawn to this unpalatable threat and ignore the following part concerning love to a thousand generations. The threatening words are intended to be a deterrent against becoming ensnared in ways that will have a negative impact on one's children, grandchildren, and even possibly great-grandchildren and beyond. We know that one person's alcohol abuse does not just affect that individual, but there is always a negative impact on others who are closest. Children suffer, and so can grandchildren. It is not uncommon to see several generations caught in a trap that is difficult to escape from. The same can happen with any serious behavior problem. This is not a curse that God is applying, but a sober consideration of impact. There is, however, always a way out. If one person stands against the family pattern, and turns to God sincerely asking for his help, the legacy can be broken, and the richness of God's love can be found. There are many examples of individuals in the Old Testament, and today, who do just that. God the Leader warns strongly, but if we read the story carefully, we find his forgiveness being offered readily to any who turn back to him.

CREATIVE PLANS FOR WORSHIP

The details of the tabernacle and the furniture and fittings for this worship tent may not, at first sight, appear to relate to the Ten Commandments. But these matters do relate to the first two commandments. Even though we are no longer in that particular context and do not need to follow the details of these instructions, we can learn a lot about God the Leader by taking time to go through the instructions in these areas carefully.

The narrative of Exodus gives considerable space to how God directs acceptable worship: to the materials, colors, and decorative motifs on items used in worship, to the appointment of specific personnel for particular duties in worship, and to the needs and behaviors of people as they come to worship. Within the freedom given to these people to be engaged in a truly interpersonal relationship with God there are directions given for keeping and restoring that relationship. There are also boundaries in worship: boundaries of design, place, personnel and practices.

In Exodus 25–30 and 35–40 many of the tabernacle design details are spelled out. I confess to having often skipped over these details, as they seemed tedious and irrelevant to my life thousands of years later. However, I was once asked to speak in a church for their annual Temple Day (something I had never heard of before). I became curious about what the temple and its predecessor the tabernacle (the version detailed in Exodus) might have looked like. It was before the days of being able to find pictures on the internet, so I decided to make a model of the temple. For the first time, I studied the details of both the tabernacle and the later temple which followed a similar pattern (1 Kings 5–7; 2 Chr 3–4) and began to be absorbed in the details. I found that God was surprisingly artistic! I was amazed that he was so interested in details of color and cloth! My reading led me to reflect on his care for the details of the lives of his people, and for the details of my life. Perhaps the details in the tabernacle design were to encourage people to engage with God concerning details in their lives.

But it was only when I tried to make my model that I discovered there is still considerable room for human creativity in carrying out the design. In some respects, the instructions are not detailed enough! I understand why different artists and sculptors, following these instructions precisely, do not end up with exactly the same image. It is similar to being in an art class where the instructor gives the colors and motifs to be used. I have seen, from experience, that no two results are alike! The range of creative imagination and expression can be staggering. Worship would, like the making of the tabernacle or temple, require connection between God as leader and humans as followers in such a way that both leader and follower contribute to the expression of that relationship. God the Leader outlines the big picture and invites us to work with him in making human-influenced details of beauty. Bezalel is the man appointed to head up the team who execute the design, not only because he has expertise in craftsmanship but also because he has been filled with the Spirit of God (Exod 31:1–11 and 35:30—39:31). God the creator invites us, whom he has made in his image, to use our God-given creative imagination and skill as we approach him.

A few years ago I asked a class I taught in India to create a drama on the book of Ecclesiastes. At first, some were shocked. Most of these students had no experience in creative drama. I wanted the drama to speak to nationals of their country and to connect themes from the book with issues in their land, so I was obviously not the person to create the drama. They were the ones with local knowledge and untapped gifts. But they needed help to begin, and they needed some framework. That is where my leadership came in. As leader, I began the process of imagining. I then heard ideas and gave some basic direction. Then I gave them a time framework for creating the drama, rehearsing it, and performing it. I formed the class into subgroups to work on specific sections. Soon we had a production that amazed the community. It had all the marks of local humor, color, and costume. Who could have written this? Certainly not me. The answer was not at first believed—it was, indeed, all of us. Leadership is required to help people to begin a difficult-to-imagine project, to provide sufficient directions to enable the imagination and skill of others to be aroused, and to know when to hand over to others to do what the leader cannot or should not do.

PICTURING GOD'S PRESENCE

Motifs based on plants and cherubs (a kind of angelic being) abound in the tabernacle (Exod 25, 26, 30), and will become even more prominent in the gold-covered walls of the future temple. Imagery of nature, in particular of flourishing gardens, is reminiscent of the Garden of Eden and invites thoughts of life and hope. Motifs of destruction and death are ruled out. Representations of angels bring the spheres of heaven and earth together. The transition from life outside the tabernacle into the inner sanctum where God's holy presence is symbolized, is signified by the different values of metals used along the way: bronze is replaced by silver, then finally by the most precious metal, gold. Offerings of sweet fragrances representing prayer are given a welcome reception by their divine leader.

This tabernacle, or portable worship tent, says a lot about God's leadership being integrally related to his presence. He does not lead from afar, from some ivory tower, as many leaders and governments do, admittedly often by necessity. He is not a distant bureaucrat. In some ways, the image here more closely resembles a village leader who knows the names, the characteristics and the histories of every person in the village. It resembles a pastor of a small church who is part of every individual's triumphs and tragedies. In our age of bigger businesses, larger areas of government jurisdiction and mega-churches, we can easily be deceived into thinking that God's leadership is at least as distant as the leadership of those organizations. The tabernacle, right in the midst of the people, shows us that it is not.

Yet, this leader who is close, who knows the daily journeys of the people, may not be presumed upon. He can rightly claim a level of holiness that humans may not. It is the more remarkable that this leader, who has a perfect right to run the universe from a concealed, lofty, distant sphere, chooses to make his presence known through a homely tent. Yes, it is a carefully designed tent, intended to communicate many things, but a tent that is made of materials similar to those of the tents lived in by ordinary people. The garden motifs remind people that following this leader brings the best of life's fruits and a hope-filled life touched by the resources of heaven.

MEETING THE HIDDEN LEADER

A heavy curtain separates the realm of human worship activities from the inner sanctum. Although the presence of God is known in often obvious and dramatic expressions throughout the Exodus narrative, the tabernacle design also suggests that God is, in his inner workings, hidden. He invites relationship, but there is a barrier between his realm and the human realm. This barrier will need to be addressed, again and again. Yet there is hope. Right in the center of the inner sanctum is a special box, called the ark. Not only is it magnificently overlaid with gold, but it has two golden angels (cherubs), with wings spread outward and upward, joined onto the cover of the ark. Here, in a resplendent image of royal leadership, God indicates that his throne is not a place of isolation but of meeting and communication. He says, "There, above the cover between the two cherubim that are over the ark of the covenant, I will meet with you and give you all my commands for the Israelites" (Exod 25:22).

The tension between the approachability of God and the unapproachability of God (represented by the curtain) is built into the symbolism, yet this symbolism offers clear hope that meeting is possible. Leaders everywhere create, and need to create, lines of time and space between approachability and unapproachability. Yet, too often these lines are drawn on the basis of games relating to ego and power, pretense, deception and suspicion. In this narrative I see, rather, lines based on truth and reality, on the genuine needs of people and the genuine requirements of God. These lines are designed to foster healthy and honest relationship.

THIS LEADER HAS NO FAVORITES

The placement of the tabernacle is important. It is not located within just one tribe but is placed right in the middle of all of the tribes of Israel (Num 2:1). As the group travels, the tent is packed up and moved with them, to be set up again in the midst of the people in their next location. This placement excludes the idea that any tribe has special access to God. He is leader of all and will not show favoritism to any of the Israelite tribes.

I have often spent part of each year teaching in India, where the influence of the caste system is still prevalent. A very good college where I have taught has a wise egalitarian policy which, in that context, is countercultural. Rules are set to reinforce that policy. They include a prohibition of meetings of caste-based subgroups. The placement of the tabernacle speaks against the elevation of one tribe or one caste. All worshippers are to have equal access to this leader.

The tabernacle is placed inside the camp, not outside, where it would be disconnected from daily life. What the people say to God and to the priests is within the context of normal life. The checks and balances of witnesses who know each other in their human activities and relationships keep worship honest.

God's leadership in carefully planning and setting out the placement of tribal camps and the division of labor for setting up and taking down the tabernacle (Num 2–4) shows concern for order (thus reducing potential time and energy lost through confusion and conflict over inconsequential matters), for fair distribution of work (so that some are not overloaded while others loaf) and for efficiency (enabling rapid setting-up and pulling-down on short notice, in familiar, well-trained teams).

It is important for leaders to be able to distinguish between decisions that genuinely need the input of all parties involved and those that do not. Many of the decisions in the latter category are best made by a single person or a small group, and then accepted as a service to the larger group. Perhaps this should be obvious. However, valuable meeting time can often be misspent because the chairperson has failed to make this distinction.

THE LEADER PROVIDES WAYS TO MAKE AMENDS

God's appointment of Aaron as the first of the tabernacle personnel (Lev 8–9) is, in one vital respect, surprising. Aaron has recently made the most foolish and disgraceful mistake of his life! And it was public! Aaron had been given responsibility to look after the people while his brother Moses was away on Mt Sinai receiving instructions from God. Aaron succumbed to pressure to allow the people to build a golden calf and to conduct idolatrous worship around it (Exod 20). God and Moses became angry. But eventually this man finds forgiveness from both God and his brother to cover his public shame. Perhaps it is not accidental that God the Leader selects a man who cannot hide his own imperfections for a position as high priest, in which he will daily deal with the imperfections of others. God's calling of the Israelites to be a "kingdom of priests" (Exod 19:6) may also suggest that their human weaknesses may suit them well to identify with the weaknesses of those beyond Israel and lead them towards the worship of God their leader.

In Leviticus 1–7 various sacrifices and offerings are described for a range of different personal situations. The priests need to determine which sacrifice or offering is appropriate for what need. What kind of a leader would demand such things? It is clear elsewhere that God is not actually interested in blood or sacrifice *per se*. Certainly other deities of that world were understood to require a range of offerings, including blood sacrifices, so it was not an uncommon idea. Whether the particular god was pleased or not was not always easy to determine, for many other gods seemed to be capricious. The God of the Israelites is not. Clear guidelines are given as a way to help people to get past their known and confessed sins in order that relationships (vertical and horizontal) may be healed. Priests have authority to facilitate the process and to convey confidence that God accepts the offerings.

Later writers in the biblical story are adamant that going through the actions without the corresponding attitude shift is entirely meaningless. Obedience is better evidence of true worship than sacrifice (1 Sam 15:22). However, a wise leader knows that it is therapeutic for people who have done wrong to be able to apologize and make amends themselves to the extent that they can. All of these laws provide opportunities and achievable processes, in an agrarian society, to allow healing in the relationship between humans and God, and they also provide the comfort of a human priest to walk beside them through the process.

QUESTIONS FOR REFLECTION OR DISCUSSION

1. "Unlike human leaders, God requires absolute loyalty and absolute obedience." How do you feel about that?
2. What is the value of rules? Can they ever help people to stay free?
3. How do the Ten Commandments inform your style and practice of leadership?
4. In dealing with others whom you lead, where do you place the balance between authoritative control and the gift of freedom to be creative?
5. We are naturally more comfortable with some people and some cultures than others. How might God's lack of favoritism direct us?
6. How can we provide and accept ways for people to make amends?

Chapter 7

Blasphemy

The third commandment (Exod 20:7) shows the need to respect the Leader, God.

> You shall not misuse the name of the Lord your God,
> for the Lord will not hold anyone guiltless who misuses his name.

First, people are not to misuse God's name, or misrepresent his character to others. God the Leader, as we see in other parts of the story, allows open questions and candid, even heated, conversation and argument. However, he will not tolerate abuse of his name, which implies abuse of his character and untruthful representation of who he is. That has particular implications for those who claim to be his people. There is no corner he cannot see around, so each participant in hidden disrespect will be held to account.

To whose benefit is the third commandment? Surely, God is large enough to cope with lies being said about him, and with his people behaving in ways that he would not approve. However, abuse of God's name will adversely affect the group. It will loosen their trust, poison their relationships and paralyze their mission. It will also erect barriers for others wanting to follow God the Leader.

ALLEGIANCE TO THE LEADER

Commandments Two, Three, and Four relate ostensibly to the vertical relationship between an individual and God. However, they also have social ramifications because they are spoken or acted out in the public space. So there is a need to address these in terms of the more specific laws relating to the functioning of the Israelite society. The matter of identifying and dealing with blasphemy can be delicate and difficult to discern correctly, and yet, if it is ignored and allowed to flourish, it can be outright disastrous.

A specific case of blasphemy is presented in Leviticus 24:10–16. A half-Israelite, half-Egyptian man, during a fight, blasphemes God's name with a curse. Moses is unsure about how to treat this man; the blasphemy is clear, and does go against the God who is leader of the group, but what should the penalty be? The answer is given by God himself to Moses and passed on to the people. The blasphemer is to be taken outside the Israelite camp and stoned to death by the people who are in this group, irrespective of their ethnic origin. It is made clear that the penalty is not related to any prejudice (e.g., his half-Egyptian origin) and that everyone who is functionally part of the group (even those of foreign families) must stand with their leader in supporting the guilty verdict and the administration of that punishment, which would act as a deterrent to other potential rebels in the group. in our multi-religious contexts this sounds shocking, but we need to look at the context.

It is not difficult to imagine that in the desert journey blasphemy would lead to people splintering off from the group, and that would put them at risk of death. Blasphemous words and actions inevitably work out in rebellion. They not only put the blasphemer at personal risk of death, but also put any others who would be influenced by that person at risk of death. In the light of that risk, the punishment of death can be seen as confining the death-consequence to the person who deserved it, rather than risking its spread to other vulnerable people.

As Moses prepares the people for their future life in their new land without his leadership, he imagines various manifestations of blasphemy and idolatry, particularly where there is explicit inciting of others to follow suit (Deut 13). Even if the blasphemer claims to be a prophet, and even if he is a member of their own family, the penalty must be the same. When the people become settled, dangers of rebellion will look a little different. As a pioneering and still novice group, they will need the strength of united will and action to resist being taken over by foreign peoples. Any breakaway people will forfeit the protection of the larger group. So, issues of life and death will continue.

It is of the utmost importance to God, as leader of this new and initially nomadic people group, that the group work together as one. And that unity is found in allegiance to the one leader who has rescued them and is now sustaining and guiding them. God can survive if blasphemy occurs; the people may not.

If the people of other communities, which they will inevitably meet, incite them to follow other god-leaders or to incorporate religious practices that violate the instructions regarding the relationship that God has founded (Deut 18:9–13) they must *not* be followed. However, there is no authority given to the Israelites to enact the same penalty on blasphemous or idolatrous people from other religious communities. These laws apply only to the people who are under the leadership of God.

When I was a child I remember hearing many words expressed in anger that I came to learn later had blasphemous origins. When I was a young child I copied a neighbor's word and discovered my mother's anger. In my two-year-old defiance, I repeated that word over and over again to see the reaction! When I was fourteen, I used another word I had frequently heard my father and other friends of the family saying. This time the strong reaction was from a nun who was my music teacher. She marched me outside, and up to the weather shed in the back of the school playground. She asked me whether I knew what that word meant. I didn't. She told me in no uncertain terms what it meant, why it dishonored God so much, and that it was actually blasphemous. I was shocked. I walked home very slowly, to let what she had told me sink in. Eventually my shock turned to gratitude. I began to think of the other words she mentioned that were also dishonoring to God. I knew them all very well. They were common parlance in my family circle. That nun prodded me to make a decision never again to merely copy the unthinkingly blasphemous words of others, especially words spoken in anger. It took a while to eradicate these words completely from my thoughts and speech, because they were there by habit. I understand that most people who use them have no blasphemous intent, so they are not deliberately being blasphemous. But I am the one who has control of my own speech, and I can choose not to dishonor God in this way.

In today's world blasphemy laws are sometimes misused to settle grievances over minor issues or to have people put out of the way on account of prejudice, envy or greed. God did not invite or authorize that kind of abuse. Many cases of horrifying violence, mistreatment and killing of people of differing religious faiths bear no resemblance to even the strictest interpretation of these Old Testament blasphemy laws. Asia Bibi, a Pakistani Christian woman, was convicted of blasphemy and sentenced to death by a Pakistani court in 2010, but fortunately she was eventually acquitted in 2018 and subsequently released. The Muslim accusations did not stand up to any of the criteria of the biblical blasphemy laws, even if she had recently converted from Islam to Christianity. Eventually that was recognized. But there are many hardline Muslims who are angry about her release. And there are currently many serious misapplications of Muslim blasphemy laws around the world.

It is understandable that people's emotions are rooted deeply in their allegiance to the leader they believe in, follow and worship. People will be offended, angered and perhaps be tempted to take revenge if they feel that the object or person of their worship is not respected. Similar emotions may occur following the murder of a loved one, a theft of property, or any other act of violation. However, all of the biblical laws are given to provide leadership on a more objective basis, and to curb the instinct to react on the basis of emotions. Personal or family revenge has no place. There must be a fair trial and any punishment implemented under the specific direction of the governing human leadership. Even if one person is found guilty of blasphemy, there is no justification for bringing further punishments on villages or tribes, or for waging war.

Blasphemy against God needs to be very carefully defined and assessed. If the person concerned belongs to a different community or faith, there is no justification for even putting the person on trial, let alone accusing them of blasphemy. Blasphemy is public, disrespectful, offensive and outright hardened rebellion against the God who has been one's leader, and incitement of others to follow suit. The example in Leviticus expresses it as cursing God. It is not an act of questioning or even disagreeing with God as leader—Moses and plenty of other human leaders do that and find acceptance. It is not just grumbling against God as leader—the Israelites do that in the wilderness; it causes their journey to be lengthened, but God still does not reject them. It is a blatant public act that does not merely offend someone's feelings about God, but attempts to have his presence obliterated.

Within many Christian circles the tendency is often towards leniency. Within some more closed Christian groups and certain other religions, the tendency can be towards harshly over-reactive punishments. In our multi-cultural and multi-religious societies of the global village, how can leaders find a way forward?

One solution is the separation of church and state. Old Testament Israel was a theocracy, a nation ruled by religious laws. Not even the modern nation of Israel is in that position, as it is intentionally formed as a democracy. Its leadership must care for Jews (religious and secular), Muslims, Druze and Christians (Palestinian and others). In the Old Testament theocracy, the blasphemy laws were fitting to keep the society strong and healthy under its common divine leader. It is no longer appropriate for modern government leaders to apply them to modern societies, because these are composed of various religious groups. In most modern countries, larger nation-states made up of many smaller tribal groups have been brought together, so they need a basis for governing a much larger and more mixed society than was even envisaged in Old Testament times.

What is then appropriate for religious leaders within their own religious communities? For Christians, there are disciplinary procedures outlined in the New Testament, where the most serious punishment for public offences, which can include blasphemy, is excommunication. While most churches try to avoid this assiduously, it can be a valid strategy when genuine attempts to discuss the problem fail. However, I have seen harsh excommunication misapplied to settle grievances over minor issues, and I have also seen it totally avoided, so that the poison of a lone, divisive rebel is allowed to spread and wreak havoc for many years. Good leadership is needed to avoid both extremes, and to assess where and how discipline may be applied in order to keep the group in a strong and healthy position, and for individuals to be treated fairly.

In other religious groups the most controversial application of blasphemy laws occurs when a person chooses to change their religion, that is, to convert. Some religious leaders do not regard this as permissible, so a charge of blasphemy is laid. However, it may reasonably be questioned whether a quiet, conscientious pursuit of truth, evaluating claims of their own religion against claims of another, is the same as blasphemy. A peaceable conviction to change is not the same as rebellious, public mockery and cursing of the God of the original religion.

While the third commandment prohibiting blasphemy is obviously against spreading slander about God the Leader, it may be compared to the ninth commandment, which prohibits the spreading of slander about other people.

QUESTIONS FOR REFLECTION OR DISCUSSION

1. Why does God not allow his name to be misused?
2. Are genuine questions about God forbidden?
3. Some religious communities have "blasphemy laws" that allow killing of people who have different religious views. What is the difference between this and the biblical prohibition of blasphemy?
4. What is acceptable to say behind a leader's back? Does that necessarily conflict with loyalty?
5. What is the difference between unity in an organization and unanimity under a dictatorial boss?
6. When might action need to be taken for criticism of a leader?

Chapter 8

Sabbath Rest and Work

COMMANDMENT FOUR

The seventh day is a gift day for rest instead of for work. In the Creation account, God is pictured as resting for a day after creatively working for six days. This gift day of leaving work aside is a mark of kindness in God's style of leadership and contrasts with the relentless demands for work that Pharaoh imposed. This policy also encourages people to have enough self-respect to ensure that their needs for rest and refreshment have adequate space in their calendars.

> Remember the Sabbath day by keeping it holy.
> Six days you shall labor and do all your work,
> but the seventh day is a Sabbath to the Lord your God.
> On it you shall not do any work, neither you, nor your son or daughter, nor your manservant or maidservant, nor your animals, not the alien within your gates.
> For in six days the Lord made the heavens and the earth, the sea, and all that is in them. (Exod 20:8–11)

The tendency towards workaholism is endemic in leaders, and many organizations virtually demand that their leaders be workaholics. Another form of this problem also occurs in some who are so engrossed in their hobby, their computer screen, or some other habit to the extent that others find it extremely difficult to call them to do something else or simply be with them. God knows our weaknesses and has built into our systems the need for a regular, weekly break and time for refreshment.

God's sabbath law functions well for those who would not take a rest unless it were imposed. Others, of course, are lazy and naturally choose to work as little as possible. The law for keeping just one day in seven assists people to avoid both extremes.

What is more, children, servants, foreigners staying with them, and animals, are all given the same amount of rest time. Compared with the working conditions of neighboring lands of the period, this was considered generous. Having the same rest day in common enabled people to find refreshment in both worship and recreation together.

In our day, many of us imagine that we no longer need to follow this instruction, treating it as an antiquated rule that smells of restrictive legalism. However, the high levels of stress in present societies, workplaces and family life should lead us to question the wisdom of abandoning this gift of rest from a kind and wise divine leader who knows what is good for his people.

Although we may think of work as a means to an end, that is, income to live, we may act as though work is our goal, our end point in life. Then, when we reach retirement, we can lose interest in life because we have lost our work, our motivation, our very goal in living. The seventh day rest tells us that work is not the final goal of life. There is something more to enjoy, to value, to find life in and to look forward to. The New Testament book of Hebrews picks up this theme of sabbath rest and applies it to a future rest (e.g., Heb 4:1–7).

TIMES FOR REST AND CELEBRATION

The subject of the sabbath (the seventh day) takes up a significant amount of space in the biblical laws. Sabbath-keeping was the most distinctive visible mark of the people group who belonged to this God. Because Israelite society was more communal than modern Western societies, work was performed communally. If an individual decided to break the sabbath, it would directly impact his work community as well as his household. People worked together and rested together.

In addition to the weekly day of rest, God the Leader gave other breaks. Three times a year all men and whichever women and children were available were to go up to Jerusalem (Lev 23). These were holidays or, more correctly, holy days. In agricultural societies, there is always a rhythm to the year. The times for sowing seed, watching over tender shoots, and harvesting fruit are different. God gave holidays that fitted the seasons and that also reminded the people of his role in this great teamwork between leader and followers. People looked forward to the special foods and colorful ceremonies, to the different aspects of worship, and of journeying beyond their home villages. As they walked in the company of relatives and friends, with children playfully darting in and out of the crowd, they told stories and sang songs. The songs of ascent (Psalms 121–134) were favorites. Celebration was always in the context of connection—connection to God and connection to each other. It fostered the embrace of reality—reality in relationship to God, to their produce, and to their human relationships. It called for a refocusing of attention beyond the daily grind to a renewed vision of the Giver of life in order that the next season of work could be rightly invigorated. And once in fifty years (after seven times seven years) a whole year was to be taken as a kind of sabbath, when people were to return to family, clan and land. This "jubilee year" also set boundaries around self-centered consumerism of time and required that the needs of others be placed center-stage.

I remember having parallel conversations in the same week with two men who were both in very similar leadership positions in Christian organizations. I asked each of them how many hours they worked each week for their organizations. One said 70 hours, and the other said 40 hours. I enquired further and also learned more about how each person worked and related within their organization. The productivity and efficiency of the one who worked fewer hours was, surprisingly, significantly greater. The relationships that each fostered in his respective organization could not have been more different. The one who worked 70 hours was so intent on his personal work achievements that he had little space or time for the needs or successes of others. The atmosphere which he fostered was detached and cold, nervously busy without the satisfaction of accomplishment. The atmosphere of the 40 hour-a-week man was warm and energizing, where achievements occurred in the easy flow of forward movement.

The second man also had space in his calendar to give extra time. If an extra need occurred, or an accident unexpectedly disabled a colleague for a time, or an important conversation opened up in the parking lot, his time was not so tightly bound that there was no extra time to give. He left margins, and he frequently gave additional time whenever necessary. The over-committed man had no such margins. Only the second of these men functioned as a leader in the truest sense of the word. When we overspend ourselves, and when we demand the same of others, we are not following the leadership of God, and the whole group suffers the consequences.

Although the benefits of rest are not stated overtly in the Old Testament, they become self-evident to those who practice this principle. Our weeks are cyclic. So, as well as seeing rest as a goal for the end of the week, we can also discover that a period of rest generates energy and motivation for the next season of work.

LIMITS ON WORK AND REST

The sabbath rest principle applies to time, to income, to produce, to servants, workers, and employees, to animals, and to land, as can be seen more clearly in the other regulations in the Pentateuch. God is not the kind of leader who "squeezes the last drop of blood" from his people, and nor does he want the people to do that to each other or even to themselves. And so he asks that a minor portion of time, income, produce and animals be given away. It is to be considered as belonging to God. Otherwise, there would be a high risk of others claiming it for manipulative or pressurizing purposes. At the same time, this minor portion is a reminder that the whole of a person's time, income, produce, animals and workers also ultimately belong to God. When the sabbath principle is practiced, unbridled obsession with work is checked, greed is disempowered, and the values of generosity and kindness are promoted. In short, relationships between humans, as well as with God benefit.

We find in the Old Testament many passages (e.g., Lev 27:30) referring to the giving of a tithe (a tenth of one's income) to God. This guideline not only checks ravenous attitudes towards wealth, but provides a living for one twelfth of the people, the tribe of Levi, who are wholly dedicated to the fostering of worship. This is their only income. It enables people to recognize the interdependence that workers and priests have on each other and to think beyond their own pockets. Additional tithes and offerings of various sorts are also directed. Those who are poor and needy are to receive special help. Giving the first fruits to God (e.g., Exod 23:19) channels the natural excitement of the early harvest outward, away from self-centered rewards, and upward. Giving for fellowship meals and holiday festivals encourages families not only to see the importance of sharing worship time together, but also to value holiday time together. Income is to be apportioned so that the income earner is not consumed by purchasing power but balances essential needs with generosity.

When a landowner is harvesting, he is not permitted to go back a second time to pick up overlooked sheaves of grain or fruit that is left on his trees. Instead, he must leave it to be found by the needy, who are classically expressed as the foreigners, the fatherless and the widows (e.g., Deut 24:19–22). He must not reap all of the harvest, not to the very edges of his field.

The portion that is left must be available for the poor to come and harvest for themselves (Lev 19:9-10). By leaving a portion for the poor to gather, all people, whether rich or poor, can participate in the work that they need in order to eat. Limits on the work of one person fosters the enablement and satisfaction of work for another.

There are limits on the rights of masters over workers. All workers, whether they are slaves bonded to the household or not, whether they are Israelite or foreign, are to be given the same day off work, the same sabbath rest. Although foreigners can be bought as slaves (common among people of these lands) masters do not have authority to rule over them ruthlessly (Lev 25:43). Israelites may choose to be voluntary, temporary slaves in order to lift themselves out of poverty. However, they must be set free after six years of service and be sent away with plentiful provisions for their new lives (Deut 15:14). In the laws of many other lands, slaves have no rights. But God gives attention to the rights of workers and slaves; offenders against them are to be punished.

There are also limits on the rights of creditors over debtors. First, no Israelite is to charge interest on a loan to a fellow Israelite. Then the loans must be cancelled at the end of every seven years (Deut 15:1-11). The ideal is to have communities without poverty. Repayments are expected, so responsibility is encouraged. However, creditors must limit their demands, based on a higher principle of generosity, arising from a heart that is not grudging.

Animals are not to be worked seven days a week. They, too, receive a sabbath rest (Exod 23:12). If a domestic animal falls into a pit, people are permitted to work to pull the animal out, even if it is the sabbath day. Care for animals is an extension of care for people. The instruction not to plough with an ox and a donkey yoked together shows that the strengths and weaknesses of each animal must be understood and respected. The weaker animal will inevitably feel that the pace of work is too much; the stronger animal may feel frustrated by being slowed down. They will not be able to walk in rhythm with each other and neither will do their best work. God's care, as leader of people and animals, is for each to be given work that fits their capacities. The teaching on care for animals is extended in Proverbs 12:10 and 27:23-27.

The land, too, is given rest time. Although it can be worked, it may not be overworked. Later, in Proverbs 24:30-34, diligence in working the land and keeping it free from weeds is commended. However, every seventh year the land must not be worked (Exod 23:10-11 and Lev 25:1-7). In this year any food can be eaten by the family and needy people; any leftovers can be food for the wild animals. Each fiftieth year any land that has been sold is to be returned to the original owner. This is to be understood in the context of fair distribution of land to each tribe in proportion to its size. Yet, the larger context is that the ultimate owner of all land is God himself (Lev 25:23).

Food laws will be mentioned here because they call for boundaries in the consumption of food. Here the restrictions are not by quantity but by kind: foods are divided into "clean" and "unclean" (Lev 11; Deut 14). No reasons are given, but many modern observers suggest that these clear and straightforward guidelines, for an unscientific people, are for the purposes of keeping the people in good health. Calling for people to think before eating, to make a conscious decision to accept or reject food on the basis of directives from a wise leader rather than on the basis of impulsive desire, serves to check human tendencies towards greed.

One unusual food law deserves special mention. It is the instruction not to cook a young goat in its mother's milk (Exod 23:19b; Deut 14:21b). Practicing Jews to this day take this to mean that one should not eat milk and meat in the same meal, so they separate cooking utensils into those used for milk dishes and those used for meat dishes. I suggest, rather, that this law places a restriction on eating even "clean" food (young goats) if a natural living bond between a mother and her young is violated. In this case, the mother's milk given for the purpose of nurturing the life of the kid may not be misused to cause the death of the kid, by boiling her young in it, no matter how good the resulting meat may taste! This is congruent with an important thrust in the Old Testament, that God is for life, and not death.

THE LEADER'S VOLUNTARY SELF-RESTRAINT

The sabbath principle has first been exemplified by God himself, in resting on the seventh day after his six-day labor of creation. However, we understand that the narrative portrayal of God's voluntary cessation of work shows us two important aspects of his leadership. The first aspect is that he does not ask his followers to do something that he is unwilling to do. The second is that he willingly engages in self-restraint, self-discipline and self-limitation.

At a recent funeral of a well-loved and effective leader it was said that this man would never ask his workers to do something that he had not done or would not himself do. He was certainly not a Pharaoh! His people had confidence in his directives precisely because of this attitude. As a result, they complied willingly. As a tradesman and businessman, as a volunteer leader in his church, as a friend and mentor to a large number of younger people, and as a father and grandfather, he inspired people to follow him by his example. He, in turn, was consciously following the example of God his leader, and called others to do likewise.

The second aspect of willing self-restraint, self-discipline and self-limitation is one that is sometimes overlooked in leadership manuals. We often hear the call to work towards your vision, your dreams. There is truth in that call. But that drive to work, even for the very best of goals, must be checked by strategically timed periods of pulling back from that work. Obviously, we do need rest breaks (even if God did not actually need them for his own sake). And these ought ideally to refocus on the bigger picture, on finding the heart of God himself, from whom new vision and new energy can flow for the next phase of work.

Looking at the above sabbath-related laws, we discover that setting limits on our own self-directed use of resources creates an opportunity for others to gain. Self-restraint can be an indirect means of developing others. And that is an important goal of leadership.

It is sometimes difficult for me to step back in order to allow someone less competent to step in. I don't mean that I should do that to allow someone incompetent to take over an important leadership function when they are ill-equipped to do so. But I do need to intentionally create spaces for people to develop. I do need to take risks in letting go, in appropriate increments. I do need to step back from micro-managing, to allow others to create their own patterns and rhythms.

Self-restraint includes a voluntary limitation of desires and even what we might call rights. Consumerism in all its forms is to be checked. And leaders can be particularly prone to various versions of it. Consumerism (preoccupation with the acquisition of goods) is graphically presented many years later by the prophet Ezekiel as he portrays leaders taking the best produce of the land for themselves before ensuring that their people have enough (Ezek 34:1–4). It is *not* the prerogative of a leader to take all that he or she can get. Leadership is to be directed outwards, to the wellbeing of others. That cannot be properly achieved without a measure of self-sacrifice.

Perhaps we may even be able to read God's example of self-restraint in the light of these laws, as they obviously reflect his character. Since these sabbath-related laws so frequently point to care and consideration of others, we may infer that God's own self-limiting is likely to be, quite intentionally, for the good of others. Perhaps, as the larger biblical story unfolds, we may even see a preliminary hint of God's voluntary self-sacrifice for the good of humankind, which becomes more obvious in the sacrifice of Jesus in the New Testament.

A leader needs to provide seasons of rest so that the people and the system do not wear out. As an engine needs the lubrication of oil to keep cogs and joints connecting smoothly, the human system needs the oil of God's Spirit as its lubricant (e.g., Zech 4:6, 12). Human kings and priests are anointed by oil as a sign of God's appointment and enabling (e.g., 1 Sam 16:13; Lev 8:10).

As parched ground needs water to soften it and to enable it to nourish plant life, God's people need the cleansing and refreshing power of water, which is another image of God's Spirit (e.g., Joel 2:22-29; Ezek 36:25-27). God's provision of sabbath and holy holidays enables people and systems to find renewed energy.

QUESTIONS FOR REFLECTION OR DISCUSSION

1. What are some of the benefits of God's sabbath, or rest day?
2. How can leaders implement this principle themselves, even if they have to work on Saturdays or Sundays?
3. What are the implications of the sabbath principle for our leadership of others?
4. Have you worked under a leader who did not respect your rights to legitimate time off?
5. What is your experience of workaholism? What are the dangers?
6. Are times of celebration important? Why or why not?

Chapter 9

Respect for Parents, Life and Marriage

Having looked at God the Leader's position as the one to be worshiped and respected, we discover that most of the laws (Commandments 5 to 10) require respect and care for other people. We see God's deep concerns for his people. His desire is that people are also respected so that they can flourish.

We can see these laws as protecting the rights of others, fostering a society where a man is not riddled with fear that a neighbor is likely to kill him, take his wife or his property, or defame his character. These laws urge particular care in guarding the rights of the poor and vulnerable (usually expressed as fatherless, widows and foreigners).

These laws are not just concerned with justice (prescribing proportional punishments), but with the restoration of relationships (which also requires restitution). Good leadership needs to be concerned about both aspects, so that the community is able to thrive and move forward without becoming bogged down, sidetracked or distracted by hurt, anger, guilt or shame.

COMMANDMENT FIVE: HONOR PARENTS

> Honor your father and your mother, so that you may live long in the land the Lord your God is giving you. (Exod 20:12)

The fifth commandment calls for parents to be honored. They are, of course, leaders. There is no requirement here to treat parents or other leaders as if they are gods. They are not to be worshiped or assumed to be perfect. Much later, in the New Testament, parents are advised not to treat their children harshly, implying that love and care must take priority in parent-child relationships. In both the Old and New Testaments, parents are to train their children in God's ways (Deut 6:4–7; Eph 5:4). Inevitably, parents will make mistakes. But the command to honor them does call for children (including adult children) to do good to them and to refrain from bringing public shame upon them. Back in Genesis 9:18–23 one of Noah's sons, Ham, had taken advantage of his father's vulnerable state and treated him shamefully. For that he was rebuked particularly severely. Open disrespect militates against the possibility of parents and children remaining in the same part of the country. This would hinder the possibility of living long lives in an intergenerational community, which, by implication, is God's ideal.

We all know that some parents do treat their children harshly and, in fact, do evil acts to their children. Because God has such a high priority on the preservation of life, it is clear that issues of safety for the children must be balanced with the call for respect of parents. If safety is threatened, then children need to be kept safe, and that may mean that they are to be kept away from parents, for a short or a longer period. But the modern trend for young people to cut parents off for trivial reasons, or even for hurt feelings, is not justified. Treating parents disrespectfully, or even shamefully, is never condoned for any reason.

Is it ever right to question, challenge or even disobey a parent? A child may respectfully question and discuss. The child's abilities and desires need to be considered. Many things can legitimately be negotiated as the child becomes old enough and realizes that the task set before him or her is too difficult or impossible to fulfill for some reason. But in some cases, a parent acts criminally and puts strong pressure on the child to do something that is wrong. Probably the majority of children in this very unfortunate situation do as the adult asks, likely out of fear. But sometimes a child chooses not to engage in the same behavior. Under God the Leader, who is the ultimate authority for what is right and wrong, a child still under parental care may disobey a parent if the parent's command goes directly against a command by God. In fact, kings are actually condemned if they continue in the wicked ways of their fathers or grandfathers. So honoring parents does not imply following them if their ways are wicked. God as leader creates a system of respect, but not a system of compulsorily following ways that are wicked or foolish.

However, outright rebellion, even from a grown son or daughter, against good directives from a parent, is considered disgraceful in God's community. In fact, persistent rebellion from an adult son, who is stubbornly disobedient, a profligate and a drunkard, is to be treated with utmost seriousness: he is to be stoned to death (Deut 21:18–21). A serious parent-abuser will become an abuser of society. Protection for others takes priority. This matter, as for all capital punishments, is not to be acted on secretly by family members. The problem must be brought to the elders for their decision, and the stoning must be done publicly.

For an adult child, the responsibility to literally obey parents in every aspect of life no longer applies, because the context is different. Where a nomadic patriarch had responsibility for his family of several generations, he had stronger reasons to require conformity. The whole family unit needed to live and move together. But today there is now a greater freedom for adult children to assess the wisdom and appropriateness of the parents' words for themselves and make their own decisions. However, advice can and should be listened to and respect must remain.

Today we hear of honor killings, usually of young women who do not want to marry the person of their parents' choice. That kind of disobedience is not what is envisaged here. In the Old Testament we see many examples of adult children marrying against their parents' wishes. The parents are upset but there is no punishment, and there is no suggestion that it is worthy of capital punishment. The family certainly has no right to carry out such a punishment privately, or to rid the family of this kind of dishonor in such a way.

This command has implications for respecting all who are in positions of leadership, including teachers, police, bosses at work, government officials and church leaders. In life, there are and there will be difficult leaders. Some are unfair, some incompetent, some vindictive, some micro-managing, and some are bullies. We may need to negotiate or even challenge some troublesome issues. Whatever we do, we must still recognize that the leader is a person with their own needs. And we must address the issues respectfully.

COMMANDMENT SIX: DO NOT MURDER

> You shall not murder. (Exod 20:13)

Each person's life is to be respected. The text of this sixth commandment does not say, "You shall not kill." When these commandments are applied to specific cases (as case law), there will be rare occasions, with very specific and limited criteria, for killing in capital punishment and warfare. But the general principle, from which these deviations are special exceptions, is that humans do not have the right to take other human life. Even leaders, like kings, are to be subject to this law.

The issues of personal, family and tribal revenge were very important to keep in check then, and it is important to keep these in check now. I have taught quite a few murderers in prisons. I have heard the stories of some of the women who killed and can see that their situations were tragic. One woman was sick of the repeated abuse of her stepfather, not only towards her but especially towards her mother. She hated seeing her mother trapped and trodden into the ground as if she were dirt. So she took justice into her own hands—and ended up with a long prison sentence. I think of a man who was hurt, humiliated and angered by his wife's blatant unfaithfulness. He took justice into his own hands and murdered his wife in a most gruesome way. There is something within each of us that can understand the emotions these people felt. But their way of solving the problem was wrong. And in each case it brought far greater tragedy to their children and damaging impact to a very wide range of people.

In one place, I taught in the prison in the morning and in a nearby adult community center in the afternoon. Very soon after meeting with some "murderers" on the "inside," I met with some on the "outside" who had attempted murder but failed. That showed me that the distance between being a "normal" citizen and a "murderer" is far closer than I had imagined. They were all people like me with feelings of hurt and anger, and all had an acute sense of justice. But self-control was poor and there was very little thought given to options and consequences.

If we want to prevent murder, we need to check our attitudes and reactions and not allow them to get so out of control that we find ourselves committing an act that we may normally consider despicable and impossible for us to do. Jesus extends this in the New Testament to a prohibition against being angry with someone (Matt 5:21–26), indicating that we should not just stop short of committing the actual crime, but examine the steps that can lead to the crime.

We do get angry. Many of us in leadership positions feel blocked, frustrated, ridiculed, slandered, even at times tormented. Anger in itself is a signal emotion. It can indicate that we need to take action to rectify something that is unjust or wrong. Jesus discusses ways of settling relationships, instead of allowing that anger to grow unabated. In the light of God's high value on life, even the life of those who wrong us, we need to take steps that will lead us away from any risk of doing them harm. And we need to acknowledge and deal with attitudes of hatred and revenge, the latter being strictly prohibited.

If this law reflects God's character, and I believe it does, we can rest assured that he does not deal carelessly or heartlessly with human life.

COMMANDMENT SEVEN: DO NOT COMMIT ADULTERY

You shall not commit adultery. (Exod 20:14)

The seventh commandment creates a firm place of respect for marriage between a man and a woman. Sex is not a commodity to be aroused on a whim, but is to be kept within a publicly declared, bounded relationship on which other relationships depend. Children are born into a bounded place, belonging with a male and a female parent, each related to other members of extended families, clans and tribes. There is order in the community. Inheritance rules will follow, in order to give all of the people a fair share in the land. Adultery not only violates a bounded relationship between a man and a woman, but disturbs extended families, and, if a pregnancy results, may mess up tribal inheritance of land.

LAWS RESTRICTING SEXUAL BEHAVIOR

The primary reference of the word "adultery" is to a man engaging in sexual intercourse with a woman who is married to another man (see also Prov 6:27–29). For this crime, the two people involved are to die (Deut 22:22). However, each principle in the Ten Commandments is an "umbrella" principle, in that it includes other related laws. So "adultery" is also indicative of other sexual sins that are made clearer elsewhere.

A sexual act by a man with an unmarried woman holds the man accountable (Deut 22:28–29). He may not abandon her but must provide for her all of his life. That is the real thrust of the instruction for him to marry her. For many men, this would serve as a deterrent. Sex is never free but requires responsibilities. I must say that I would not like to be a woman being compelled to marry her rapist! This is still under debate in some countries. But the point of this law is really to compel the man to take responsibility. Perhaps a suitable application today, in preference to a forced marriage, might be that the man has to pay for all consequences of this act, for the rest of his life. So, he should pay to provide housing and other needs for the woman, especially if she now carries a stigma that makes it difficult for her to marry (which in many cultures is still the case). He should also pay for any medical or emotional treatment that the woman needs as a result of this unwanted sexual act and its trauma. If a pregnancy ensues he must pay for all provisions for the child until he or she is independent.

If the woman is engaged to be married to someone else and screams for help by the man's rapacious advances, but others are too far away to hear her, the man is put to death but not the woman. If the act is consensual, both are to be put to death (Deut 22:23–27). This equal treatment for equal sexual responsibility has not yet been recognized in the laws of many nations, where the woman is punished severely and the man is let off freely. Even Jewish leaders sometimes misapplied it, as occurred in New Testament times when some Pharisees brought a woman, caught in adultery, to Jesus (John 8:1–11). In that case the obvious unspoken question is, "Where is the man?"

If a bridegroom finds that his bride has had sex before marriage he can accuse her and she is to be stoned to death (Deut 22:13–21). This contrasts sharply with a Facebook post I read recently in which the question was asked whether a one-night stand, even during a committed relationship with someone else, needs to be confessed. I wonder what commitment really means in that context? The possibility of pregnancy is not explicitly mentioned, either in Leviticus or in this Facebook post, but it is certainly a cause for concern to people before contraception. If a bride is actually in an early stage of pregnancy when she marries, the bridegroom will be the person who has to bear the cost of providing for a child that is not his! Again, sex comes with responsibility.

It is clear that sexual acts between men and women outside the boundaries of marriage are unacceptable, even though there are differences in how they are handled judicially. There are restrictions on marriage and sexual activity between various family members who are directly related or are related by marriage (see Lev 18:6–18). Offenders are to be "cut off" from their people (Lev 18:29).

A man may not marry a woman and her sister, in a polygamous relationship (Lev 18:18). However, other forms of polygamy, although not meeting the desired pattern of marriage (see Gen 2:24) do not attract such explicit prohibitions and punishments. Strong evidence against polygamy in the Old Testament occurs in the narratives where patterns of rivalry between wives and children within polygamous families demonstrate the acute difficulties that humans have when they try to live in a way that goes against the desired pattern. Perhaps polygamy is accommodated, to some degree at least, on account of the need for women to have male protectors when there are shortages of men, often after wars. However, it is never condoned, is always negatively portrayed, and by the time of the New Testament polygamy is simply out of the question.

Homosexuality is only ever mentioned in terms of its condemnation (Lev 18:22; 20:13). It is considered detestable and its participants must be put to death. Male and female cult prostitutes are also considered detestable, and their financial earnings are not to be accepted in places of worship (Deut 23:17–18). Sexual acts with an animal (bestiality) are also detestable (Lev 18:23; 20:15–16). The human and the animal must be put to death.

Human sexual capacity is carefully bounded to be used for the procreation of life within an unambiguous marriage relationship that does not violate other prior family relationships. This God is a leader who fosters life. Sexual engagements are envisaged to be within marriage and undertaken responsibly, where new life is welcomed and nurtured.

QUESTIONS FOR REFLECTION OR DISCUSSION

1. Why does God as Leader want to protect parents, life and marriage?
2. When might it be difficult to honor parents, bosses and other leaders?
3. What standards of respectful speech are in place in your sphere of leadership?
4. Western societies have largely devalued marriage and pushed to liberalize other sexual expressions. How do we uphold God's commandment in a secular society?
5. What "commandments" would you put in place if you were the leader of an organization?
6. Identify some important boundaries that you recognize in your life.

Chapter 10

Boundaries and Punishments

I remember a conversation with a man who supposedly gave me his reason for wanting to do an action that would cause hurt to someone else. He said, "It's because I want to." When questioned further, he would not admit that there might be any higher consideration that whatever he wanted to do. The concept of boundaries around other people was not there. Empathy for the effects of violating another's boundaries, whether land, possessions, money or even person, was entirely lacking. For all the idealistic talk about how children will become kind if they see kindness modelled, it doesn't always automatically happen. God the Leader is no such idealist; he knows human weaknesses. So he names boundaries that should not be violated, and in other case laws gives examples of appropriate penalties for violations.

COMMANDMENT EIGHT: DO NOT STEAL

> You shall not steal. (Exod 20:15)

This eighth commandment means that each person's property, animals, farm produce, workers is to be respected. Someone might say that the person would have given it to him anyway. We may not presume on another's generosity, as all gifts must be freely given. This rule applies, in the first instance, to whatever is understood to be "owned," but it also implies the obligation to respect the needs of others in the group when using common property. Respect for property includes respect for the plans that the owner has for it, including any plans for generosity. Even kings will not be given the right to claim what belongs to another.

I remember the shock and pain of betrayal when I discovered that I had been secretly and systematically robbed by someone I trusted implicitly. It was not only a matter of the money or the things that were lost, although that caused definite and significant hardship which was difficult enough to recover from. But stealing fundamentally involves a violation of the relationship. Something has changed, trust has gone. The loss of a trusted relationship brings enormous pain and damage into a community.

Many of us live in countries where fixed weights have been required to be used by sellers for a long time, e.g., a gram of produce measured on one set of scales is the same amount as a gram measured on another set of scales. But in many places where we have been, individual sellers can easily falsify weights to make a greater profit. Transactions are to be clean and honest, and the practice of deliberately using incorrect weights and measures not only constitutes stealing from neighbors but is also detestable to God (Prov 20:10, 23). It is usually the little people who are hit hardest by these dishonest businesses.

The positioning of physical boundary markers still causes conflicts in many communities. While doing some family history I read of a notorious ancestor who chronically and severely ruptured the harmony of his small village in the Shetland Islands, and was eventually prosecuted, because of his nightly habit of moving his boundary stones to gain greater advantage of land. This, too, is stealing (e.g., Deut 19:14).

The thief who engages in outright stealing of animals (e.g., Exod 22:1–4) must pay back not only the equivalent of what he took, but extra—up to five times as much. When the New Testament character Zaccheus faces Jesus, he instinctively knows that he needs to pay back restitution money and decides to return four times the amount to anyone he has robbed. This goes some way towards offering an apology and compensation for lost time, lost work and lost peace.

In some situations, then and now, one may claim to have just "borrowed" property belonging to a neighbor, so if that property is lost or damaged while under the borrower's care, is the borrower liable? Responsibilities of a borrower are also outlined (e.g., Exod 22:7–15) to avoid unfair charges and careless borrowing.

All cultures allow for some property to be owned by individuals or families while some is shared by a larger community. The boundaries between what is owned and what is shared differ between cultures. Some cultures have few rules regarding individual property rights, and are stronger on sharing, adopting an approach which tends towards "What's mine is yours, and what's yours is mine." Conflict can easily ensue when people of such a culture co-exist with people of another culture who are very guarded about every tiny thing that they "own." People of the sharing culture will too readily be accused of stealing, and people of the ownership culture will be too readily accused of meanness. However, the principle expressed in this commandment can still be understood and applied contextually.

It was a shock to see the familiar face of a well-loved family friend on the front page of the newspaper with the word "Thief" above it. He was in a highly responsible position in his work and had been quietly taking money as he closed up the shop after other employees had left. He claimed that he was just trying to help his family. I'm sure he was, but he was robbing other people! I know of several terrible cases of church treasurers siphoning off church funds for their own use. It is far worse when people who claim to follow God betray trust in such an unthinkable way. The damage is extensive and long-lasting. And none of this should be swept under the carpet.

COMMANDMENT NINE: DO NOT SLANDER

> You shall not give false testimony against your neighbor. (Exod 20:16)

In this ninth commandment, the problem of stealing is extended to taking something from a person himself or herself: a valid reputation and replacing it with something maliciously distorted and untrue. Each person's reputation is to be respected and spoken of honestly.

We probably all fail to show sufficient respect for our neighbor and the truth when we distort a story, ever so slightly, in a way that puts that neighbor into a less favorable position, particularly if we are angry with that neighbor or if we want to bolster our own sense of righteousness or importance. God decreed that the Israelites must not damage another person, even by distorting their reputation, because he or she is important in the sight of God the Leader.

Political and media messages are often laced with significant quantities of "spin." Persuasion is legitimate but telling untruths about opponents is definitely not legitimate. I am horrified to see magazine headlines about celebrities that are not based on facts, but merely on what someone thinks will sell their magazines. In the lead-up to Australia's plebiscite on same-sex marriage, there were countless disgraceful untrue reports and false accusations of opponents, all in the name of winning votes.

In the Old Testament, two or three witnesses are needed to convict someone of a crime; one witness is insufficient. However, if a witness is found to be maliciously falsifying the truth, then the penalty that was to be done to the person lied against must be done to him (Deut 19:15–21). How we speak about someone is serious.

I was once in a job where blatant untruths were spoken about me by a woman in a position of authority. Those lies were spread around and led to many people avoiding me. After some time one courageous woman asked me a direct question: "Where were you on [a certain date]?" I thought, and answered honestly that I was away from there, in fact in a different country. She then considered my answer and worked out that I was indeed not in that country on that day. Then, to her credit, she sent word around that the story about me must be false, because I was not even in that location. Gradually the people realized that this story and several other stories from the same source were pure slander. The woman who spread the lies was exposed, and when she realized that she'd been found out she left her job.

God speaks truth and desires truth. A society where truth is honored and spoken is much more respectful, orderly and open than one where it is not.

COMMANDMENT TEN: DO NOT ENGAGE IN ENVY OR JEALOUSY

> You shall not covet your neighbor's house. You shall not covet your neighbor's wife, or his manservant or maidservant, his ox or donkey, or anything that belongs to your neighbor. (Exod 20:17)

The last, tenth commandment is different from the preceding commandments. It addresses an attitude rather than something which can be externally assessed. It deals with the closely related human problems of envy and covetousness. Envy is a feeling of discontentment that is aroused when someone else has qualities, possessions or opportunities that I don't have. Covetousness occurs when I long to possess something that another person has. These roots contort the inner life of a person and may result in violating boundaries between neighbors. Envy and covetousness are such common, but under-diagnosed, components of human conflicts that God thought it good to place this boundary in a prominent position in the list. Gratitude and contentment run counter to envy and covetousness. It was, perhaps, only through suffering that Paul, in the New Testament, said he learned to be content, and indicated that it was a prerequisite for joy (Phil 4:11, 12).

Both the first and last commandments relate to the heart, even though that term, "the heart," is not yet used in the Old Testament. They both are concerned with each individual person's placement in relation to God and self. All other relationships in this society, and in the commandments sandwiched in between, are rooted in and affected by these two commandments. The first commandment gives an obvious orientation toward God as leader. The last commandment, in a more indirect way, also relates to God the Leader, as it can only be achieved through adopting a position of receiver, focusing on what has been given instead of on what is lacking. Since God is the ultimate provider in this narrative, the last commandment also orientates the individual towards God as giver.

The worship of God alone (the first commandment) will be expressed externally through prescribed rules regarding tabernacle, priests, offerings and sacrifices. However, the root meaning of this commandment calls for the worship of God in the heart. The externals are aids, but, without the heart, they will not meet the requirements.

The last commandment may seem unnecessary, considering that other commandments deal with life, marriage and property. But this commandment addresses a root that is able to spread its leaves and fruit into behavior that is externally observable and assessable by other commandments.

Any leader who sets rules must have the capacity to assess whether the rules are kept or broken and to set consequences. The first and last commandments pertain particularly and exclusively to God as leader, as he is the only one with the capacity to assess whether they are kept or not. Human leaders may not demand worship, and they do not have jurisdiction over the hearts of their people. Human leaders, under God's leadership, may and should exhort people to orientate their hearts towards God and demonstrate gratitude and contentment. They may even detect signs that suggest disorientation in these areas and call for change publicly or talk to people privately. But they are fallible in their judgments. They do not have the capacity to make ultimate assessments of the heart.

Commandments two to nine deal with phenomena that can more easily be assessed through speech or action. Since idols are made in visible form, bowing down or otherwise worshiping created beings is observable. Speaking God's name in vain and working on the sabbath day can be heard and seen. Dishonoring parents is shown through speech or actions; murdering, adultery, stealing and giving false testimony against a neighbor can be examined and judged. These areas can more easily relate to rules that human leaders in charge of tribes and governments need to make in order to give protection to the innocent and to foster social harmony.

God the Leader sets requirements for the internal and external lives of his people. Requirements that lead to healthy living for both individuals and communities. Requirements that he is able to watch over, for people he is able to help, not as a measurement for acceptance, but as guidelines to keep people out of slavery and living in freedom.

PUNISHMENTS

Cases need to be brought to justice swiftly, given fair trials with witnesses, and have consequences applied decisively. In all punishments, there is proportionality. This is referred to as "eye for an eye" (e.g., Lev 24:19–21) meaning that the punishment must be the same as whatever the person has done to another. So, the punishment for stealing a sheep is not the same as for murder. There are many nuances in punishments, as can be seen in the case laws, indicating that consideration is given to the crime, the intention, the location, any other relevant details and the condition of the people involved. This is the basis for modern Western judicial systems.

Israel's laws required that, besides punishment, restitution was also needed. This goes beyond many modern laws in its compassion and compensation for the victim. A man who steals one sheep must pay back four sheep (Exod 22:1). So, the victim is compensated for the loss of sheep plus loss of work time in looking for the sheep and discovering the thief, and the resulting breach in the relationship. This principle, often called restorative justice, has now been successfully applied by police dealing with young offenders in several countries, if the young offender shows willingness to be involved. The offender and victim are brought together with an intermediary, the victim speaks of the impact, the offender speaks, and, importantly, a scheme of restitution is worked out.

Where the wellbeing of the community is most seriously threatened, a greater punishment is needed, both as a means of damage control and as a serious deterrent. The aim is not only justice but restoration and the health of the community.

The question of capital punishment raises many alarm bells for modern readers. However, we often fail to consider that these laws were made for people who were nomadic or had a fairly marginal hold on a new land. Nomadic people have no prisons. Tents are not effective means of confining anyone against their will. There are no walls, no guards and no bureaucrats with government money who can keep people alive if they are not productive members of society. The whole camp may be required to move at a moment's notice. There is absolutely no capacity to luxuriate in the unreality of a prison system of any description.

In many modern societies prisons are overfull and their effectiveness is often questioned. I have taught in several prisons for adults and in one Young Offenders Institution. I have met a few prisoners who have used the opportunity inside to rethink, learn and prepare themselves for a crime-free, productive life on the outside. Unfortunately, I have also met many whose values have not changed and who would readily commit the same crimes when they next have opportunity.

The closest thing to a prison system is planned for the time of settlement in the promised land. That is when Cities of Refuge are allocated on both sides of the Jordan River (e.g., Deut 4:41–43). These towns are, however, not for the guilty to be kept away from society in order to protect society, but places where the innocent can stay so that they can be protected from false charges.

SETTING BOUNDARIES

In setting these boundaries, God the Leader is concerned for the wellbeing of the community. He will not tolerate outright rebellion, divisive behavior or violation of other people's rights. His instructions are clear, yet with sufficient flexibility to consider the variations in particular cases. He is fair, and his punishments fit the crimes. Action is taken swiftly in accordance with the laws which people have been told. While some specific instructions (in the case laws) are appropriate for a people in that historical and geographical context and not necessarily for us now, the general principles underlying these ten major laws still merit attention.

God the Leader's purpose is to build a society where trust and trustworthiness are strong, and where life is valued and fostered. We often wonder why modern life seems to be so much more stressful than the lives of our ancestors, even if they suffered wars and other tragedies. The more chaotic life is, the more stressful it becomes. Could our problems be due, in part, to the loss of clarity and the loss of some of those boundaries that were intended to protect us from undue chaos?

If a leader errs on the side of harshness, the outcome will be crippling fear, as we saw under Pharaoh. However, it is less well recognized that if the leader errs on the side of softness, the outcome will be chaos. We need the boundaries to be sufficiently clear, protected and enforced. Otherwise we will discover that others who do not have our wellbeing at heart will jump into the power vacuum and violate innocent people who should have been protected.

QUESTIONS FOR REFLECTION OR DISCUSSION

1. What were God's motivations as a Leader in setting these Ten Commandments?
2. Have you ever been robbed? Or slandered? How did you feel?
3. How serious a role might envy and jealousy play in conflicts you know about?
4. As a leader in your family or organization, what strategies would you put in place to limit damage?
5. How far might these principles be applied in a secular society?
6. Do we need punishments? What kinds work best today?

PART 3

Ethical Issues in Leadership

Chapter 11

Ethnicity

There are three issues—ethnicity, land and war—which can be fraught with difficulties for many national political leaders. These issues also have more subtle implications for many other non-political groups. This chapter will look at God's leadership in relation to ethnicities and other separations between insiders and outsiders. The subsequent chapters will look at issues relating to land and war.

Some people tell me that they have never considered or experienced ethnicity as an issue. Perhaps it is because they have never experienced rejection or conflict on account of ethnicity—something to be thankful for, indeed. Or perhaps they have been blind to the issue because they were settled and accepted members of the dominant "insider" group. However, people who belong to minority ethnic groups, or who experience regular racial or tribal tensions, or who have been displaced from their former home, are acutely aware of ethnicity issues.

Was God's leadership tainted by ethnic favoritism? Did he make decisions that only supported the needs of the insiders in his group, without regard to the needs of outsiders? Did he place a curse on some racial groups? Did he rank people according to their family origins? These questions arise in many contexts.

When I was a student in an international, multi-ethnic college, I attended a class led by a professor who, although a good lecturer, continually gave illustrations from his own country's sports and media personalities and events. Over half of the class, including me, had no knowledge of these people or events, so we missed many of his main points and were therefore unable to contribute to those parts of the discussion. In addition, I noticed that the professor made eye contact only with white Westerners, mostly with males. The non-Westerners, who numbered a third of the class, never received his eye contact and never spoke in class. Ethnicity and related issues were present but flew under the radar of this well-intentioned professor and the students who were from his own country.

When I taught in Ethiopia, I was asked to coordinate a class on the subject of "Ethnicity Issues" and teach a section from the Old Testament on the subject. Perhaps I was asked because I was an outsider to the tribal resentments simmering only barely under the surface in that land and affecting every student to some degree. I also discovered that many Ethiopians and other Africans suffer from the very alive notion that Africa's poverty and lowly place on the world stage arise from the outworking of the curse of Ham (or more accurately a misunderstanding of the curse of Canaan in Genesis 9:24–27). Are dark-skinned people under a curse by God, a curse that they cannot break free from?

We have probably all experienced an invisible wall that keeps us as "outsiders" to a group. Sometimes we can't find an obvious explanation for this. Is it because we are from another part of the country? Or went to a different kind of school? Or come from a different kind of family background? Or are simply not related to anyone in the group? Children can be experts at keeping anyone who looks a little different out of their "insider" groups. As a redhead I experienced this, but I also recognize that anyone who is too fat or too thin, too tall or too short, too bright or too dull can also feel excluded. The same human factors that were at work against me as a child in Australia thrive in other places, in more exaggerated forms, as the ethnicity issues that fuel violent wars.

We may have leadership experience in one ethnic group. Then the integration of people from several ethnicities and cultures creates an element of stimulation and excitement, but also some new challenges and new conflicts. How do we really understand our leadership and God's leadership in relation to multiple ethnic groups?

How does God as leader deal with outsiders coming to settle among the Israelites? Some think the Old Testament picture of God is that he is for the Israelites (or Jews) and against everyone else. But a closer look at the story demonstrates that God is not a one-eyed nationalistic leader who encourages a kind of supremacy thinking. In fact, there are various statements indicating that God assesses all peoples evenhandedly (e.g., Jer 18:7–10), even though the story of his leadership of only one particular people group is recorded.

BELONGING

Belonging to a family, to a tribe, or to a nation fulfills our need for connectedness. Genealogies may be boring to those outside the family group but create identity and sometimes roles for insiders (Gen 5, 10, 11). Traits of ancestors turn up in succeeding generations (Gen 4, 5) for good or ill. But even within the same family, brothers of the same parents have quite different attitudes and behaviors (Gen 4:1-12), warning us against a monochrome view of any racial group.

The leader of a family, tribe or nation confirms the people's sense of belonging, and fosters cohesion of the group. God as Leader confirms his people's special relationship to him through a covenant, likened most often to a marriage covenant where both the leader and the people have responsibilities towards each other.

God does not commit himself to any automatic action on behalf of this group of people and against their enemies. His loyalty is not blind. His actions of blessing are conditional on the people's loyalty to him and on their good choices. In fact, there is a warning that certain serious acts of disobedience to his leadership will cause his blessing to be withdrawn, thus allowing them to experience curses (Deut 28). It may be helpful to view these blessings and curses as consequences built into an orderly system that God created. They are not at all like the magical notions of blessings and curses, which are prohibited practices (Deut 18:9-11).

THE CURSE OF HAM

Because of African ethnic sensitivities, the question of the "curse of Ham" needs to be carefully considered. But the implications of this story are wider. Is God truly cursing a particular family or ethnic group? Is there justification for us to treat some groups as inherently entitled and others as beneath us?

In this story (Gen 9:25-27) the words of curse are pronounced by Noah, not by God, just as words of blessing and curse are pronounced elsewhere in the Old Testament by other fathers over their future generations (e.g., Gen 49). Usually such words are given near the end of a patriarch's life, but Noah's words come after a specific incident that Noah considers a marker in the life of his family. In this incident Noah's son Ham behaves distinctly differently from his two brothers, Shem and Japheth.

Noah gets drunk. Every other reference to drunkenness in the Bible condemns it. But here the focus is not on drunkenness but on how Noah's sons deal with finding their father in a weakened, vulnerable state. The narrative suggests that Ham, who finds his father naked, brings shame on his father by failing to cover him and by telling his brothers, most likely in a mocking way. Shem and Japheth do not join in the mockery but choose to cover their father respectfully by walking in backwards with a garment.[1] With this understanding, the behavioral problems demonstrated by Ham are: 1) showing and enticing disrespect for a father, and 2) exploiting and shaming a person in a weakened condition (irrespective of the cause).

This is not the only place in the Old Testament where exploiting and shaming the weak is regarded as a serious issue. A more generalized statement of Ham's offence is given in Habakkuk 2:15–16, where God condemns the person who gets some kind of pleasure from making another person drunk so that he/she can look at their nakedness—perhaps even gloating over their own apparent righteousness (their desired "glory" v.16) for not drinking and getting themselves into a similar vulnerable state. The consequence will be shame, because they have put another person to shame and have tried to gain "glory" for themselves at the expense of another.

Returning to the "curse of Ham," we see that it is actually placed on just one of Ham's sons: Canaan. There is no explanation given here as to why the curse is on only one branch of Ham's family. (Was Canaan with Ham when this happened?) Later the Israelites are told of the extensive and hardhearted wickedness of the Canaanites and God's decision to destroy them and give their land to Israel. Perhaps it was Canaan's family that perpetuated the sin of Ham, and most likely many other evil practices, but other branches did not.

Through the centuries many interpreters have not read this passage accurately and have said that 1) the curse was on all of Ham's descendants; 2) it was related to the color of his skin. This interpretation has been misused to justify racism against African and dark-skinned people, even though it is clear that Ham's descendants also spread towards the east of Israel and include a much wider range of skin color than this interpretation allows. There is absolutely no link in the Bible with skin color, only a link with sinful behavior. Nor is there instruction or even permission to try and make a curse happen.

---

1. Some suggest that the sin is sexual relations by Ham with Noah's wife (Ham's mother). Several verses use the same expression (uncovering a man's nakedness) to mean illicit sexual relations with his wife, e.g., Lev 20:11, 20–21; Ezek 22:10. This is obviously a much more serious sin which violates all biblical teaching about marriage and the prohibition against sexual activity outside marriage, as well as showing contempt for both father and mother. However, the action of the other two sons (covering their father's nakedness) would not make sense with this interpretation.

As we have seen, an Old Testament curse is not a magical curse, because all magic was forbidden. Rather, it expresses the consequences of repeating the same offending behavior, or the consequences of specific sins, which can often be perpetuated down family lines. And a curse can be broken by people who change their behavior away from that which gave rise to the curse. The example of Rahab (Josh 6:25) shows that someone who comes from a family that was supposedly bearing a curse (Rahab was a Canaanite) can be released from the curse. By her own faith and actions (protecting God's people instead of handing them over to be destroyed) she became an exception to the Canaanite pattern of behavior. She was saved instead of destroyed; she joined the people of God and became an ancestor of Jesus.

THE ETHNIC FORMATION OF THE HEBREW PEOPLE

Does God's leadership of one ethnic group imply his rejection of other peoples? In order to assess this, we will look at the nature of this covenant people and relationships with people of other ethnicities.

The formation of the Israelites as an ethnic group was unique on account of their covenants with God their Leader. Their particular call was not a sign of being against other people, but a sign of being, in a special way, with God. And it was for the ultimate purpose of bringing blessing to other peoples (Gen 12:1–3). However, they could not fulfill their specific purpose if they mixed their religious beliefs and customs with those of other people.

Every ethnic group has an unseen boundary around it, with boundary markers.[2] For Israel, the most important boundary markers were the signs of circumcision of males and the whole community's keeping of the sabbath, together with some dietary laws. These related to purity—to holiness before God. Those who did not keep these signs were outside the group. There is no mention of any boundary of language or physical features or specific clothes, as there might be for other groups.

Although there is a common family history of the group, coming from Abraham, Isaac and Jacob, it was always possible for those who did not have this ancestral origin to be integrated into Israel if they submitted to the signs of belonging required by God. This is because their submission would show their respect for Israel's God and Leader. So Hebrew ethnicity is not based on ethnic purity as such but on purity (holiness) in relation to God.

---

2. Pitkänen, "Ethnicity, Assimilation and the Israelite Settlement."

FOREIGNERS LIVING AMONG THE ISRAELITES

There is evidence that some non-Hebrews chose to travel with the Hebrews from Egypt (Exod 12:38). Although some of these people became complainers, they obviously shared life with the Israelites (Num 11:4–6). Moses' brother-in-law (a Midianite) was invited to join them (Num 10:24) as he could provide help from his knowledge of the desert and in return he would share in other benefits. It seems that some of his descendants remained with Israel. Caleb's background is not purely Israelite—he is called a Kenizzite, but his family had established themselves among the Judahites and so he came to belong to the tribe of Judah (Num 13:6), even becoming a leader of the tribe.

In Exodus and Deuteronomy, the Israelites are often told to give specific care to the foreigners among them and not to mistreat them. The main reason given for showing them particular care is that the Israelites had themselves been aliens in Egypt (Exod 22:21). Boaz is a good example of a righteous Israelite who showed commendable compassion towards a foreigner (Ruth), and actively helped her to get food by offering protection as she gleaned.

FOREIGNERS WORSHIPPING WITH ISRAEL

When the first Passover was celebrated in the land of Israel, no foreigners were to participate. These foreigners seem to have been temporary residents, so probably would not have known God or the significance of Passover. However, slaves bought by Israelites could eat Passover if they were circumcised (Exod 12:43–45). Later, foreigners living among the Israelites were to celebrate Passover with them. Exactly the same regulations applied to them as to the Israelites, because by now these people would have joined the group and understood its significance (Num 9:14). The same regulations for offerings and penalties for sins applied to foreigners as to Hebrews (Num 15:14–16, 26–30).

There were, however, restrictions on foreigners entering the assembly of the Lord. Ammonites and Moabites were restricted to the tenth generation. These two groups had created serious difficulties for Israel. People of Edomite descent (from Esau's family) or of Egyptian descent were not considered as hostile; they could enter the assembly in the third generation (Deut 23:1–8). Differences in these rules suggest that it took longer for people of some groups to integrate and worship Israel's God. However, there were always exceptions. For example, Ruth, a Moabitess, was fully accepted in Israel from the time of her arrival. Her intention in coming into Hebrew territory, as stated to her Hebrew mother-in-law Naomi, was that "Your people will be my people, and your God my God" (Ruth 1:16). Identity with God's people is of greater significance than an identity based on genetic ties.

INTERMARRIAGE

There is an awareness in Genesis that marriage is better within related people, rather than with neighbors who do not share the same faith and values. For example, the servant in Genesis 24 goes to find a wife for Isaac from his own kindred. This is particularly on account of the covenant which God has made with Abraham and his family, which will include Isaac and his son Jacob. When a clear instruction is given not to marry outside the group following God as leader, the reason given is always religious and never on tribal or racial grounds. The ban on marrying people from the seven specific tribes whom God will drive out from the land that will become Israel is given because "they will turn your sons away from following me to serve other gods" (Deut 7:3, 4).

Moses himself married a Midianite (the daughter of a Midianite priest) and may have also married a Cushite wife (scholars disagree over whether this could be the same person). Although his siblings complained about his foreign wife, God vindicated him (Num 12:1), so there was no blanket rule against all intermarriage.

There is plenty of evidence in the historical books of the Old Testament that intermarriage did often cause people to turn away from following God. In the north the wicked Jezebel, daughter of the pagan king of Sidon (1 Kings 16), had a particularly evil effect on her husband King Ahab, who clearly turned away from following God as leader and committed an untold number of atrocities.

When the Jews return after the exile, Ezra is extremely distressed to hear of this kind of intermarriage and calls it unfaithfulness (Ezra 9:1–4). This is unfaithfulness to God rather than mere unfaithfulness to the ethnic group. The same problem occurs again in Nehemiah 13 where many of the children of these mixed marriages do not even know the language of Israel. Since language is the medium of instruction concerning God their Leader, it means that the foreign mothers would be teaching them religious views that stand in direct opposition to God their Leader.

However, there are other examples of mixed marriages that are blessed, e.g., with both Rahab and Ruth who become part of Jesus' family line. In both cases these "foreigners" respect and accept Israel's God. So, the ban on mixed marriages is a religious ban, not an ethnic ban, even if the instructions are sometimes summarized in a shorthand form as a ban on mixed marriages.

RELATIONSHIPS WITH OTHER GROUPS

Under God's leadership, the Israelites are to have different kinds of relationships with different ethnic groups. With some peoples, there are to be friendly and cooperative relationships. Isaac makes a covenant with Abimelech, king of the Philistines, for peaceful and respectful coexistence (Gen 26:28, 29). The Israelites are not to fight with certain peoples who have shown kindness and respect to Israel, or with whom a treaty has been made (e.g., the Gibeonites, Josh 9). Later, King Solomon has agreements with Hiram, king of Tyre, for the provision of materials and skilled men for the building of the temple. Jeremiah tells the Israelites to accept Babylonian leadership in Israel and, while in exile, to seek the peace and prosperity of the cities in which they now live (Jer 29). However, God directs that some groups are to be treated as enemies. These are people who pose a continuing threat to Israel's safety and to the ability of Israel to stay true to its purpose as a holy people.

It is apparent that God as Leader does not promote a monochrome view of ethnicity. However, ethnic identity is secondary to behaviors and to relationship with God. God is not a Hebrew supremacist who is against the incorporation of foreigners into his people; nor does he promote antagonism towards other ethnic groups simply because they are "other." His concern, as Leader, must be for the safety and security of his own people, and to keep them spiritually and relationally wholesome.

God the Leader is no ethnic bigot. His leadership of Israel is no excuse for tribal prejudices, or for looking down on people who are not quite like us. The people of God have their primary identity rooted in relationship to God, while descriptors of nationality, tribe and language take a lower place. This sets the scene for the New Testament, where God's leadership is more clearly shown to work across all ethnic and tribal divisions.

QUESTIONS FOR REFLECTION OR DISCUSSION

1. Have you grown up with ethnic or cultural or social prejudice?
2. How relevant for you is the issue of "insiders" and "outsiders"?
3. What experiences do you have regarding prejudice and discrimination in leadership?
4. What are some characteristics of "safe" leaders?
5. How do you deal with issues of ethnic, cultural and social diversity in the sphere of your leadership?
6. Is intermarriage between different ethnic or cultural or social/caste groups an issue in a community you know? If so, why?

Chapter 12

A Place to Settle

All humans, and indeed all creatures, have a need for place. Whether this is a physical place on a piece of land, or a place for us to find in a new social group, workplace or neighborhood, the need is universal. Yet place is so frequently under threat. And leaders of all sorts need to deal with it.

Conflicts between old settlers and new refugees, both claiming their needs for place, erupt in every continent and in every age. Establishing, maintaining and protecting physical places lies within the jurisdiction of national and tribal leaders. Establishing, maintaining and protecting emotional and/or spiritual places lies within the jurisdiction of certain other kinds of leaders. Large sections of the Old Testament relate to God's leadership in the realm of physical place, of land, for his people. Yet, this is always integrated into his wider care for spiritual and other kinds of place which his people also need.

The quest for physical place, often has the potential for conflict. In this chapter we will look at God's leadership in the area of the provision of land. The next chapter will examine God's leadership in difficult situations of conflict and war. The two are obviously linked. Both of these issues are often entwined with ethnicity issues, which were outlined in the last chapter.

LAND RIGHTS

From an Old Testament perspective, God's authority over land is beyond that of any other leader. He owns it all. He can give it to any people group he chooses, and he can take it away. He can make conditions of occupation of land and can decide when a particular group has forfeited their right to stay there. This means that any claims to ownership of land are always relative and temporary, even if long-term. If we do not accept this Old Testament premise, we may falsely invest individuals or the human leaders of communities with ultimate rights of land ownership. This would be detrimental to our ability to read and interpret this body of writing on its own terms.

Promises of land made by God to Abraham were not fulfilled in his lifetime but only hundreds of years later. And that was only after periods when his people were nomads, settled aliens, slaves and refugees. The community ideal is for each man "to sit under his own vine and fig tree" (e.g., Micah 4:4; Zech 3:10), to spend enough time in his own place for vines and trees to flourish and bear fruit to share in hospitality and friendship. God as Leader recognizes the importance of this ideal but chooses to lead his people through a range of relationships with the land. Settledness is an important need, but not the only need.

TIMES OF UNSETTLEDNESS

The one situation that was ultimately intolerable for both people and God was the period of slavery under harsh overlords in Egypt. Previously the Hebrews had been given a place in the area of Goshen in Egypt in which to settle as aliens. The fact that they did not technically "own" the land was not regarded as a problem, as they were invited, welcomed, treated respectfully and allowed, in all respects, to live there well. They had a legitimate place. A later Pharaoh, however, viewed their thriving as a threat, and placed slave-masters over them, working them ruthlessly (Exod 1). At this time the place of the Hebrews was being demolished, in terms of their presence in that land, and in terms of their safety and security. As a result of being required to work long hours on the Pharaoh's projects, their ability to use the land to produce food for their families, through crops and livestock, was also diminished. We might also infer that other aspects of place were impacted—for example, a place to think, to rest, to make choices, to relate freely, to be respected, to be heard, and a place to worship.

God's leadership of this displaced people (displaced within the place that had been allocated to them) becomes known. He hears their cries, demonstrates that having their place eroded so forcibly and cruelly is not acceptable, and promises to lead them to their own new place. But he has reasons for leading these refugees through a lengthy period of nomadic existence first. Here he establishes relational place, founded on his love demonstrated in his rescue, signified by the establishment of a covenant between God as Leader and his people. Since the fundamental cause of the people's loss of place was the loss of a mutually respectful relationship between them and the Egyptian leader, this aspect of displacement needs to be addressed first. Otherwise, the people may not be able to settle, even if given land.

The most obvious establishment of place in the desert is not of a physical place, but of a place in relationship with God—a spiritual place. This, in turn, strengthens their communal identity as the people of God. In this narrative, spiritual place takes priority over a settled physical place in the land, even as the story moves towards the latter. Their place in relationship to God is the basis on which a place in the land will be established.

In order to provide a new land in which the Hebrews can settle, other peoples will need to be unsettled and removed. We hear the story only from the perspective of the needs of the Hebrews, so our imaginations tend to fill in the gaps regarding the peoples who were previously settled in that land, and our imaginations may not be accurate. Across most cultures in past ages, stories of conquest were told without any reference to the needs, losses and feelings of conquered peoples. Questions of justice and injustice for the vanquished did not belong in the telling. But in our post-colonial age we are more aware of and more interested in the underside of the story, in the lives of the underdogs. If we don't have information, we tend to presume the innocence of whoever is in the weaker position and presume that they have been sinned against.

OLD AND NEW SETTLERS

There are, indeed, legitimate rights and needs of old settlers. There are also rights and needs of new settlers, especially if they are asylum seekers or refugees who have been wrenched from their previous settled places. If both old settlers and refugees are seeking to live in the same land, whose rights and needs should take priority? It is always a complex question.

My ancestors moved across the globe in several directions. Sometimes they were forced to move. For example, the Puritan group who made their way to America in the *Mayflower* were already displaced from their homes by religious persecution. Other ancestors convicted for petty crimes of theft were transported by the British Government to the new penal colony in Australia. Others moved for economic reasons or to escape relationship difficulties and went to India, when it was under British rule, or as free settlers in other colonies. Further back in my family history, I discover ancestors from all over Europe moving to other lands because they were fleeing from wars, or because they were conquerors. Each of these people had needs. And so did the peoples who were already in the lands to which they went.

The biblical perspective of God as ultimate owner of all land can be very helpful in attempting to balance the needs of old and new occupiers, as human ownership is relativized—not ignored—and arrogance is checked.

DIFFICULTIES IN JUDGING OTHER PEOPLES ACCURATELY

God is not only the leader of the Hebrew people, but the rightful judge of all peoples. Human leaders looking for land for their people do not have the capacity to judge other groups with accuracy. For this reason, the biblical narrative implies that God alone knows why seven specific tribes are to be ousted from their land (Deut 7:1). Perhaps they had crossed some line of injustice in terms of their persistent, serious and arrogant mistreatment of people, similar to the line that Pharaoh had crossed in his mistreatment of the Hebrews in Egypt. We don't know and guessing will not be productive. God is, however, able to make judgments concerning the needs and conditions of all peoples. Taking land from one group and giving it to another is one such act of judgment.

As a leader, God chooses not to disclose matters that pertain to other people. Otherwise it could easily provoke attitudes of arrogance, scorn and perhaps misplaced pity. It would also certainly cause confusion about their future actions, and that confusion would interfere with their ability to take the land God is giving them. While there is a consistent biblical call to show pity and exercise justice, it applies to relationships and situations in which people have some knowledge and responsibility. In this situation, God, who has knowledge and responsibility, has made a judgment about which the Hebrews have no knowledge. He chooses to give his own people only the information that is useful and relevant to them. His approach reminds me of Jesus' rebuke to Peter, who asked, "What about him?" (John 21:21). The reply was effectively, "Mind your own business!"

LAND-GRABBING NOT ALLOWED

For whatever reason, God declares that the land of the seven tribes is now to be given to the Hebrews. It is worth noting that there is no permission given for the Hebrews to take the lands of any more tribes than these seven. There is no encouragement for them to initiate any other land conquests. They may only take what God has made a prior decision to give them. This stands in stark contrast to the mentality of some of Europe's kings and queens. For them, owning more land meant greater prestige, so they plotted to increase their land through wars or marriage. The relative needs of people on both sides of the boundary were of little concern to them.

Conquest of land is usually perpetrated by the strongest people group, not necessarily the most deserving. In some parts of the world that is still seen as an acceptable basis for land transfer, rather like the survival of the fittest and the weeding out of the weak. When God leads his people to their new land he announces that the unexpected will occur: they will defeat those who are much stronger than they are (Deut 7:7–8; 17–23). This land conquest will be different. The aim will not be to prove which people group is the greatest or strongest. However, the power that is involved in effecting this land transfer is the power of the God of the Hebrews, the owner of all the land. That power will be seen by both the Hebrews and the surrounding tribes. It is he who will give land to the Hebrews to meet their need for a settled place.

God sets the boundaries of the land, even before the Hebrews enter it (Num 34). Each Hebrew tribe is to be allocated their piece of the land, rather than being allowed to grab whatever they can. The distribution of land is to be orderly and considered, with appointed tribal representatives working together with the human leader of the group and the high priest. The size of each tribe is an important consideration. Some land is negotiated. The leaders of two and a half tribes (Gad, Reuben, half of Manasseh) approach Moses and are given the first land on the east of the Jordan, on the condition that they will continue to help the other tribes to claim their land. Later, Caleb asks Joshua for his share on the basis of a previous promise by Moses. Some years later, after many battles have been fought and won in this land, Joshua and his team cast lots for the remaining allocations for nine and a half tribes; the use of lots implies that they are reliant on the leadership of God for direction (Josh 14).

God instructs Moses that the tribe of Levi is to be treated differently (Num 35). They will not be allocated tribal territory, only towns with pasturelands, which Joshua later allocates by lot (Josh 21). Their presence within the Hebrew people, now called Israel, is a reminder that those who are settled should always be mindful of those who do not have that same security of land and are necessarily dependent on them. The Rechabite clan follows a family vow to live as nomads, without the security of settled land (Jer 35). They are commended by God for keeping to this vow, and for not drinking wine, which can only come from the fruit of a settled existence. The prophets Isaiah and Amos point to the social dangers in being settled—dangers arising from overcrowding, lavish homes and lifestyles, and drunkenness (e.g., Isa 5:8–12).

FEASTING AND CAMPING

An annual week-long festival is appointed by God as a call for the Israelites to leave the security of their settled homes in the land. For the Feast of Tabernacles (also called Feast of Booths or Sukkot) the people must build temporary shelters and live in them for seven days (Lev 23:33–43). Today, people who celebrate this festival often sleep and cook in the comfort of their own homes and visit the shelter for meals. But the original idea was for people of all social classes to leave their comforts, rank and signs of their wealth, and come to be on the same level as everyone else. It was a time of intentional self-denial and of bringing various offerings to God, a time of living more simply and being covered only by a rough and insubstantial shelter. Yet it was also a time of wholesome fun, a productive holiday. The Feast of Tabernacles is an exercise in remembering the time when God led the people through the wilderness. In order to live well as a settled people, it is necessary to hold settledness somewhat lightly. There are relationships and values that are more foundational to life than being comfortably placed in the land.

I appreciate the image of "God the Camper" given by Robert Banks,[1] picturing God leading his people on a giant camping trip through the Sinai Peninsula. In fact, for modern settled people, going camping is, in some respects, a similar exercise to that of the Feast of Tabernacles. I remember one camping holiday with our children on the east coast of Tasmania. As I watched the children playing readily with unknown children from neighboring tents I wondered if some of the campers might hold important positions in society and live in big, fancy houses back at home, and if others might struggle on very little income. It was impossible to tell. Everyone wore the same kind of casual beach clothes; everyone slept in a similar kind of shelter—a tent; everyone cooked on a simple camping stove. Camping is a great leveler. Some people refuse to go camping because the idea of going without home comforts seems too hard. But for those who do it, the benefits of refreshed perspective are well worth it.

During the Exodus journey, the primary relationship is between leader and people, not between land and people. As leader, God allows the use of land, for shorter or longer periods, to meet legitimate needs of food and rest.

CAN LAND BE OWNED?

There is another significant factor in the land debate, and it may lead to misunderstanding. A conquering people may think in terms of ownership

---

1. Banks, *God the Worker*.

of specific plots of land, and the vanquished people may have less clearly defined boundaries to mark its ownership, especially if they are nomadic or semi-nomadic. This has been the case in the settling of Europeans in North America and Australia. Indigenous groups often naively and hospitably welcomed the newcomers and made treaties with them. The newcomers often did not keep the treaties and showed great disrespect to the indigenous people. There were misunderstandings on both sides, and part of the misunderstanding concerned relationship to the land. Europeans viewed land as a commodity which could be bought and sold. The indigenous people saw land as a place of belonging, a place that could never be traded.

In Fiji, land is held by the native Fijians, who arrived from Melanesia around 3,500 years ago. However, nearly half of the population is Indian. Most of these Indians are descended from indentured laborers, whom the British colonial rulers brought to work on Fiji's sugar plantations between 1879 and 1916. Many Indians have fought for equal treatment, but with very limited success. Even though their families have lived in Fiji for a hundred years or more, they do not have the land rights of native Fijians. Land rights issues evoke plenty of emotions, as well as thorny questions of justice.

GRATITUDE, GENEROSITY AND PRESUMPTION

A place in the land is not to be taken for granted. An attitude of gratitude to God for providing it is to be fostered (Deut 8). God knows the human tendency towards greed, complacency and competition. God instructs the Israelites to offer to himself the first fruits of any produce, and, when they are harvesting, to leave grain at the corners of the fields for the poor to pick. In these things he is reminding them that occupation or "ownership" of the land does not mean *carte blanche* permission to squeeze every last drop from it for personal profit.

In fact, a place in the land means a place to offer hospitality. The Israelites are frequently reminded of their days as slaves, aliens and nomads in order to call them to show particular compassion to others who are now in these categories. This hospitality opens the possibility of foreigners settling in the land, under certain conditions, and becoming part of the Israelite people. The land itself needs to be observed, understood, cared for and periodically rested.

God's gift of land comes with a warning: if the people do not continue to be faithful to the covenant made with their leader God, they may eventually be expelled from the land, just as other groups before them have been expelled. Over time, the people become over-reliant on the land and the temple built within it (Jer 7). When they are eventually taken captive and forced out of the land they assume that they have lost the presence of God their leader. But God demonstrates his mobility and shows up right where they are, in Babylon, far from their land (Ezek 1). Furthermore, he surprises them by saying that he has been with them, even in their punishment—their "time out" away from their land (Ezek 11:16). And he encourages them through the prophet Jeremiah to settle down as aliens on foreign soil (Jer 29:4–7). Even so, through the period of exile in Babylon, the land of Israel is still regarded as "home" for this nation, by the people and by God. And eventually they are called and enabled to return.

CONCERNS FOR PROVISION

God's leadership in providing land for his people is for the purpose of meeting their foundational needs for food and shelter—their physiological needs. As it is written in other places, it is reproachable to ignore such basic needs when it is within one's means to meet them (Prov 3:27; James 2:15, 16). Another need is for people to work, to be productive; the provision of land enables work that connects humans to the land in the quest for both food and shelter. And in the labor there is to be enjoyment (Eccl 3:12, 13). All of these things contribute to another foundational need: health.

Although it might seem obvious that people should have their foundational needs met, and, ideally, with some sense of enjoyment, it is not obvious to all human leaders. That is why governments enact legislation regarding the rights of employees, and health and safety in the workplace. It is, unfortunately, *not* obvious to leaders who are preoccupied with financial or production goals that workers need adequate breaks for food, bathroom, and rest. Nor is it obvious to some that enjoyment of work, through meaningful productivity and congenial relationships, has anything to do with the function and purpose of leadership. Pharaoh-behavior inflicts harsh treatment that serves the leader's own personal goals and ignores the need for the provision of a legitimate and suitable place so that a worker has freedom to be creative and productive.

We once lived in the suburb (originally a village) of Bournville, in Birmingham UK, the home of Cadbury chocolate. In the late nineteenth century, the Cadbury brothers, who were Quakers, needed to move their factory out of the city center, so they decided to create a model village, one where the needs of their workers would be the prime consideration. This idea was, at the time, totally counter-cultural and counter-intuitive. They wanted to alleviate the compounded stresses of living in cramped and unhealthy conditions. So they planned acres of green space for relaxation and sporting activities, schools and free community facilities, and built houses that not only looked very attractive (and still do) but also had enough backyard garden space for fruit trees, vegetable gardens, and a safe place for children to play. It is still a very delightful place to live and Cadburys still strives to look after its workers. The Cadbury brothers serve as one human leadership example that, to my mind, follows God's leadership in seeking to care for legitimate basic human needs, for health, recreation and beauty, for belonging, community and work, all in the physical place of land that is developed for this purpose. The success of the outcome is not just in assisting with those particular needs, but in fostering greater enjoyment and loyalty and, of course, increased productivity.

Christians follow God as Leader too. There are some promises and creations of "place" for God's people in the New Testament, but it is not of land. The question of land for the Jewish people today is a different issue. They have been unjustly persecuted to an extreme degree and do need a place of safety, just as any other people group does. But contemporary questions around the modern state of Israel go beyond the scope of this book. The character and principles of God's leadership remain but the context, where people of every nation and tongue now join in following this God, is different. Ethnic boundaries no longer cleanly separate those who follow this Leader from those who don't.

QUESTIONS FOR REFLECTION OR DISCUSSION

1. How important are considerations of land in your situation? Are there any issues?
2. How does an understanding of God as ultimate owner of all land affect your thinking?
3. To what extent should a leader encourage a sense of "settledness"?
4. If God is concerned to care for the basic human needs of place, health, work, recreation and community, how might this influence our own leadership?
5. How can going without our normal comforts, whether camping or not, realign our priorities?
6. How can we foster gratitude?

Chapter 13

War

God's quest for land for his displaced people—a good and worthy aim for peaceful existence—may involve conflict. That conflict at times may even involve bloodshed. I would much prefer that it did not. I would like it if God, who has so many more resources available to him than to any of us, could find ways of solving problems without battles, especially those risking loss of life. Yet, we do see several important differences between God's ways of leading his people into battles and the ways of most human rulers.

If God did, as a matter of principle, avoid all conflict, there would be no possibility of him ever rescuing innocent people from the clutches of wicked tyrants. There would have been no deliverance from the Pharaoh of Egypt. There would be no point in any of us calling to him for help in the face of cruel enemies. He would effectively place his people at the mercy of every other army who was ready to exterminate them! God is a leader who takes his responsibility of protection seriously, so avoiding conflict is not an option. Assessing and dealing with threats and conflict is always a component of leadership and it is naive to imagine otherwise.

In a recent conversation with a pacifist friend I asked him, "Why do you think people go into the army?" His immediate reply was, "To kill people." That may be seen as an acceptable motivation for those joining some terrorist armies, but it is not seen as an acceptable motivation for people joining the armies of most democratic nations. Rather, the primary purpose of the latter kind of army, and a legitimate motivation for people wanting to join it, is for defense and for peace. Military forces aim, or should aim, to save, deliver and protect. They should not choose to initiate aggression, and they should be mobilized only as a last resort.

However, war is messy and it is simply not possible in most wars to defend one group of people without stopping another group from taking them over. Nor is it always possible to do so without using violence and inflicting serious wounds and even death. Inevitably people who are not directly involved in the conflict will suffer.

I am no fan of warfare. Neither am I a fan of passivity in the face of cruel and unjust aggression. And I am very aware that pacifism is not passivity. While a certain level of verbal conflict is normal and can even be healthy and productive, too much conflict at any level runs a high risk of poisonous spin-offs. I have benefited much from living among Mennonites. They have contributed a wealth of thinking and practical advice on conflict resolution without resorting to violence, and this wisdom should be much more widely known and utilized than it is. But some aggressors seem to be highly resistant to whatever means we try towards cooperation, understanding and peace, because those things are simply not on their agenda.

It is clear that God's way is to pursue the way of peace with all other groups, if at all possible. Warfare is engaged with great reluctance, severe caution and clear boundaries. As we look at God's leadership in war in the Old Testament, we also need to recognize that he led a theocracy, not a democracy. God was the leader of a nation, not, as is the case today, in charge of scattered people within different nations, often on different sides of conflicts led by their opposing governments. There is no longer any nation (not even Israel) that is in the same position in regard to God's leadership as what we see in the Old Testament.

GOD'S HEAVENLY ARMIES

As a young person, I heard of "God's heavenly hosts" and imagined innocuous angelic beings wafting around the sky in nightdresses, the kind I associated with the shepherds on the hills at Christmas. But I had overlooked the fact that the shepherds were terrified of these beings (Luke 2:9). In fact, fear is the most frequent reaction of anyone in the Bible who recognizes the presence of an angel. That is why the most frequent command in the Bible is, "Do not be afraid." However, there are reasons for both the fear response and the counter-command. The fear response is due to the presence of incredible power. The counter-command is due to the power being used *for* the person, rather than *against*.

The Message version of the Bible talks about "God of the angel armies" instead of "the heavenly hosts." That, I think, is more accurate, because the heavenly hosts are none other than a super-charged, mega-powerful on-duty but normally invisible army. They can, however, appear anywhere at any time, as necessary—on the ground or in the sky, looking like normal people or more obviously like supernatural beings. God is the leader of this army. God is, therefore, far from being a passive, helpless onlooker, as we may sometimes surmise.

I recall that Aslan the lion in C. S. Lewis's *The Lion, the Witch and the Wardrobe*, presenting an image of the biblical God as Leader, is not called "safe," even though he is called "good." God as Leader is never referred to as safe or harmless to those who defy him, even though he is said to work for his own people's safety. On the contrary, he is fearsome and dreadful in his ability to destroy and demolish. God as Leader has power—immense power within himself and the power of being able to command a heavenly army to travel and act as he wishes. In addition, he has the power of command and persuasion over his people and their army. He has the power to create life, and he also has the power to destroy life. Yet that power is very carefully controlled.

GUIDELINES FOR HIS PEOPLE

God gives humans the capacity to both procreate and to kill. However, he puts careful safeguards around both of these powerful acts. Killing humans is highly restricted. There is to be no murder. No one has the right to take the life of another for any personal reason. The right to take vengeance belongs to God (Deut 32:35) and is not given to any individuals. A court must assess whether a person's criminal action deserves a death sentence, and it must follow God's instructions in making that assessment. Cities of refuge provide protection for those who kill accidentally or are at risk of revenge when they are innocent.

When it comes to the topic of war, we have already seen that the Israelites are not to fight with whomever they please. They have no permission from God to fight with the Edomites, and because the ruler of Edom will not allow them to walk through his territory, they have to go the long way around instead of fighting him (Num 20). When the Israelites try to go into the Promised Land after God says they may not, they are defeated by the Amalekites and the Canaanites (Num 14:44–45). Going into their new land at the wrong time, and without God's instruction to do so, only leads them into battles they are not authorized to fight. Unfortunately, lives are lost unnecessarily. At other times they are attacked by hostile tribes when they have no plans to fight; in these cases God gives them victory over those enemies (Num 21).

The Israelites have been promised specific land—they are not permitted to take any other. We are told that the seven tribes that live there already have forfeited their right to live in it any longer because of their wickedness (Deut 9:5). While we know very little about the precise nature of their wickedness, we do see evidence of the continuing Canaanite practice of sacrificing children to the god Molech (e.g., 2 Kings 23:10; Jer 32:35). This detestable practice was even adopted by some in Israel. God's abhorrence of this practice is very great.

In Sabah, North Borneo, the practice of head-hunting is still within living memory. But the Christian gospel took root in that place and whole tribes laid down their weapons. When I teach there I often smile when I observe students from different tribes learning and worshiping together in peace, instead of killing each other for their heads, as their grandfathers would have done.

It seems that God is the one who knows best whether a peaceful encounter with the reality of his presence and authority will be accepted, and therefore lead to a peaceful change and radical move away from such evil practices. For some groups, a peaceful encounter will be sufficient; for others it will not be accepted, so stronger measures are needed. The ensuing wars are, then, for the dual purpose of giving land to the Hebrews, and for confronting and demolishing the evil practices of highly resistant, corrupt peoples who would not be open to negotiation. However, the seven tribes who are to be displaced are not the only corrupt people. Considering that the focus of the warfare is so limited, it is clear that there is no blanket mandate here for going to war against any other people just because they are deemed to be corrupt.

GUIDELINES FOR WAR

In Deuteronomy 20 God gives specific, important guidelines regarding warfare when the people enter the new land. They are to go into battle only out of obedience to God's command, and for no human desire for conquest or vengeance. They should not be afraid of their enemies. God does, after all, have the authority and the power to bring victory. The battle and its outcome is ultimately his and not theirs alone. There is kindness shown to men who have just become engaged to be married or have just built a house or planted a vineyard; they are exempt from warfare. These battles are not to squeeze the last drop of manpower and energy from the group. After all, the outcome is not merely dependent on the number of fighters. These are no ordinary wars.

There are two different rules of engagement. The first is for any cities that are outside the seven specific tribes that have been previously mentioned; the second is for the seven tribes whose lands they are to inherit. These rules can be summarized like this:

> Case 1: Outside cities
> Offer of peace (v.10)
> If accepted: forced labor (v.11)
> If refused: lay siege to city, kill males, spare others, take women, children, livestock and everything else as plunder (vv.13–14).
> Case 2: Seven Canaanite cities
> Offer of peace (v.10)?
> If accepted: forced labor (v.11)?
> If refused: lay siege to city, kill everyone, otherwise they will lead you astray.
> Do not destroy the trees (vv.16–17).

Scholars disagree about whether the seven tribes are actually given an offer of peace.[1] But whether they are given it or not, it seems extremely unlikely for those particular tribes to entertain any offer of peace. So, there is little difference in practice. There will be some battles in which God allows plunder to be kept, and others where it may not be kept. This, too, reminds them that war for the explicit purpose of personal gain is not permitted. Women from the other cities may sometimes be taken, implying that not all intermarriage is banned. But the killing of all women and children of the seven cities to be taken over is specifically for the purpose of precluding intermarriage. This is because the risk of these women threatening the safety of the community and leading the Hebrews astray is dangerously high.

HOW ARE BATTLES FOUGHT?

Once the Jordan River has been crossed, the first battle is against the city of Jericho (Josh 6). The strategy is highly unusual: marching once around the city each day for six days, and on the seventh marching seven times around the city with the priests blowing trumpets and the people shouting. Then the city walls collapse, and the Hebrews charge in with trumpets and the

---

1. Gordon J. Wenham, *Exploring the Old Testament: A Guide to the Pentateuch* (London: SPCK, 2003), 137.

Ark of the Covenant in front. One woman, Rahab, who has helped Hebrew spies, is saved, but nothing is to be taken in plunder.

Two problems emerge to check their overconfidence with this initial, miraculous success (Josh 7). First, some of them assume that, on the strength of this victory, they can simply send a small army to conquer the neighboring city of Ai, but they fail miserably. Going into any kind of warfare presumptuously doesn't work. Second, it soon becomes apparent that there is another obstacle in their midst: one man has taken some of the plunder from Jericho and hidden it inside his tent. Greed cannot be allowed in warfare. This internal problem is shown to be serious. God directs that this greed must be stopped. No more battles can be won until he is put to death. If his behavior were overlooked, a dangerous precedent would be set. Obedience in God's way of warfare must be complete.

God does subsequently give instructions for going against the city of Ai, but this time the approach is to be different: they are to set an ambush (Josh 8). As the king of Ai marches out to attack one group of Hebrews, his city is captured and burnt by those in ambush. And this time the people can keep the plunder. Looking to God the Leader for specific strategies for each battle is essential.

Next, five Amorite kings (from the named list of seven tribes) join together to attack. God throws them into confusion and they flee as they are pelted with large hailstones from the sky. More are killed by the hailstones than by the swords of the Hebrews. In addition, extra time is given by the sun standing still (Joshua 10). God's way of doing warfare is not limited to traditional army maneuvers.

After the death of Moses and his successor, Joshua, the people ask God for guidance concerning which Hebrew tribe should attack their remaining enemies (Judges 1). God indicates that it is to be Judah. One king is captured and his thumbs and big toes cut off. It turns out that this king has done the same to seventy other kings, so he realizes that God is paying him back in the same way. Perhaps that gives us a hint that some other battles may be showing God's punishment against other people for their cruelty in the past.

In time, the people become battle-weary and decide to simply coexist with many of the peoples from the seven tribes they were to fight. The result is that the people forget God and even serve the gods of their enemies. But life does not simply continue on in the same way. They become weak, and another king captures and oppresses them. But when they cry out to God he sends them a deliverer (the Book of Judges calls him a judge) who leads them into victory in war. This warfare is followed by a lengthy period of peace, which is, of course, the aim. The Book of Judges shows this cycle being repeated many times over (e.g., Judges 3:7–11).

In the time of the judge Gideon, the enemy Midianites are terrified by a dream of a loaf of barley bread entering the camp of the Midianites (Judges 7). God instructs Gideon to drastically reduce the number of fighting men, and to have them carry trumpets, jars and torches. The noise causes confusion and the Midianites turn on each other. The battle is won with very little fighting by Gideon's men. Did God give the dream, and primarily use tactics causing fear and confusion among the enemy instead of attack?

The Israelite kings are always to seek God's counsel, through inquiring of the priest or sometimes a prophet, before engaging in a war. While the stories and outcomes are often less than straightforward on account of the varying extent to which the Israelite kings follow God's leadership, we can see that God's directions often bring victory with minimal fighting. His purpose in battles is always peace and his methods may be surprising and even counter-intuitive. The engagement is ideally as short as possible with the minimum number of casualties.

The Old Testament battles are often spiritualized in the New Testament to show God's leadership in the spiritual realm. Paul does this in 2 Corinthians 10:3–5 and Ephesians 6:11–18, since God is still Leader of the angel armies, and enemy forces continue to harass God's people. At a personal level, there never was, and there is not now, any justification for revenge or for any kind of personal aggression. In fact, God is the only one who is authorized to act in vengeance (Deut 32:35; Rom 12:19).

WAR TODAY?

Some thinkers have drawn on these Old Testament principles of war to create a Just War theory. Criteria have been developed for going to war, and also for the conduct of war. Oliver Barclay gives four criteria for going to war:

1. There needs to be a just cause against evil, so going to war can only be to resist unjust attacks.
2. There needs to be a just intent, that is, to restore a just peace for all.
3. Force must be used only as a last resort, after trying persuasion, negotiation and even, if necessary, compromise.
4. There needs to be an official declaration of war by the lawful government, not by private individuals.

In terms of how a war may be conducted, the following four criteria apply:

1. The objectives for peace mean that destruction of an economy or totally crushing the national spirit are unjustified.

2. Non-combatants should be protected, as far as possible.
3. The force used must be limited to what is necessary to secure a lasting peace.
4. There must be a reasonable hope of success.[2]

In this view, there is a distinction between personal responses to evil, which cannot include revenge or the taking of life, and the God-given duty of governments to protect their people.[3]

Many conscientious Christians cannot conceive of the possibility of a Christian engaging in any activity that is violent or that could lead to someone's death. This view finds a stronger basis in the New Testament and relegates the God-led wars of the Old Testament to a past that is not repeatable in the present. In this view, an individual Christian is not at liberty to work in vocations that could involve violence, like the military or the police.[4]

Whether we are pacifist or whether we agree with Just War theory, either way we are left with dilemmas which neither choice fully solves. Both sides are more complex than they appear. But looking at God's purposes, strategies and methods shows us that his leadership in war is often very dissimilar to the patterns and motivations of the many human leaders who go to war, now and in the past.

QUESTIONS FOR REFLECTION OR DISCUSSION

1. Do you agree that dealing with threats and conflict is always a component of leadership?
2. How difficult is it for you to think of God being involved in warfare for the protection of his people?
3. Is there anything comforting in God's willingness to engage in warfare for his people?
4. Have you lived through a war? Is there anything you would like to say about it?
5. What controls does God place on warfare for the Israelites in this context?
6. The ideals of Just War Theory and Pacifism are both difficult to keep in situations of extreme threat. Do you lean towards one or the other?

2. Barclay, *Pacifism and War*, 27–30.
3. Barclay, *Pacifism and War*, 213.
4. For a fuller discussion representing both sides of this debate see Barclay, *Pacifism and War*.

PART 4

Images of God as Leader

Chapter 14

God the King

Many images are used in the Bible to describe God. Of these, several describe aspects of his leadership. But no single image describes the whole of God's leadership. This is because images are drawn from human functions (e.g., king, father, shepherd) or inanimate objects (e.g., rock). In addition, our own associations of these words with people we know colors these images. For example, if we were raised by a cruel father, we will need to acknowledge that God is likened to an ideal father and cruelty is not part of that ideal. If we have been working to build a road, the image of rock may represent a huge obstacle that needs to be blasted away. However, we can see that the likeness of God to a rock is never used to indicate an obstacle.

An image evokes a wider range of associations and emotions than a list of attributes. It compresses many ideas into one and is far more easily remembered than words. In these chapters we will seek to decompress these ideas in order to gain a richer understanding of God's leadership and so we will use words. However, my hope is that the images themselves will remain, hopefully with more detail. In this chapter we will look at the image of God as king. In the next few chapters we will discuss other images of God's leadership.

GOD THE KING

God the Leader is very frequently referred to in the Old Testament as King, and spoken of as having a kingdom. It's widely understood that the title "king" refers primarily to the person holding the highest position or rank. In biblical times, is understood to refer to sovereign power expressed in both political and military arenas. No one has more power than the king. God is often called King, but God's rank, rulership and power extends beyond that of any other king, and so he is sometimes called King of Kings.

A lot of royal imagery is applied to God. Visionary language refers to his throne and even the pavement on which his throne sits (e.g., Exod 24; many psalms; Ezek 1; Dan 7), his kingly robes (Isa 6), and his multitudes of royal chariots (Ps 68:17). He is pictured being carried by angelic cherubim (e.g., Ps 18:10; Ezek 10) and riding on the clouds or covering himself with clouds and light (e.g., Ps 18:10, 11; Ps 104:1–3). His presence is often marked by precious stones, fire, radiant light or glory (e.g., Exod 24; Ezek 1). His clothing and hair are pictured as being brilliant white (Dan 7:9, similar to the imagery of Jesus in Rev 1). This language portrays God not just as an earthly king but as the cosmic King, a cosmic military commander, the Lord of Hosts, leading out the stars like a mighty army (Isa 40:26), the one who presides over the heavenly council (e.g., Ps 82:1; 89:7).[1]

We are used to associating kings and queens with pageantry, with robes and thrones, precious stones and gold, decorated attendants and ornate chariots. But the British queen, who is my queen, in reality has severe limitations to her expression of power. That is not to deny her extraordinary global influence. Many other kingdoms, not only in Europe but also in Asia (e.g., Malaysia, Thailand) have also placed limitations on the powers of the monarch because of previous abuses of power. The king in biblical times has no such limits, and God as King has even wider powers than would belong to a human king in Old Testament times.

For many systematic theologians, the sovereignty of God (we might say kingship of God) features as a foundational attribute of God. Louis Berkhof sees God's sovereignty rooted in his role as Creator, in his absolute authority over the beings of both heaven and earth, and in his will as the ultimate cause of all things.[2] What does this sovereignty or kingship entail? King David expresses a cluster of relevant aspects: he is from everlasting to everlasting, he has greatness and power, glory and majesty, owns everything in heaven and earth, is head over his great kingdom, and dispenses wealth and honor, strength and power (1 Chr 29:10–13). As Creator, God has higher rights of kingship than any earthly leader.

However, God also has an earthly kingdom—the people of God. This simply means the people who have God as their king. The same idea

---

1. Block, "Leader, Leadership, OT," 621.
2. Berkhof, *Systematic Theology*, 76.

is brought over into the New Testament, where people can choose to take God as King and enter his kingdom (e.g., Mark 9:47). In the Old Testament this kingdom is generally identified with the people of Israel, also called a kingdom of priests (Exod 19:6), because this nation began as a theocratic kingdom. We have seen that God defends this kingdom, as particular people with their particular gift of land, and stands against the enemies of this kingdom.

Yet there are others outside of Israel who, for various reasons, also choose to follow the God of Israel and turn away from other gods (e.g., Naaman the Syrian leper who is healed by God's prophet Elisha in 2 Kings 5, and the pagan sailors in Jonah 1:16). These people do not become part of the nation of Israel but indicate that their new allegiance is to Israel's divine king. Might they not also be considered part of the people of God, part of God's hidden, scattered kingdom?

God is also understood to rule over the nations (Ps 22:28; Jer 10:7). He has the power to appoint human kings under him to rule his kingdom Israel (1 Chr 28:5) and also to appoint foreign rulers to do his bidding for rescue or for destruction (e.g., Cyrus in Isa 45:1; the Babylonians in Hab 1).

However, as ultimate King, he chooses to set some limits on his own powers in order to give certain powers to humans. He does not merely set up the Israelite kings, or even the foreign kings, as puppet kings under him, but allows them certain freedoms, reflecting the freedom that he, as King, has. Sometimes they act in accordance with his good desires and are commended. Sometimes they do not and are rebuked.

The idea of voluntary limitation of one's own powers can be difficult to accept, especially if the level of power is high and time is short. It is much easier to get things done by yourself, and to know that they will be done properly. There are certainly times when this is necessary. But how will others be trained if there is no room for them to try, to fail, to learn and to succeed? Our perfectionist pride becomes a hindrance. God has no need to prove his excellence and creates space for the learning, creativity and leadership of others.

We have already seen how God's kingship in the Exodus journey is in stark contrast to that of Pharaoh. God acts as King in giving basic provisions to the people: food, water, safety (including protection from enemies) and eventually land. In contrast to Pharaoh, he listens to petitions, is open to negotiation and changes his mind about certain plans. He gives instructions that will enable people to live well and find justice in matters regarding neighbors, thus promoting a harmonious community. He warns of dire consequences for disobedience, as any king has the right to do, but ensures that the people know very clearly that the consequences are directly related to their choices and behaviors and will never be based on God the King's whim and fancy. His kingship is never oppressive.

We discover that not all kings use their powers in identical ways. Israelite kings, who are intended to express some of the character of God's kingship, are not simply to mimic their counterparts in other nations, for God, the original King of the Hebrew people, sets the primary pattern of kingship for this nation and it is not the same as other patterns of kingship given by any other deity.

God gives Moses instructions regarding the appointment of human kings over his people (Deut 17:14–20); this reflects God's understanding of kingship. The king is to be from his own people, not a foreigner. This implies sympathetic understanding of the people he governs. He is not simply to impose ideas from the outside, without first really knowing the people. He must not sacrifice the freedom and honor of the people to support his own schemes for self-aggrandizement or to horde excessive riches or women for his personal pleasure. There is no justification for him to bend the rules, as if he is an exception. In fact, the king has a greater responsibility to know, read and govern by just and right principles given by God, the ultimate king. He is not to make decisions based on personal interests, on cold detachment from needs, or on impulsive or impetuous emotions. His attitude should be humble, showing respect to God, his law, and the people.

How does this relate to the kingship of God? We find repeated examples of God sympathetically knowing and listening to his people. His rulership follows transparent principles which even he chooses to follow. However, he is not merely a bureaucrat who is enslaved by petty rules but is willing to be somewhat flexible out of consideration to matters brought to him by people. His kingship is both principled and relational.

My home is in the island state of Tasmania, across the 250 miles of rough sea that constitutes the Bass Strait, between Tasmania and the mainland of Australia. I was once an outsider and a newcomer to this beautiful state, even though my father grew up here. Over the years I have seen many newcomers arrive, and quite a few of them depart after just a few years. Sometimes they come in order to take over a position of management. An appointment in Tasmania is often a ladder-climbing exercise. They come to make a mark, and often that mark is for themselves, so that they can become a "bigger king" somewhere else back on the mainland. They come with bright ideas that may have worked in another context. But they fail to realize that Tasmania is not the same as anywhere else. Actually, nowhere is the same as anywhere else. Yes, there are similarities, and yes, there are some ideas that have wide application. But until they pause and look and listen to the people, to the social fabric, to the needs and gifts and wisdom that are already there, they will be like a foreign king who never earns the true allegiance of his people and wonders why his bright ideas don't take root.

When the Israelites crave a human king, the prophet Samuel warns them of the corruptions common to kingship in neighboring lands (1 Sam 8:10–18). An Israelite king may begin well but may succumb to the pattern of kingship that is prevalent in the area, which will mean that many people will find themselves torn away from their own labors to compulsorily serve the king, to fight in his army, to farm his lands, or to work for his extended household. In fact, he may take possession of traditional family lands, animals and produce, institute burdensome taxation, and cause hardship so that his own sense of self-importance is fed. Yet God, as King, has given the protection they need without any such onerous demands.

In Psalm 72 we find many aspects of the responsibilities of an Israelite king: justice, prosperity, stability, security of land, victory over enemies, and care for the needy.[3] God as King has been involved in all these things. He also has a responsibility to bring divine blessing to the land and people, and so kings of Israel establish places of worship and are required to act in obedience to the commands of the divine King. Even in neighboring cultures, kings stand and fall in relation to their gods. Daniel Block summarizes the three major functions of a king in this way:

> to defend them against external threats (leading the nation in battle),
> to defend them against internal threats (administering justice),
> and to defend them against divine threats (serving as patrons of the cult).[4]

The last religious function was, in practice, delegated to the priests, but the king still retained the responsibility for maintaining a relationship with the divine King.

Kings of biblical times enter into various covenants and treaties with kings of other nations, and are obliged to be faithful to the various promises made in those agreements. If they are indeed faithful, there is peace. If not, there is a high risk of serious conflict and loss of life. One of the dominant and persistent descriptors of God's kingship is that he is faithful—faithful to the covenant he initiated, and faithful to all of the words he has spoken. His kingly character is reliable.

It is not difficult to find plenty of historic examples of kings on any continent who used their powers greedily, harshly and abusively. In fact, it often became the expected norm. I think of a tenth-century duke of

---

3. See Stevens, *Leadership Roles of the Old Testament*, 18–31.
4. Block, "Leader," 622.

Bohemia, named Wenceslas, who was posthumously given the title of King. He dared to act against the prevailing model of kingship. His motivation to rule differently arose from his Christian faith, still new in that land at the time, which gave a radically different model of leadership. An English Christmas carol conveys the essence of his approach:

> Good King Wenceslas looked out
> On the feast of Stephen,
> When the snow lay round about
> Deep and crisp and even.
>
> Brightly shone the moon that night
> Though the frost was cruel,
> When a poor man came in sight,
> Gathering winter fuel.

The rest of this carol tells a tale of exceptional humility and generosity. The king and his servant trudge more than three miles through deep snow, carrying food, drink and firewood to the home of the poor man. Along the way, Wenceslas encourages the servant to step in the footprints that he, as the leader, has made so that he will find some warmth there. The carol ends with a reflection for contemporary leaders.

> Therefore, Christian men, be sure
> Wealth or rank possessing,
> Ye who now will bless the poor
> Shall yourselves find blessing.

The end of King Wenceslas's life came far too soon. His brother Boleslaw murdered him and grabbed the throne. Boleslaw and others in that privileged circle were enraged that a king would stoop to help the needy at the expense of the rich. However, Wenceslas understood the leadership of God the King and followed well. Today he is regarded as the patron saint of the Czech Republic and his statue provides the focus for Wenceslas Square.

The image of God as Judge is closely related to the image of God as King, so it will not be dealt with separately. One crucial aspect of his role as judge is his defense of those who are marginalized—the oft-repeated triad of the "fatherless, widows and foreigners" (e.g., Deut 10:17–19). God as Judge exercises positive discrimination towards those whose power is inadequate and who need protection, and rebukes those who are exploitative. Wenceslas was following this example.

Kings are also those who have the capacity to bless and give, since blessing flows from one who is considered superior and has greater bounty to give. With a high position comes the obligation to be generous to those who are in need, and to those who can be helped or encouraged. People in such positions generally have wealth, often from taxation, and so they have a responsibility to use that money for the public good.

God is pictured as having bountiful riches—the cattle on a thousand hills (Ps 50:9-12). He is never in need of our offerings and sacrifices, as some other gods may be. He does not need the *things* we offer, as he has abundantly more than he needs. The purpose of his riches is to share them.

In British history there have been traditions of monarchs giving to the poor. Queen Margaret, wife of King Malcolm III of Scotland, is remembered as a saint because of her piety and her great generosity to the poor, hosting them regularly for meals. Since the thirteenth century, British monarchs have followed a custom of distributing money and gifts to the poor at Easter. In addition, the Royal Family is well known for its involvement with charities. While some of this may be a mere token of what is needed, it is, nevertheless, a frequent reminder that people in kingship and other related positions are meant to use their leadership wealth generously. As King, God is generous to all who follow him.

GOD THE KING'S EVALUATION OF SAUL AND DAVID

God's evaluation of human kings says a lot about the character of God as King. The first two of Israel's kings, Saul and David, provide an extended contrast. Saul initially appears to be a good leader. He not only looks the part, but calculates the threat of being attacked, moves to defuse panic in his men, rallies them together, takes charge of pre-battle procedures, and assertively leads his troops forward (1 Sam 12-13). However, he fails to understand that God's way of being king needs more than this. He lacks patience, wisdom and humility and is motivated primarily by fear. He will not wait for or adhere to divine orders and often acts foolishly.

Another disturbing pattern emerges in Saul's jealousy of David. It begins mildly enough but gets out of hand, leading to mental disturbances, paranoia and eventually attempted murder. For the rest of Saul's life, we see a marked pattern of failing to discern communication from God, ending with a frustrated, last resort attempt to get forbidden advice from the banned witch of Endor (1 Sam 28). He dies the next day, a lost and lonely man. The twin evils of fear and jealousy have weakened and ultimately destroyed the good potential that he showed at the beginning. They bear out the seriousness of Samuel the prophet's rebuke.

In contrast, David exemplifies patience. Although he knows he has been chosen by God to be the next king, he will not force the issue and will not act impulsively or out of fear, as Saul has done. Even though Saul is bent on murdering David and needs to flee, he does not take opportunities in which he could easily kill Saul (1 Sam 24 and 26). He places himself under divine direction, care and timing, and waits. His attitude of humility before God becomes a steady character trait, even when he is shown to be wrong.

After David commits adultery with Bathsheba, falling prey to the prevailing stereotype that presumes kings are exceptions to normal sexual laws, he is roundly rebuked by the prophet Nathan. He genuinely repents and accepts the consequences (2 Sam 11 and 12). At another time of failure, David is once again rebuked by a prophet, this time Gad, for taking a census for the wrong reasons (1 Chr 21). David realizes his foolishness and is very accepting of negative consequences. David is far from being a perfect king, but his willingness to accept legitimate rebuke and the serious consequences of his misdeeds contributes to the assessment of him as "a man after God's own heart" (1 Sam 13:14; Acts 13:22). He will listen, receive truth and submit to justice. The many prayers attributed to, or at least associated with, David confirm his ongoing humility towards God and show him focused on seeking obedience to God's direction and avoiding a fear-governed path.

Whereas the biblical narrator portrays God's assessment of David as "a man after God's own heart," God's assessment of Saul is portrayed as foolish, a man who moves further and further away from God. From this we can deduce some things about the character of God's own kingship. God will not act on impulse or out of fear. His ego is not fragile, so he is not ultrasensitive or easily threatened. Timing is important, so he is very willing to wait for the most appropriate time. His attribute of patience is often commended; his responses are steady. He is concerned about doing what is right and righteous, so he will not react on a whim. God acts in accordance with laws and principles, rather than on egotistic agendas.

Fear and jealousy plague the inner life of many human leaders. However, these are very rarely on display and are not often guessed as being the driving forces behind other behaviors. I once worked under a CEO of a non-government organization. On first meeting, she made a positive impact, being attractive, articulate and sociable, with the right background and skill set for the job. However, her tendency to be more controlling than was appropriate soon became apparent, along with her frequent and unnecessary statements of her own power. A new member of staff joined the team. He brought considerable experience from a different organization and was better qualified in certain respects than the CEO, not that he ever flaunted his qualifications. He worked diligently and cooperatively, putting creative energy into all projects he was asked to take on. Soon some were singing the praises of this newcomer and the new projects became more successful than ever before. The CEO made a public announcement that one successful project would close. Then there was another—and another. Soon followed a secret meeting of the CEO's inner circle, and they kicked the newcomer out of his job, riding roughshod over the procedures laid down by their organization and spreading untrue rumors. Some others knew the inner dynamics but were too fearful to speak out. If they did, they might be next! Several employees quietly moved on.

The exercising of over-the-top control can mask the inner fears that drive it: fears of being toppled off their own pedestals, fears of having their weaknesses exposed, fears of losing respect, fears of what certain others may think, fears of being compared with someone else and found wanting, fears of losing their own jobs and suffering financial loss. And these fears can easily fuel a jealousy that is crippling. Leadership based on personal fears leads to losses rather than gains, including loss of cohesion in the organization. This CEO eventually lost friends, as people slowly saw through her false facade of confidence and came to recognize more of her self-centered motivations. She left that job a lonely woman.

The kings who follow David are a mixture of wise and foolish, humble and arrogant, serving the people and serving themselves. Those kings who follow the ways of God the Leader foster communities that flourish and live in peace. Those who don't suffer division, injustice and bloodshed, and eventual vulnerability to takeovers by enemy leadership.

QUESTIONS FOR REFLECTION OR DISCUSSION

1. How do you respond to the image of God as King?
2. In what ways does King Saul's rulership provide a negative example of leadership?
3. What aspects of King David's rulership are helpful for leaders today?
4. What kinds of damage can be done by a leader's arrogance?
5. As a leader, what do you fear most?

Chapter 15

God the Shepherd

Among the many images used of God as Leader, the Shepherd is probably the most popular. The picture of a shepherd carrying a cuddly, hurt lamb can bring us comfort when we see ourselves as that distressed lamb in need of tender care from God the Shepherd. And because the image of shepherd is also assigned to Jesus in the New Testament (e.g., John 10), its force is strengthened for Christians. This image, in fact, evokes a much wider range of connotations than mercy to the needy. Anyone who has been engaged in shepherding or in any kind of animal husbandry understands this.

The term "shepherd" is often applied metaphorically in the Old Testament to kings and political leaders in Israel. Some of these shepherds are commended, like David. Many others are rebuked. Ezekiel 34 uses this extended image to great effect, showing the stark differences between the recent human shepherds of Israel and God as Shepherd. This serves as a warning to us not to unthinkingly transfer to God what we have experienced from human leaders. Although we cannot press every aspect of an image for meaning, the shepherd image is useful if we look at its ideal characteristics.

Ezekiel 34 begins with a description of what God is *not* like as a shepherd and what he denounces in the bad shepherds, the leaders of Israel. The essence of bad shepherd-leadership is self-centeredness or narcissism. It is a shepherd taking care of himself or herself instead of taking care of the flock (v.3). Shepherding is, by definition, taking care of sheep, and this necessarily entails paying attention to their needs and not neglecting or abusing the sheep through self-absorption. A human shepherd has some legitimate rights to produce and profit, since shepherding is a working occupation;

he also has a legitimate need for resources to do his job. God condemns shepherds and kings for going far beyond their legitimate rights and needs and neglecting the real work they should be doing. God's shepherding is not like that!

Shepherding involves continual observation of the sheep and goats in care, to know the condition of their fleece or hair, their eyes and mouth, their bellies, their tail areas, their feet, their limbs, their strength and agility (see Prov 27:23–27). Watching must be a primary activity of any shepherd but watching is not enough. Watching must issue in responsive action. Those animals that are sick, weak, injured or lost must not simply be left in that condition; the shepherd has a responsibility to heal and care for the sick, weak and injured, and must search for those who are lost. The bad shepherds here are said to be not only neglectful in these areas of responsibility but also harsh and brutal. They don't care about the wellbeing of the sheep. In their view, sheep only exist to serve the needs of their shepherd. Instead, the ideal shepherding image evokes a relationship between shepherd and sheep whereby both sheep and shepherd have their needs met in mutual dependence.

The outcome of bad shepherding is a scattering of the flock and vulnerability to ferocious attacks by wild animals. In human terms, the vulnerability may be to leaders who are even more abusive than the first. God's anger is acute: he will remove them from their posts of responsibility so that they can no longer benefit from the produce of the sheep. Zechariah 11:15–17 is a shorter passage that uses the same imagery. Here there is a pronouncement of woe against the worthless shepherd, showing the severity of his crime: "May the sword strike his arm and his right eye! May his arm be completely withered, his right eye totally blinded!" (v. 17). These words may appear to be overly harsh, but if we place them in the context of the cruel mistreatment of his flock—not caring for the lost, not seeking the young, not healing the injured, not feeding the healthy (v.16)—then the judgment falls into the category of an "eye for an eye" punishment. As he has mistreated those in his charge, he will be punished.

There was a movement in some churches in comparatively recent years nicknamed "Heavy Shepherding." While it may have begun as a well-intentioned desire to see people grow and mature in their Christian faith, the model of shepherding used by church leaders in this movement became overly controlling and abusive. These "shepherds" were too idealistic in their view of themselves, thus becoming blind to their growing arrogance. They did not pay close enough attention to the true condition of their "sheep," not listening to or recognizing their truths and gifts and not seeing the damage that their own harsh treatment was doing.

I think of another man, not in that movement, who was eventually elected into a position of lay leadership in his church. He had his idiosyncrasies, but people naively assumed that he meant well. He said he wanted to protect the church from various threats that he saw through his knowledge of the law. Once elected, his so-called protection turned into bullying. His supposed expertise in the law, with which he hammered people relentlessly, turned out to be a sham. The slander which he spread about other leaders was eventually exposed as lies. Although he said he wanted to protect the people in the church, his constant intimidation of those people brought greater damage inside the church than any supposed threat from the outside. It was fortunate that the people woke up and, at the next election, voted him out. He could not tolerate defeat and left.

I do feel angry when I see how the effects of bad shepherding, whether political or spiritual, affect the most vulnerable people the most. I think of young people, eager in their quest to learn more about God, some who have been injured by previous abusive relationships, and elderly folk who can become very confused. Oppressed. Scattered. Disillusioned. Such toxic shepherds get in the way of people connecting to the Good Shepherd and can cause severe damage.

We see the characteristics of God as the Good Shepherd of his people in Ezekiel 34:11-31. First, he pays attention, then seeks for his sheep and looks after them when he finds them. If they are scattered and therefore unsafe, he will rescue them and gather them into a place of safety. He looks for, finds and provides good, healthy pasture for their nourishment. They will be able to lie down in peace, being satisfied and secure. God will continue to search for other lost and hurting sheep, bring them in and take care of them also.

The same image of God as Shepherd appears in the most famous of psalms, Psalm 23. The ideas of provision, guidance, security, comfort, restoration and abundance are emphasized. Quiet waters appear beside the green pastures, the paths along which the sheep walk are carefully selected, steady and true, even if dangers lurk nearby. The shepherd goes ahead as the leader, moving the sheep on paths that the sheep have not chosen. Their choices may well have led them to stop moving, or to stay in the same ruts, or to take a path that would prove dangerous. Yet the shepherd's paths lead to refreshment and are said to be paths of righteousness. The choice is wisely considered and is right for the sheep. The shepherd's two sticks—the rod and staff—are to fight off threatening, wild animals, or to discipline erring or fighting sheep (the straight rod) and to pull a straying sheep out of a danger spot (using the hooked top of the staff). Emotional language—restoration of soul and feelings of comfort—is used to stress the inner wellbeing of those under the shepherd's care.

The person under this shepherd's care is not treated as just a nobody, as a generic sheep. He or she experiences the head being anointed with oil by the shepherd. Anointing oil combines images of chosenness, calling and a specific role for an individual in community. It also indicates that the person is not alone, but has the resources of the presence, power and healing of the Holy Spirit of God. The shepherd prepares an abundantly laden table even while jealous enemies look on, unable to succeed in their attempted attacks. This kind of shepherding results in a flow of goodness and love that never dissipates and leads to everlasting security in the home provided by this good Shepherd.

I did not grow up with sheep. Born and bred a city slicker, I remember the excitement of first seeing real sheep being shorn and real cows being milked. I knew cats and dogs and am grateful that my parents valued and taught us about the relationships and responsibilities involved in keeping animals. I can't say that I always fulfilled my "shepherding" responsibilities well, so it was fortunate that my mother took her "shepherding" role with our pets more seriously and ensured that there was always a healthy food supply and that sick animals were treated. I enjoyed relating to our pets, patting them and playing with them. I can't count how many times I felt too discouraged to be bothered with the dog, only to find him wedging his nose into me somewhere, determined not to let me stay in my discouraged state and inviting me to resume my rightful place and take him on a W-A-L-K that would put us both into a position of good cheer. I'm glad that God the Shepherd is a more conscientious carer than I was, and also that he genuinely enjoys a mutual relationship with us.

Later, when our four children were young, we learned a lot more about caring for animals when we had angora goats and a donkey. I was constantly looking at the state of each paddock, its feed-mix and water supply, and making decisions about when and where to move our animals. We were not ideal shepherds in many ways, because we did not live on site. But we knew every goat by name. A slight difference in the curl of the horns or the shape of the nose, the expression in the eyes, or the angle of the ears was enough to distinguish them. Subtle differences in color, curl and texture of their coat, the shape of their body, and the particular stance of their legs could help if they were at a distance. No two goats looked the same, and no two had the same personality. We knew which ones were easily scared, which ones were more phlegmatic, which ones were on the lookout for escape routes through, over or under fences, which ones were leaders and which were followers. I looked over our herd with delight, enjoying something special about each creature, and pondered how much more God the Shepherd must know and enjoy the uniqueness of each of us, his creatures.

Because many of us who come from cities are unfamiliar with what is required to care properly for sheep, we can gain much from the writing of Phillip Keller, who draws from his practical experiences of shepherding to fill out this image of God as Shepherd.[1] He points out that sheep will not lie down unless four requirements are kept: they must be free of the fear of enemies, free of friction with other sheep, free of pests, and free of hunger.[2] This means that the shepherd must be ever vigilant in these four areas. The sheep's enemies must be known, understood and kept at bay. Sheep, like other animals, have a "pecking order," and often sheep that are more dominant bully other sheep that are lower down the hierarchy. However, Keller notices that friction between sheep is very often dispelled when the shepherd walks into the midst of the sheep. His presence gives peace from conflict.

Keller also speaks about "cast" sheep, who end up on their backs, and cannot get up.[3] These sheep are in acute danger of death, and vulnerable to attack by predatorial birds. The risks for becoming cast can be too much wool, too much fat, too much comfort—choosing a nice hollow to lie down in, rather than on the grass. The image of the shepherd in Psalm 23 restoring the soul suggests to him the role that the shepherd plays in searching for and finding a cast sheep and holding it upright until it is strong enough to be restored to the rest of the flock with a future of life instead of death.

Green pasture does not grow readily in the best sheep-growing areas of the world as they are semi-arid. In order to provide green pasture, a shepherd has to clear the land of rocks, root out dry stumps, plant special grains and legumes and irrigate them. If good, clean water is not provided, sheep will likely drink at polluted potholes where they can pick up infections from internal parasites, so shepherds work hard to locate and, if necessary, provide a safe and refreshing water supply. Finally, the table that is prepared in Psalm 23 is likened by Keller to the sheep's summer grazing in abundance on the tablelands. There the vigilance of the shepherd in keeping away flies and other tormenting insects, and scabies (especially on the head) is vital.[4]

There will be many times when sheep may feel alone or distressed, e.g., through injury or sickness, through becoming lost, through lack of food or

---

1. Keller, *A Shepherd Looks at Psalm 23*.
2. Keller, ch. 3, p. 1. The remaining comments in this paragraph refer to Keller's remarks in this chapter.
3. Keller, ch. 5.
4. Keller, chs 9 and 10.

water. Humans have parallel difficult times of distress for many different reasons. It may seem that the shepherd doesn't care or can't see, or perhaps has abandoned the sheep. The sheep cannot know what will happen next. Yet the kindness or the cruelty of that shepherd will determine the response of that sheep when the shepherd does appear. Animals do have memories for both kindness and cruelty. From my experience with dogs, even if a dog is very sick he will show a warm, grateful response when a caring owner appears. Trust has been built and loyalty is retained. That will help the sick dog to cooperate and to heal. But if someone who has been cruel to the dog appears, even if it is an owner, there will be no trust. The dog will cower further in fear and avoid cooperating.

We as humans have a greater ability than animals to understand and also to look ahead, either in panic or in trust. Some people claim that God their Shepherd does not see what is happening in their situations (e.g., Ps 94:7). They panic. They forget that God is the Good Shepherd who is ever on guard, ever on the lookout and ever working to help his sheep in need. Others are able to wait because they trust the Shepherd's character. They know he is not neglectful or cruel. They don't understand the situation, the reasons or the injustice in their circumstances, but they know him. More waiting may be needed, but they know he will come and that when he comes he will, as is his character, rescue and help and bring new hope.

Another well-loved portrayal of God as Shepherd occurs in Isaiah 40:10-11. We warm to the picture of the shepherd tenderly carrying vulnerable lambs, perhaps sick or injured, in his arms and slowly guiding and reassuring the ewes, as he brings them all to a safe shelter where he will no doubt be better able to give medicine, apply ointments, and bind up broken limbs. Yet there is another side to this shepherd. He is also the same one who comes with power (v.10). Actually, there is power in being able to heal and to rescue. But verse 10 also uses the word "rules." A shepherd is, indeed, the powerful ruler of his flock, and the rulership aspect has long been the reason that ancient kings were often referred to as shepherds. However, God the Shepherd is a tender ruler, one who is gentle with the most vulnerable of his people, but he is also a ruler with awesome power.

Coming back to Ezekiel 34, God the Shepherd is not only the one who searches for the lost and brings back the strays, he is also the one who shepherds the flock with justice. He attempts to cajole and discipline the wayward sheep with his rod, and on occasion has to destroy some stubbornly arrogant sheep who refuse to share the gifts of good pasture with other sheep, or in some other way have a destructive influence over the whole flock (vv. 16-22).

We did get annoyed by the behavior of our animals at different times. Sometimes it was simply their obstinacy in refusing to be moved to better pasture. Sometimes it was their strenuous objection to the treatments of toenail clipping, vaccinating and drenching that would enable them to walk without crippled feet and to be free from infections. But sometimes it was their cruel treatment of others lower down the "pecking order." Our angora goat Carmel was such a pretty creature. Beautifully proportioned, yielding high quality mohair, with the cutest twist of her dainty horns. But I never knew that some animal mothers could be so cruel to their offspring. Consistently bearing twins, she killed each one. We attempted to keep some kids alive at home for a time, but as soon as she would be let loose in a paddock with them she did something to cause each to die in no time. I grieved to see such harshness in a mother. I felt angry, and after giving her chance after chance, we decided to let her go.

The shepherd's justice demonstrates that his mercy extends to all of his sheep, and especially to those who are mistreated by bully sheep. His desire is that all of his sheep will be strong, well fed, and well built. But that strength must not be abused through violence towards weaker sheep. Although he has worked hard to give health and strength to his sheep, he will not tolerate the abuse of those gifts.

He will not ignore those who always push and shove to get an advantage at the expense of others. He will not be satisfied to provide excellent pasture just for the aggressive sheep and fluke-infested muddied grass for the others. He will not tolerate the chronic rejection of some sheep by others. In order to be fair to all of the sheep, he has to observe how the sheep behave towards each other and make judgments about what is going on. If there are fences, he can separate sheep into different paddocks. He has to discriminate positively, perhaps deliberately allowing weaker sheep access to better pasture. And he has to discriminate negatively, perhaps keeping the strong sheep away from other sheep and away from the good ground. But, as fences were and are not part of shepherding in biblical lands, there comes a time when the only way to stop the bullying is to stop the bullies. And that can only be done with the killing knife.

When our first angora kid, our pride and joy, was but a few hours old, she naively and falteringly wandered in the direction of the donkey's feeding trough. Suddenly, from out of nowhere, our normally gentle donkey Gemmy appeared in an angry dust storm and used her strong back legs to give this tiny kid a forceful kick that resulted in broken bones. I was really angry. There was no real threat to the donkey or to her food, and the force in the kick was way out of proportion to what was needed to keep the tiny kid away. Shepherding can be heart-breaking work, as sheep and goats and donkeys and humans mistreat each other in more ways than we want to think about. God the Shepherd keeps on keeping on, mingling mercy with justice, joy with judgment.

Shepherding was also a nomadic activity, an occupation that required movement in order to meet the needs of the sheep.[5] A shepherd could not afford to be sedentary, to stay in the place of personal comfort, or in some detached "ivory tower" away from the working face of earthy needs. The nomadic leadership of God through the Exodus journey can be seen in terms of shepherding. Security for the people lies in their willingness to move as the leader directs. Trust can be placed in a shepherd who is flexible enough to perceive all the factors in a situation and to use his knowledge and experience to predict the best path. He must move confidently ahead, without becoming bogged down, in order to keep resources fresh.

Shepherding is still a good image of God's leadership and human leadership, even though the term has been sometimes abused. God the Shepherd is still worth contemplating, not only to know him better, but also to follow his model of shepherd leadership more closely.

QUESTIONS FOR REFLECTION OR DISCUSSION

1. What is most helpful in the image of God as Shepherd?
2. What is the essence of good shepherding?
3. How have you been hurt by abusive leaders?
4. How might a good leader deal with bullies?
5. "Mingling mercy with justice, joy with judgment." How might these things be kept in balance in your situation?
6. How might your leadership become more like that of the Good Shepherd?

---

5. See Laniak, *Shepherds after My own Heart*, for a helpful examination of this image throughout the Bible.

Chapter 16

God the Father, Mother, and Husband

GOD AS FATHER

While God is not often explicitly referred to as Father in the Old Testament, the imagery is often implied much more widely. God's fatherhood is established through his role as Creator (Deut 32:6). However, God is also said to be, in a more specific sense, the Father of the Israelite people. In fact, Moses tells Pharaoh that the people of Israel are collectively God's firstborn son (Exod 4:22–23), inferring that God is their Father.

God is likened to a father who has carried his son (Israel) all the way through the wilderness (Deut 1:31). The Israelites are to identify themselves specifically as children of God in front of other peoples (Deut 14:1). And this same father disciplines the people he provides for (Deut 8:5).

The idea of a father disciplining his child is universally understood. The father wants to ready his child for taking on greater responsibilities—for moving towards adulthood, for developing skills, for making wise decisions, for caring for others. This idea is picked up again in Proverbs 3:12 and repeated in the New Testament (Heb 12:5, 7, 11). A father who cares is also willing to discipline. God's discipline of us arises from his love for us.

King David later understands God as Father of the nation (1 Chr 29:10) who shows fatherly compassion to those who have respect for him (Ps 103:13). Where there is no human father, God acts as Father (Ps 68:5). David also thinks of God as Father to himself personally (Ps 89:26), and then to his son King Solomon who will build the temple (2 Sam 7:14; 1 Chr 17:13; 22:10; 28:6).

The image of God as Father is continued in the writings of the prophets, often making more explicit the emotional aspects that are implied in a father-child relationship. God has raised the Israelites as a father raises children, loving them, teaching them to walk, bending down to feed them, healing them when they are hurt, tenderly taking them by the hand and guiding them (Isa 1:2; 63:16; Hos 11:1–4). Yet the people have rebelled and show no respect to God their Father and he is understandably angry (Jer 3:4; Mal 1:6; 2:10). As Father, God has the power to make choices about his children, just as a potter has power over the clay (Isa 64:8, 9). But he delays any punitive action on account of his love and his long-held hopes and dreams and takes time to plead with them and call them back to a healthy family relationship (Jer 3:19–20, 22). His fatherly desire is to spare them from punishment and to lead them back onto a level path, nourished and refreshed (Mal 3:17; Jer 31:9). In the New Testament Jesus repeatedly speaks of God as Father and even invites us to address God that way in the Lord's Prayer (Matt 6:9).

Our personal experiences of our own fathers or father figures can either enhance or block our ability to accept God as Father. In the New Testament (Eph 3:14) it is clear that human fathering derives from God's fathering, but, we must admit, imperfectly. Every human father has limitations, but a trustworthy father can certainly help his children to know that the heavenly Father is trustworthy. A seriously untrustworthy father can make it very difficult for a child to even imagine that a heavenly Father could be trustworthy. And so on with other attributes. So we parents, fathers or mothers, carry a serious responsibility of representing God, at least for the early stages of our children's development.

But if our fathers have serious impairments, we can still discover the ideal model of fathering and come to relate well to God as our Father. When I was a young child, I had a sudden realization one morning that my father was limited, for some reason that I didn't understand, and that he couldn't fulfill some of my expectations of how a father might treat me. It was helpful. It enabled me to accept that he simply couldn't do certain things or behave in certain ways. I began to see that he was struggling. My understanding of his struggles grew as I grew, but that early realization helped me not to depend on the image of my own father for my understanding of God as Father. I am thankful that I came to know God's fathering as separate from my biological father when I was eleven, even though there were aspects of my father's fathering that I appreciated and could apply.

I know now that my father's idea of God as Father was filled with fear and dread. That contributed to his struggles. In his mind God had a big stick and was out to hit any naughty boys—and he still saw himself as a naughty boy. It was only when he was dying of lung cancer that he found God and was amazed to discover that the heart of God, the heart of God's fathering, was love. Our relationship as father and daughter was transformed.

GOD AS MOTHER

The image of God as Mother occurs less frequently in Scripture but is not insignificant. This is not about the gender of God. He is not gendered yet both males and females are made in his image. The Bible consistently uses the masculine pronoun to refer to him, but that is not to say that he is literally masculine in the human biological sense. He is never referred to as a goddess, but many aspects of his leadership are likened to that of a human mother.

In Deuteronomy 32 God is described both as the Father who created the nation (v. 6) and the Mother who gave them birth (v. 18). Like a mother in childbirth he gasps and cries out in pain, and like a mother God promises to comfort the people whom he collectively calls his child. God as Mother can never forget the child she has borne (Deut 32:18; Isa 42:14; Isa 66:13; Isa 49:15). The Psalmist writes that the appropriate position for him is to sit still and quiet with God, just as a young child can settle with its mother (Ps 131:2).

These words evoke many related images and emotions. A mother suffering labor pains in order to bring her child into the world. A mother holding, cuddling and comforting her child. A mother cherishing memories of things about her child that most others have forgotten. A mother holding a vision of hope for her child when others write him off. A mother's calming effect in the midst of fears, tensions and obstacles. A mother's thinking to plan a way forward for her family.

I love the picture of God likened to a mother eagle who rustles her young out of their high nest when she perceives that they are ready to learn to fly. She allows them to fall for a safe distance, but not too far, because she spreads out her wings in flight underneath to catch them if their wings are not employed. After taking them to the nest to recover in safety for a while, she stirs them up so that they fall out of their nest again. She is constantly vigilant. Once again she flies underneath and rescues them if their wings are not yet strong enough to enable them to fly. She repeats this process until they learn to fly (Deut 32:11–12).

As a child, I was extremely hesitant to take on certain kinds of new challenges. One of these was swimming. I really did want to learn to swim, but I needed to be sure that I would not be at risk of drowning. Two different female relatives, who were also mothers, tried to teach me at different times. The first was stern Aunt Mary. She decided it was time for me to learn. I knew it was time, but I was scared. Her method was to hold me in rough water that was quite deep for me, while I lay on my stomach to become used to the position. But I was afraid of being let go without any support. She promised emphatically not to let me go, so I allowed her to hold me. But she very soon did let go and didn't catch me. The water was deep and rough, and I was soon in difficulties. I would not try that again or allow her to teach me to swim. The second was Aunt Sylvia, who took me to a quiet pool. She came alongside me, showed me what to do, watched me and stayed close enough to catch me whenever I needed to be caught, all without fuss and drama but with a quiet reliability I could count on. I began to swim.

Even as adults we periodically need to learn how to ride a new challenge. If we haven't faced it before, we may be ill-equipped and may panic. Perhaps we metaphorically 'flap our wings', but not yet productively. God, like the trustworthy mother eagle, is watching and is ready and eager to catch us. He has no desire to see us crash out or to be destroyed. As a type of mother leader, he still sets safety limits and offers nurture even as he challenges. We may miss finding the nurture if we refuse to accept the help that is offered with the challenge, and we may find ourselves in bigger trouble if we refuse to face any challenges. God watches and intervenes, gives pauses and new learning, enables us to become stronger and rejoices when we succeed.

Also like a mother bird, God will provide refuge for her young under her feathers (Ps 91:4; Ps 57:1). This image also recurs in the New Testament in reference to Jesus' desire to gather his people like chickens under his wings (Matt 23:37; Luke 13:34). Yet, in another mothering image from the animal world, God can be likened to a mother bear robbed of her cubs. She is fiercely protective of her young, so her anger is quickly stirred into vengeance (Hos 13:8). A maternal instinct to protect her young, to keep them safe, is a foundational feature of good mothering. The same mother who gently shelters and comforts her own can appear hostile to those who threaten her own. God's tender love for his own, and his fierce anger against those who unjustly threaten, fit this image well.

Like fathering, our own experiences of being mothered can affect our ability to relate to God as a parent. My own mother lost her mother, by divorce, when she was two years old. The court gave the children into the care of the father, with no access to the mother. Mum had no recollection of what her mother looked like and was not shown any photos. She had no understanding of why her mother abandoned her. Mum and her siblings were subsequently placed in a Children's Home. Throughout her childhood she carried a longing for her Mummy, a gaping hole that her institution could never fully fill. Her perception of God was as the leader of an institution, not as a parent. Not as someone who would know her personally, who would notice her simply for being herself, who would observe her needs and listen to her cries, who would hold her hand and lead her along the way, who would discipline her fairly and in love, who would never disappear or desert her.

Sadly, her ability to mother her own children was impaired. She fulfilled her duties in domestic chores very well and was certainly a very interesting and productive person. But she much later claimed that no one had ever told her that she was supposed to love her children. I realized that she, too, was limited. Yet my understanding of God as Mother and Father was not constrained by what my human parents were able to show. I was able to discover, more and more over my long years of knowing him, that God as Mother and Father is a truly good Parent, truly reliable and truly loving.

GOD AS HUSBAND

At the heart of the Exodus story lies the establishment of God's covenant with his people. It is not an impersonal contract in order to regulate services. It is much more like a marriage covenant to establish a mutually committed relationship. The foundation is laid by the approach of the Israelites towards God, and the approach of God towards them to rescue them from slavery (Exod 3:7; 20:2). All laws are given by God within this covenanted relationship, but the covenant cannot come into effect until the people agree to the covenant. God is obviously the Leader in this arrangement and stands in the place of a husband while the people, in the place of the wife, must give their assent.

The common statement of marriage in the Old Testament—that a named man took a named woman and she became his wife (e.g., Ruth 4:13)—is also used of God taking the Israelites as his people (e.g., Exod 6:7; Deut 4:20).[1] The similarity of expression strongly suggests the analogy of marriage: God is to Israel as a husband is to a wife. This image of leadership in marriage must be held in tension with the more distant image of God as King. God is also a leader who is close, who knows his people and is known by them, who is in an intentional, focused relationship, who gives and receives, who commits to the provisions and care expected of a husband, who is motivated by and affected by emotions. Both parties are responsible to be faithful to each other.

1. Sohn, *YHWH, the Husband of Israel*, 31.

The initial period in the Exodus journey can be likened to an engagement period, when God makes his choice of bride and she willingly and lovingly agrees to go with him. The later prophet Jeremiah refers to this period with romanticized imagery and emotional color (Jer 2:2f). The agreement of both parties to the covenant ratified at Mt Sinai (Exod 24:1-8) is likened to a marriage ceremony. There is a reading of conditions and affirmative response by the people, together with the sharing of sacrificial blood (showing the life-and-death nature of the commitment) sprinkled on both the altar (representing God) and the people. Once this is established, a group of leaders is given a visionary experience of being in the very presence of God, enjoying his hospitality as they eat and drink (Exod 24:9-11). The celebratory sharing of food is common in marriage customs as people on both sides joyfully give and receive. God's provision of the land of Canaan for his people then parallels the duty of a husband to provide a place for his wife to live.[2] Later writers imaginatively picture the wearing of marriage garments (Isa 61:10).

The possibility of marriage breakdown and divorce is built into the imagery of marriage. At the renewal of the covenant before entering the new land, there is a warning against the Israelites turning their hearts away from this committed relationship with God to a relationship with rival gods. Warnings of calamities are issued if these people abandon the covenant that has been made with God (Deut 29:25). God, as the Husband, is capable of expressing his furious anger (Deut 29:28), analogous to the anger of a man whose wife has committed adultery, an image which is prevalent in the prophets (e.g., Jer 3:20; 9:2). The divorce formula used in Israel of a man to his wife, whether spoken or written, is the model for God's statement of divorce to Israel (Jer 3:8). Now he has no more responsibility to provide a home, so the predicted consequences of unfaithfulness (Deut 28:36), namely being driven out of the land God provided as home, are fulfilled in the exile. The prophet Jeremiah pleads with the people to realize this connection between their behavior and their perceived right to stay in the land (Jer 7:3-15). The God of the covenant is no mere temple, with its impersonal structures of pseudo-permanence. He is a personal God who is not deceived by outward conformity to rituals that hide the disloyalties of the heart and the abandonment of covenantal behavior. He can and will act to destroy the signs of marriage, including home and temple, if the marriage is, in fact, no longer anything more than a charade.

Yet, divorce is not the last word. God's husband-love is fiercely strong, even in the face of marriage unfaithfulness and breakdown. The prophets

---

2. Sohn, *YHWH, the Husband of Israel*, 51.

reflect God's emotive pleading, as they call for the Israelites to return to their God (e.g., Jer 3:12–14). Hosea expresses this in graphic poetry as God the abused Husband speaks with emotional force, urging remarriage (Hos 2), while Ezekiel uses a lurid allegory that is designed to shock people out of a complacent drift that has become dangerously idolatrous and ruptured the marriage (Ezek 16). These passionate attempts to draw wayward people back show that God's anger is not as deep as his love. That love will continue beyond any marriage rupture (Isa 54:5–8).

One book of the Old Testament that was, for most of Christian history, widely understood to portray the tender relationship between God the Husband and his people, the bride, is the Song of Songs. To modern readers who are regularly over-exposed to sexually suggestive and explicit material in immoral contexts, it has become distasteful to associate God as Husband with love poetry. Medieval writers generally took this work as an allegory of the relationship between God and his people and attributed hidden spiritual meanings to many details, like the fruit and the flowers. That approach is no longer helpful to modern minds, and there is no evidence that the medieval allegorical meanings were originally intended. If the book is taken to refer to a historical marriage, the idea of associating the figure of King Solomon as a model for exclusive, committed marriage is problematic at the least, when we consider that he had 900 wives and 300 concubines!

However, the Song of Songs is well worth rediscovery. I suggest that we need to read the Song of Songs at two levels: 1) the level of a healthy love relationship between one man and one woman who commit themselves exclusively to each other in marriage, and 2) the level of the committed marriage covenant relationship between God and his people, taking the first as an analogy to the second.

The Song of Songs is written in poetry and does not necessarily follow a consistent chronological story line. But we can easily recognize that both the man and the woman speak to and about each other, that both long to be in the company of the other and sometimes need to undergo a search for the other, that both invite each other, at different times, to come with them, and that both express their delight in the other.

The emotive language and poetic imagery used in the Song of Songs provide us with a vivid relational metaphor of God as Husband and his people as wife. The reciprocal ardent desires of bride and groom for each other give us the best understanding of the passionate desires expressed by God for his people. This divine Leader, like a husband, is most definitely not detached or dispassionate. His people matter greatly to him. Interestingly, the man in the poem is sometimes called a king and sometimes a shepherd, combining two of the other images of God's leadership with that of a husband.[3]

GOD'S ANGER IN THE CONTEXT OF FAMILY IMAGERY

People often express difficulties with the Old Testament portrayal of God's anger. However, it is helpful to see this in the context of God's role as Father, Mother or as Husband. Emotions are deeply embedded in these intimate family relationships. In all relationships where there is intense love, there is also a high risk of anger.

Anger will emerge when parents see someone mistreating their child. Anger will also arise when parents see the child making choices that imperil his or her wellbeing and future. If the child has love towards the parent, the instinctive dislike for parental anger should motivate the child to reassess what they are doing, at the very least. Obviously, the expression of parental anger needs to be within safe and appropriate limits. In order to provide security to the family, words and actions of discipline and judgment are needed, sometimes towards those on the outside who threaten the security of the family, sometimes towards those inside who threaten their own wellbeing.

Within a marriage relationship, emotions are rightly very strong. Committed love, when thwarted, rightly raises emotions of jealousy and anger. Both of these are attributed to God as Husband. It would only be a very impersonal kind of leadership, like that of a bureaucracy, that would not involve any emotions. But in a committed marriage relationship the full range of the more intimate emotions, including both love and anger, can be expected. Again, these emotions need to be expressed within appropriate boundaries in order to communicate but not destroy. It is important to note that the emotions attributed to God, even those of jealousy and anger, are expressed only within well-controlled boundaries.

---

3. See Duguid, *The Song of Songs*.

QUESTIONS FOR REFLECTION OR DISCUSSION

1. Can you relate to God as Father? As Mother? As Husband?
2. Which is the image that is easiest to relate to? Are there specific aspects that are important?
3. What have your own parents taught you about leadership, positively or negatively?
4. Can you accept God's anger as well as his love?
5. How do you relate anger with love in your own life?
6. Can you speak to God as intimately as you would to an ideal close parent or spouse?

Chapter 17

God as Wise Guide, Host, Helper, Rock

GOD AS WISE GUIDE

I often notice that the proportion of students who tell me that they are looking for wisdom—they are seeking to become wise—is much higher in non-Western countries than in Western countries. Perhaps this is a sign that today's media and other value-shapers no longer openly esteem wisdom. That leaves our young people more vulnerable to the whimsical ideas of peers seeking to shape their choices. Perhaps students in the West prioritize correct doctrine, so that they may more accurately understand the right things to believe. That, too, is a worthy aim. However, the latter tendency, if unbalanced, can lead to a neglect of wisdom, where what is right is balanced with and yet connected to engagement with the decisions, relationships and pathways of daily living.

Wisdom is highly prized in the Old Testament and God is its origin. Wisdom is needed to make choices that will stand the test of time, to sift through complex possibilities, relationships and arguments and make decisions that will promote the most good, to keep the balance between justice and mercy which is so characteristic of God. Wisdom enables us to resist the temptation to think only of short-term goals without taking the long-term consequences into account. Wisdom enables us to balance our own needs with the needs of others. And this wisdom is said to be available—from the Wise Guide himself (e.g., Prov 4).

The Exodus story illustrates God's leadership as a reliable guide for the people, going before them to show them the way. This image of God as Guide is picked up in the book of Proverbs. Life is pictured as a journey along a path. Many warnings are given against wandering onto crooked paths, which deceptively lead to death instead of life (e.g., Prov 2:12–18). Those who guide the young onto such paths are described as foolish, perverse or wicked. The result is that gullible youths stumble or get easily sidetracked into similar foolish, perverse or wicked ways. Those guides mock the sound guidance of the wise. Mocking here demonstrates great foolishness and has disastrous effects.

Wise guidance should come through good parents, who receive their wisdom from God. The paths of wisdom are described as being straight (Prov 4:26–27), where the rewards are abundant and precious (Prov 4:18; 3:13–18). Unwise paths are called crooked or devious and hold hidden dangers. Young people need God as a trustworthy guide who will direct them towards the straight paths (Prov 3:5, 6). But it is not only young people who need this—we all do!

In the book of Proverbs, a female figure called Wisdom is a personified form of God (e.g., Prov 1:20; 8:1–36). The wisdom that she offers is to be desired, grasped and treasured. It will lead to honor with God and people (Prov 3:4). However, in order to access that wisdom that is found in the straight path, one has to place oneself in submission to God as Leader (Prov 1:7). It will be in and through wisdom that his guidance will necessarily involve discipline (e.g., Prov 1:2–3).

In many cultures and languages, the virtues, including wisdom, are represented as feminine; here is no exception. Although the dominant imagery of God in the Old Testament is masculine, this feminine imagery (and the small number of references to God as Mother) provides a balance. God's leadership embraces characteristics that we typically associate with men, and also characteristics that we typically associate with women. This fits with the statement in Genesis that both males and females are made in the image of God (Gen 1:27). In the book of Proverbs, the guidance of the Woman Wisdom figure seems to be congruent with the teaching of both the father and the mother. God's wise leadership, then, can be likened to the wise guidance of ideal parents of both genders. However, we also see examples of evil represented in both males and females in the book of Proverbs. The antitype to God as Wise Guide is portrayed as another female figure, the wily and foolish female guide who lures the gullible by false promises, playing on their passions, to a hidden chamber of death (Prov 9:1–6, 13–18).

God's word is also referred to as providing wise guidance through the metaphor of light for our path (Ps 119:105). The image is of a guide holding a lamp to show us where to place our feet so that we will walk securely without stumbling (Ps 56:13). It also echoes the opening verses of Genesis, where God needs only to speak for light to come into being (Gen 1:3). The association of God's word with light is also said to give understanding (Ps 119:130). The light image here takes us beyond blind following. God's wise leadership encourages thinking; knowledge can legitimately be pursued, and insight can be grasped.

Even his law and his specific commandments are said to give light to the eyes and joy to the heart (Ps 19:8). Following what is right is wise for life. God is the teacher who gives wise laws to enable life to be satisfying. It is not only God's word that is associated with light; his face is said to shine (Ps 4:6; Num 6:25). God's leadership presence gives the light of goodness, grace, peace, salvation and security (Ps 27:1).

Two Israelite men stand out through giving wisdom to foreign kings in crucial periods. In both cases these kings need to know the interpretations of strange and troubling dreams that seem to contain hidden messages. The kings' wise men, trained in the best of human wisdom, are unable to help. But Joseph and Daniel (Gen 41 and Dan 1-4) turn to God for specific wisdom to give the correct interpretations that are needed and speak words that are recognized as true, that break the confusion, and that give a way forward that works. They don't claim to be wise enough in themselves to be able to give these accurate interpretations but both declare honestly that it is God who gives the wisdom for such things.

The invitation to seek for wisdom is picked up in the New Testament (James 3:13-18) and adds a description of the wisdom from heaven that issues in righteousness—it is pure, peace-loving, considerate, humble, merciful, working for good, impartial, and sincere. This is congruent with the Old Testament's understanding of wisdom. James contrasts this kind of wisdom with the wisdom from earth that issues in evil practices—this "wisdom" is envious, selfish, disorderly, and untruthful.

This image of God's leadership as Wise Guide clearly overlaps with the images of God as Father or Mother, King and Shepherd. Perhaps the most fundamental need in good leadership is wisdom. But many leaders don't realize that until, perhaps, they are faced with decisions that deal with a more complicated scenario than they had imagined. Our wisdom can and should be informed by knowledge of truth, of good principles, of human understanding, of resources, of timing and any other factors that are pertinent to our sphere of operation. But sometimes, after working through all of these, we need a more personal guide for a specific problem. King David didn't know whether to go into a particular battle, so he asked God. The prophets Jeremiah and Ezekiel, when kings and leaders pressed them for advice, waited for God's answer. There have been numerous times when my husband and I tried to make a decision by working out all of the pros and cons, using the best principles and advice we knew, but remained stuck. Through an unexpected direction from God the Wise Guide the impasse was resolved and a new, right and peaceful way ahead was opened. We still need God's wisdom!

GOD AS HOST

God is a hospitable leader, a host who draws others towards him, who provides refreshment and who delights them in his presence. There is a wonderful scene where God calls Moses and seventy-three other leaders up the mountain right into the presence of God himself (Exod 24). It is a warm experience of what the covenant between God and his people is really about—a close relationship. Somehow these men 'see' the God of Israel. The men are refreshed by eating and drinking, just as many of our good friendships are filled with memories of eating and drinking together.

God is said to be the Host of feasts. The most famous image comes from Psalm 23, where the writer says to God, "You prepare a table before me in the presence of my enemies. You anoint my head with oil; my cup overflows" (v 5). God is the one who not only provides sustenance, but also performs the traditional host's duties of anointing a hot, tired head with refreshing oil.

In another text God is likened to the woman Wisdom, who prepares well for a feast and then invites people to come and participate in the banquet, and, at the same time, to live in the way of understanding (Prov 9:1–6). It stands in contrast to the other woman Foolishness, who invites but has nothing to offer; her invitation is a snare, capturing her victims for destruction (Prov 9:13–19).

Although God is supra-human, he provides a hospitable space in which people can be honest in the full expression of their thoughts and emotions. He notices and cares about needs which he himself does not have, like food and clothing. He functions as one who is on the inside of the group, and the placement of the tabernacle in the center of the camp, rather than on the periphery, signifies that. He becomes the Host in the midst of the people, inviting the people to meet with him in his specially-designed space. A space which is designed to draw people towards himself.

In some of the prophets there is the picture of people from other nations also coming to God's house so that God can teach them his ways, so that they too can walk in his paths (e.g., Mic 4:2). As the temple was dedicated, King Solomon envisaged the gathering of people from other nations to pray there, simply because they would hear about God and his power (2 Chr 6:32). Just as a good speaker draws a crowd, God is shown as one who draws people.

Israel was also to bear God's light to shine out to the people of all nations, to be a light to the Gentiles (Isa 42:6; 49:6). God, the Leader of Israel, and the justice that he teaches (Isa 51:4) would be attractive to other peoples; he is like a warm and welcoming light, drawing people out of darkness.

The image of host is picked up in the New Testament, as Jesus is pictured, especially in Luke's Gospel, hosting meals that include many unlikely people. Holy Communion continues the image, which will find its fulfillment in a future heavenly banquet celebration (e.g., Luke 22:16, 18; Rev 19:6–9).

Hospitality is a grace that every leader needs to learn. It does not primarily refer to the provision of meals, although that may be a component. It is rather opening your heart to provide a hospitable space so that the other person can feel free to be themselves in your space. It means putting yourself sufficiently in the shoes of the other so that you can see and hear who they really are—their hopes and aspirations, their gifts and capabilities, their limits, difficulties and needs. It includes empathy and generosity, welcoming and refreshing, openness and grace.

GOD AS HELPER

The word "helper" may not appear to be a leadership word, as we often use it to describe someone who gives help at a fairly basic level in order to free another person to do more complex tasks. This usage would suggest that a helper is on a lower rank than the person or organization being helped. Yet, how many of us cry out to God to help us when we are threatened, confused or feeling powerless in the face of difficulty because we hope he can give greater help than anyone else?

A helper can be someone who is inferior, equal or superior. The most frequent use, by far, of the word for helper in the Bible refers to God. He is clearly not inferior or even equal. A helper can often provide something that the person who requests help cannot provide. It is not uncommon that someone is asked to be a helper precisely because he or she has specialized skills that are of higher quality than the skills of most other people.

God the Leader's helping role often means that God bends down low, to the level of the human, in order to hear, in order to know, in order to lift up or to walk beside. When many write of their past struggles and remember

God's rescue they often picture God as the Helper who bent down to listen to their need, and then to take action to save (e.g., Ps 116:1–8). In fact, God's help is often depicted as rescue, deliverance or salvation. In a later chapter, we will see God's leadership behind the scenes. If we read carefully, we discover that God is at work helping in many situations where he is not even named, and certainly not publicly thanked.

God promises whatever help is needed to each prophet who doubts his ability to do as asked. God promises Moses and Jeremiah that he will help them to speak. God promises to Jeremiah and Ezekiel the help of protection. All of God's help is available when he is present. There were times when Moses didn't think he could continue to lead the Israelites, because of their persistent grumbling. He certainly couldn't do it alone. God's strongest promise of help was contained in his assurance: "I will be with you" or "My Presence will go with you" (Exod 33:14).

A useful way of looking at leadership is to say that it provides help. That help is of vital importance. Without a leader, a group can easily disband, lose its vision, be lacking in certain resources, and may not have a voice to speak in strategic places. Leaders give whatever help is needed so that the group can function and thrive. Sometimes leaders provide specialist knowledge and skills, but often a good leader needs to fill in the gaps with help of a more mundane variety. His or her task is to help the people to move towards the fulfilment of their goal, and a good leader is willing to give whatever kind of help is needed to that end. Taking a posture of superiority is counterproductive in God's model of helping leadership.

Thinking of a human leader as a kind of savior can lead to an overinflated sense of a person's capacity and importance, and can encourage an extremely unhelpful Messiah complex. However, there is an element of truth in the idea that leadership saves people, so long as limits to capacity are not over-stretched or over-imagined. While a Messiah complex is distinctly unhelpful, a leader who saves a group from disaster, in any form, is one who is a genuine helper. It is part of a leader's mandate to work towards solving problems instead of creating them. Solutions may require the help of many other people, but a leader's task is to gather whoever and whatever is needed to bring solutions and find help, which may sometimes be some form of saving, for the sake of the people.

There is another image that is not said to portray God but is applied either to the idealized group of Israelites or to an individual, referred to as the Servant (Isa 42:1–7; 49:1–7; 50:4–9; 52:13—53:12). This Servant is certainly a leader who reflects God's values in leadership and so is relevant for our discussion. With God's Spirit on him he will act wisely and bring justice to the nations. He will not be one who demands attention but is sensitive to the wounded. He gives hope, light, release from captivities and salvation. Although he is severely mistreated, despised and rejected, he suffers on behalf of others. This Servant is not self-absorbed—not preoccupied with his own image—but works to help the people in a variety of ways. Some ways are quiet and perhaps hidden, some work for justice on a wider scale, some even involve him being misunderstood and publicly humiliated. Like God, his leadership task is to help others in whatever ways are needed. I, with many other Christians, take this to be a description of the Messiah, Jesus.

GOD AS ROCK

Another very prevalent image of God is as a Rock—a very solid rock, not a movable stone. Might this also be an image that relates to God's leadership? One obvious difference between a leader and a rock is that a leader moves and leads others to move, whereas a large rock will not move even though people may try to make it move. Yet there are some important ideas in the widespread use of this metaphor that do relate to and describe God's leadership.

There is an inherent problem in every image, which is that it is inexact and incomplete. The Rock image is more limited in its application than many of the others. But the compilation of several images builds a multifaceted model of God's leadership that not only helps us to consider God's leadership more carefully, but also encourages us to identify and emulate relevant characteristics in our own leadership, to the degree that we can.

The Rock idea suggests security, a place to run into, like a cave or a fortress. The leadership of God the Rock provides shelter and protection when threats abound. The Rock also speaks of the beginning, the foundation, the source of life and the giver of firm principles. Like a large rock that is very difficult to move, God is secure and steady; he is not swayed by the latest fads or fazed by the latest terrors. He is totally reliable and faithful; his character remains steady and sure. This does not mean that God is a boring leader who refuses to budge; we see plenty of movement, vision and change. But the constancy of his character engenders trust through those periods of change.

In applying the rock image to our own leadership, there are obvious limits. Even if we have founded an organization, we cannot claim to be the foundation as God can. However, the other attributes evoked by this image apply—reliability, steady character, and staying true to firm principles.

One of my weaknesses used to be that I was not good at being on time. When I first became the choir director for our musicals I was not consistent in the starting and finishing times for our rehearsals. After a few weeks one lady in the group spoke to me very candidly. She really needed to be certain of these times for several very important reasons and could not continue in the choir if I could not give her definite times. She helped me to realize the importance of reliability in the time framework. I am grateful to her for explaining her need so clearly. We all benefited from the new definite time limits. I changed and she remained.

Chronically unpredictable leaders do not have this rock-like quality. I have been under a couple of such leaders. All had charm, but their charm could quickly turn to rage. They could not be relied on to keep arrangements; sometimes they could overturn decisions on a whim. People working under them were continually frustrated, insecure, often anxious and chronically unable to plan their own work effectively. A stunning personality, good looks and great skills are not enough to enable someone to be an effective leader. Reliability, faithfulness and consistency of character are foundational. God's leadership is rock-like. Is our leadership like that?

QUESTIONS FOR REFLECTION OR DISCUSSION

1. Which of these images of God's leadership do you value most?
2. How important is the idea of God giving light to our path?
3. Are you an active seeker of God's wisdom?
4. How can one be a "hospitable" leader?
5. To what extent is a leader primarily a helper?
6. Why is it important for a leader to be rock-solid in certain traits?

PART 5

God's Leadership in Uncertain Times

Chapter 18

God and His Prophets

We pick up the story after the Exodus and the settlement of the Israelite tribes in their new land. The institutions of monarchy, priesthood and law are established and functional. Boundaries have increased, periods of peace have lengthened and there is pride in national identity. The magnificent temple in Jerusalem provides religious focus. Regular feasts and holy days create a good rhythm between work and rest. Outwardly, things are going well. God as Leader has, indeed, provided what he promised.

There are, however, some problems simmering under the surface. King Solomon does well in putting Israel on the map of "must see" places for wealthy foreign dignitaries. But there is a price: harsh taxation of the people. His son Rehoboam takes an even harsher stand and the result is a revolt by ten of the twelve tribes. Israel is now divided into two smaller kingdoms. Some of the appointed leaders maintain faithfulness to their role but many more do not.

Where is God in these times when guidance from the institutional leaders becomes corrupt? The kings of the Northern Kingdom move right away from God's designated guidelines for worship. The priests quickly follow suit and the result is widespread corruption in values and behavior, with palpable social effects, not just changes in ritual. The Southern Kingdom has periods of hope under some faithful kings, but other periods of incalculable evil.

Is God silent? No. He looks for some who are willing to listen, usually people who are outside the institutional leadership. They are not uniform in their backgrounds, training or spheres of influence. But they listen to God. As they listen and engage in conversation with him, they get to know his character, his words, his visions, his messages. God sends them to particular people and to particular places. Sometimes to kings, sometimes to priests, sometimes to people coming through the temple gates to worship, sometimes to people who are staying away from worship. They speak out of their personal experience of God. They dare to challenge the highest authorities; they dare to challenge anyone. And they suffer the huge cost of unpopularity with the powerful and those who crave their patronage, or worse.

God sends these messengers, these prophets, to speak where no one else will speak. To speak where truth matters. To speak where innocent people are affected by wrong decisions. These prophets have never aspired to such a position—they are called. They often cannot imagine themselves speaking out in the situations where they are sent. But they obey, often with fear and trepidation, but with the assurance that God their Leader will go with them.

Although there are prophets who are active in establishing Israel as a nation and kingdom (Moses and Samuel), and prophets who bring challenging messages in the days of the united kingdom (e.g., Elijah and Elisha in the north, Nathan and Gad in the south), prophecy is most needed, most active, and most rejected after the split into two kingdoms and when other human leaders actively or passively put the people at risk. God as Leader does not merely stand by, as if helpless. He watches, speaks and acts, and the activity of the prophets is evidence of that. In times when there is little receptivity by the king towards God's leadership, God continues to guide through his receptive prophets. They are the ones whom God uses to call the people back to the conditions of the covenant and to the path of life, not death.

BUILDING REVIEWS INTO SYSTEMS

Every established system or institution needs checks and balances. It needs to be maintained and periodically reviewed. God the Leader considers the needs of his people for both maintenance and review, for checks and balances. He anticipates the potential for people and systems to veer away from their intended course and function to their own detriment if certain aberrations are allowed to continue unchecked. The prophets form a vital part of the "review" component of the system. Priests are also engaged in review, in the sense that they help people to make appropriate sacrifices to put their relationships right with God and with others. However, prophets are especially needed to speak out in correction when other leaders, particularly kings and priests, fail in their respective maintenance tasks of justice and teaching.

Human leaders can be too naive. They think they can invent perfect, streamlined, foolproof systems and pride themselves that, once they have one up and running, all of the indicators they value will demonstrate its rugged superiority. And they may arrogantly bask in its success. For all its advantages, the system can, however, still be undone, much more easily than we like to imagine or admit. Even God faces that leadership problem and spots the weak points, where tension, arrogance, bullying, discouragement, ineptitude or incompetence are threatening the system. It only takes one weak spot, given enough pressure, for a system to become distorted, dysfunctional or to actually break apart. Continual vigilance is essential. Sparks must be put out quickly before they become wildfires.

PROPHETIC COMMUNICATIONS

In contrast to the period of the Exodus story, where God as Leader could speak in direct ways through Moses to declare truth, laws and guidance, God often has to find more indirect ways to speak through later prophets because of their distance from, and sometimes opposition to, mainline human leadership. This also impacts the style of communication. Because prophets are not the credentialed leaders, they may need to use provocative language or dramatic acts to catch attention. Their style of speaking is usually poetic, colored by arresting visual imagery and rhetorical force. They may include proverbial sayings and riddles, rhetorical questions, sarcasm, irony, allegories that are sometimes outrageous, and visions that are of homely or bizarre subjects. They may utter laments and use the language of cursing (pronouncing woe), or they may give enormous comfort through the language of blessing. The prophets engage the full force of their own personalities and particular expertise to give weight to the emotive appeals and warnings from the heart of God to his people.[1]

Prophets also express the forward-thinking, visionary aspect of God's leadership. It is to this group that God reveals himself as a leader who not only knows the future consequences of present actions, and who passionately urges people to make choices that will give the best outcomes for the future, but who also radically re-visions the future beyond the present limits of human thinking, in order to inspire the people to hope and faith.

---

1. See Heschel, *The Prophets*, for many valuable insights on the Old Testament prophets.

GOD'S LEADERSHIP OVER EACH PROPHET

God's leadership over each prophet is very personal. He takes the initiative to call each one in an unexpected and unique way, with words and images comprehensible to the individual. Amos is called to lay aside his secular work and move beyond the boundaries of his own kingdom; Isaiah is impressed by a temple vision of God's holiness and his own unworthiness, and responds to God's need to find someone who will go and speak for him; Jeremiah hears about God's intimate knowledge of him and God's call for him to be a prophet to the nations; Ezekiel is shown visions of God on a grand scale and is overwhelmed as he contemplates the unexpected arrival of the divine entourage in exile and his strange role as God's agent in a strange land.

These prophets are not left to rely on their own resources. A divine call is accompanied by divine responsibility and divine provision. When the prophet Elijah is afraid, discouraged and exhausted, and even gives up on life, God the Leader sympathetically sees what he really needs and provides sleep and food accordingly (1 Kings 19:3-6). When Moses and Jeremiah do not understand how they can speak convincingly on behalf of an unseen God, God provides signs, words and protection (Exod 4:1-17; Jer 1:9, 17-19). When their lives are threatened by others, he often provides a warning to enable them to stay out of danger (Jer 11:18-23; 12:6). Yet God's prophets are people under certain disciplines that are necessary for the carrying out of their mission in their particular contexts. Jeremiah is forbidden to marry or attend funerals or feasts (Jer 16:1-9); Ezekiel is forbidden to participate in the customary mourning rituals following the death of his beloved wife (Ezek 24:15-24). And even though these prophets faithfully speak warnings on God's behalf to the people, they are not exempt from the consequences of these messages: Jeremiah and Ezekiel both suffer exile with their people, and the prophet Uriah is killed for speaking the truth (Jer 26:20-23). However, God holds each faithful prophet in his inner circle, his council (Jer 23:18), where there is a level of intimacy between leader and prophet that is not often known by others.

In the following chapters I will select two prophets who speak to the Northern Kingdom before its demise (Amos and Hosea), then two prophets from the Southern Kingdom who speak in the midst of disruption and exile (Jeremiah from Jerusalem and Ezekiel from exile). God the Leader is still at work through these messengers, leading the people, if they will listen, back to what works best.

QUESTIONS FOR REFLECTION OR DISCUSSION

1. Can you recall a time when God has spoken truth to you through another person, perhaps someone unexpected?
2. Can you think of times when a modern-day prophet might be needed to speak truth from God?
3. What might the characteristics of a modern-day prophet be? How might you tell if they were false?
4. Have you ever been given a message from God to communicate to others?
5. How often do you take time to review your commitment to God?
6. What can we learn about the systems we set up?

Chapter 19

Prophets of the Northern Kingdom

AMOS

God's leadership through Amos breaks conventions of the day. This divine Leader is simply not bound by human political expectations or rigid roles and moves beyond them. God calls an agriculturist from the Southern Kingdom to speak a bald, unpalatable prophetic word of warning to the king of the breakaway Northern Kingdom (Amos 7:10–17). The incident causes understandable offense and Amos is ordered to go back to his homeland; he has no rights in that place, and the king, not Amos, is the one in charge. Yet this distasteful word turns out to have been a legitimate warning from God.

Amos is rhetorically skillful in leading the people of the north to approvingly envision God's just judgment against surrounding nations. However, this purpose is to confront them finally with their own acts of serious injustice and offense to God, their rightful Leader (Amos 1–2). Throughout the book, Amos articulates the exact issues that God identifies as problematic. There will be no room to charge God with being a leader who is uncommunicative or who gives uncertain, mixed messages.

God is concerned about abuse. Innocent, upright people are bought and sold as slaves, the poor are treated with indignity, women are used disgracefully by men, and people are forced to act against their conscience. The arrogant wealthy are castigated by means of insults and sarcasm in an attempt to shock them out of their ruinous complacency. The idle rich, both men and women, passing their time in wanton luxury at the expense of the poor workers, are addressed as cows! "Go to worship—and sin!" shouts Amos sarcastically. Such an unthinkable disjunction of ideas is intended to help them to see the incongruities in their lifestyle and to understand why God has not blessed their fields. Can such a call to reassess their habits jolt them out of their hypocrisy and lead them to turn to God in integrity?

It is much easier to warm to a speaker who oozes comfort than to one who berates us with insults. But there are times when the truth spoken with genuine care cuts to the heart with good effect and becomes healing. I remember a woman, old enough to be my mother, who was one of these cutting truth-tellers. I didn't like it when she would name some wrong attitude that I had. Perhaps it cut the deepest when she was right. I hated it when I saw that same wrong attitude in others and I certainly did not want to hear that I had a different version of the same problem. I found myself simultaneously wanting to resist her diagnosis and being drawn to her genuine care. The combination of truth and mercy is powerful. I recognized that she gained no joy in naming my problem. She spoke frankly because she wanted me to be free of the unwanted consequences of that attitude. I had spoken to her because I also wanted that, but I had not recognized the cause and didn't expect that the cause could lie within me. I am grateful that she had the courage to confront me, for my good not hers, and to do it with grace.

Proverbs and riddles are used in the attempt to alert people to what should be universally self-evident among any people (Amos 3:1-8). Israel, of all peoples, should know what their God expects and the reasons why they, even more than the surrounding nations, should be judged. God issues a cry of lament (Amos 5) to express his immense sadness that his bride Israel has fallen. These people are no longer behaving as the people he called into the intimacy of a covenanted relationship. Yet there are still signs of hope that life for God's people can be restored. "Seek good, not evil, that you may live. Then the Lord God Almighty will be with you, just as you say he is" (Amos 5:14).

The people seem to assume naively that a future "day of the Lord" will be a cozy retreat, when their God will pour out blessings in abundance on them as his favorite people. But they have not discerned the distance that is now between them and their God. In fact, their persistent perpetration of injustice in society has caused God to hate many things they do. He even hates their worship (5:21). Sacrifices might be outwardly conformist, but they have no integrity in respect of their lives. He would much prefer justice and righteousness in their human relationships over an elaborate sham to try to win God's favor. Now God is ready to pronounce curses on them

("Woe!" in 5:18; 6:1), reminiscent of the dire warnings given in Deuteronomy 28:15-68.

Yet Amos feels for the people as well as for God. He cries out to God to spare these people from judgment, and subsequently hears that God relents. God as Leader is open to negotiation. Yet there are standards, and God will make his assessments carefully (Amos 7:1-9). He concludes that the time is ripe for judgment (Amos 8-9). God who has led Israel is a greater leader than they imagined. He thinks and acts on the international stage (Amos 9:7).

Amos certainly comes out of left field. Today, those who speak outside authorized positions are, like Amos, very easily dismissed. Sometimes a young child, before learning the rules of acceptable social conversation, will prod people's conscience by innocently blurting out the truth. We need people who think outside the box. But they do need to interact with the appointed leaders graciously and humbly. Bald truth can be spoken with love. But in order for it to be received, the appointed leaders must listen in respect and humility. These people on the side may be able to observe, reflect and comment on reality in a way that others cannot see. They may be among those to whom God speaks more directly; they may even be sent by him. Their wisdom needs to be tested, as they may be very wrong. But an appointed leader must listen and test, so that they don't miss the gems, the gifts, that God may be bringing to assist them in their leadership.

HOSEA

God selects the prophet Hosea because he will be able to convey his emotional appeals to the Northern Kingdom with poignancy, because of his own painful experiences with an unfaithful wife (Hos 1-3). The often used analogy of God as Husband and the people as wife comes to the fore. Although Amos and Hosea both address the same kingdom in a similar period (the comfortable reign of Jeroboam II), their own experiences, interests and observations are sharpened in different directions. God can never be represented adequately by one prophetic voice, so he works in and with several prophets of different temperaments and experiences.

Where Amos expresses despair over matters of social injustice (horizontal relationships), Hosea perceives the breach primarily in terms of their religious prostitution, that is, unfaithfulness in their vertical relationship with God. Perhaps some people may recognize the truth in Amos's message, while others may better understand the truth in Hosea's. The problem lies with both king and people. They have rejected what they have been taught by God and have sought guidance in outlawed divination (Hos 4). In doing so, they have become vulnerable to the wily ways of foreigners and run the risk of falling captive to them.

Hosea's attention to idolatry is in keeping with his vigilance against turning to the foreign superpower of the day, Assyria (e.g., Hos 5:13). This rejection of God is expressed in terms of adultery, of trusting other lovers (Hos 8:9), alluding to the foreign gods worshiped by these other rulers and the blatant compromises of worship that would be required. The people of the Northern Kingdom are gullible, willing to believe that any other leader of promise is trustworthy (Hos 7:11), but their trust is misplaced and they will ultimately be put to shame (Hos 10:6). Israel's forebears have had to turn their backs on the leadership of both Mesopotamia (in Abraham's day) and Egypt (in Moses' day) in order to follow the leadership of God.[1] Now they are giving in to the temptation to reverse that turning.

There is a universal human tendency to look for a leader to follow. We might consider ourselves to be independent thinkers who don't need anyone to look up to—neither a god nor a human leader. We fool ourselves. We all, even those of us who are leaders, are followers of others to some extent. If we won't follow a good and wise leader, we can be vulnerable to unhealthy influences of bad leaders and even domination by them. If we are functional atheists (we may believe in God but do not follow him) we can fall prey to wherever our passions (e.g., fear, lust, greed, envy) lead us. We may be seduced by other religious or occult leaders, or we may place too much reliance on those with political, financial, academic or social power. We gradually become more like those we follow. So the challenge to identify those who have the greatest influence over us is wise. And, if we discover that some of those influencers have an agenda that is potentially harmful, we need to re-orient ourselves. God the Leader calls us because the leadership he offers is in the way of what is right, wise and good.

Like Amos, Hosea also pronounces a woe curse on the people (Hos 7:13; 9:12). But it is still not without passionate pleas to return to God their Leader (e.g., Hos 6:1) and heart-wrenching calls to recognize God's historic compassion and care (e.g., Hos 11; 13:5, 6). Within those pleas there lies a hopeful opportunity. But the people have become proud, dismissive and rebellious. They may look to the superpower of Assyria to bolster them up, but that trust will be misplaced. God has come to the end of his tolerance, so judgment will come.

It is worth considering God the Leader's use of emotional language, through Hosea, in his appeals to the people. While the pleas often focus on

---

1. Heschel, *Prophets*, 71–72.

God's unrequited love, primarily as Husband but also as Parent, they need to be seen in conjunction with his concern for the metaphorical fruit of that love (Hos 10:12). If the people "marry" another god then different offspring will be produced. God is concerned that the people use their land (the land he has given them) to produce fruit as offspring of their union with him, instead of union with idols. This reflects his desire for the fruit of righteousness, instead of wickedness. He wants truthfulness instead of deceit (Hos 12:7–8). He wants life for them instead of death (Hos 13:14). While we may often associate a leader's emotional pleading with selfish manipulation, it is not the case here. The point at issue is not God's ultimate prestige, but the wellbeing of the people. It is not about God's survival, but the survival of the people. The emotional language is definitely intended to be persuasive, but it is not deceitful or self-serving. It uses poetic color, imagery and rhetorical force in order to open people's eyes to reality and urgency but does not distort the essential nature of the true situation.

TWO DIFFERENT PROPHETS

God as leader has chosen his two spokesmen, Amos and Hosea, carefully. The serious predicament of these unsuspecting people of the Northern Kingdom is presented through both social and religious imagery. Can these people, especially the leaders, consider the effects of their behavior on those who are being abused, or on the person of God their Leader? This double-edged plea is congruent with the responsibility given to leaders, in the Torah (the first five books), to look after the interests of the vulnerable (the fatherless, the widows, and the foreigners). Appeals are made to their better judgment, to their compassion for neighbors, to their historical memory, to their sense of righteousness and law, and to their empathy for God as rejected Lover. The consequences of their failure to listen will fall primarily on the people. God as Leader wants to protect them from disaster, but if he is voted out of leadership the people will need to discover the destructive consequences of stepping out on their own.

The northern people hear from God, via these two different prophets, through both rational and emotional language. We need both. Rational language alone can become detached, cold and clinical; emotional language alone can become manipulative or be perceived to be so. Leaders must know the time and place for each, and, even when rhetorical flourishes are needed, truth must retain its firm boundaries.

QUESTIONS FOR REFLECTION OR DISCUSSION

1. How do you feel about the idea of God making people feel uncomfortable?
2. Have you been made to feel uncomfortable in a way that was ultimately right and helpful?
3. What people have had the most positive influence on you? Did they ever challenge you?
4. Might you respond best to a more rational approach, like that of Amos, or a more emotional approach, like that of Hosea?
5. What are the appropriate uses of rational language and emotional language in leadership?
6. How do you respond to the idea that God chose two very different men to communicate essentially the same message in different ways?

Chapter 20

Prophets of the Southern Kingdom and the Exile

Although the Southern Kingdom retains authorized worship centered on the Jerusalem temple and the Davidic kings, and although the social decline is slower than that of the north, attitudes and behaviors of the southern leaders and people reach an alarming state of decline. But there are few who recognize it. Most are complacently carried along in the sliding stream of cultural change, clinging to the false security to be found in external trappings, including the very temple itself. The leaders don't notice, so there is now a need for urgent warnings from others. The Northern Kingdom did not heed the prophetic warnings and succumbed to Assyrian conquest, with the result that the people were scattered. Could something like that possibly happen to the people in the south?

JEREMIAH

God knows the inevitable, unpalatable consequences of drifting in this direction. So, as the ultimate Leader, he calls Jeremiah to speak on his behalf and to challenge the false security that is prevalent in this nation. The people presume that their God is close to them because they pay outward homage to him at his sanctuary. But, in fact, they fail to *know* him. Nor do they consider that God might be interested in knowing them or seeing how they live their day-to-day lives. Their concept of God's leadership is that he has no role or interest in their lives, but that he simply has a responsibility to bless them unconditionally. The presence of his temple in their midst and their participation in certain rituals confirms that assurance. But their assurance is misplaced, and their understanding of God's leadership and person is severely distorted.

The people forget that the covenant relationship between God the Leader and his people involves mutual knowing and mutual responsibilities. Whether overtly or covertly, the people are abandoning their Leader, and any previous closeness between him and their ancestors has quietly slipped away.

This situation creates a leadership crisis. Since the people are not actually following God, who are they really following? We find that cakes are baked and incense is burned in worship to the Queen of Heaven, as well as to other idols (Jer 7:18; 44:15–25). However, these rival leaders have no genuine power to help the people with their lives. God will not uncaringly sit back and allow the people he loves to fall into traps of empty deception.

A leader needs to earn the right to speak with strong emotions. God as Leader has earned that right, just as a faithful and loving husband of a lengthy marriage has earned the right to speak his heart with strong emotions to his wife. God and this group of people have been committed to each other in a covenant which is repeatedly and intentionally likened to marriage. Jeremiah 2:2 recalls the honeymoon period, as imperfect as it was, when Israel's love for her Husband was expressed in simple, unadulterated devotion, following him willingly on an unknown path and discovering his unwavering care and provision through inhospitable, barren terrain through to fertile pastures. In contrast, some of Israel's current behavior is likened to that of an errant wife who has become a prostitute (e.g., Jer 3:3)!

God engages an emotionally sensitive man, Jeremiah, to speak for him. He is often given challenging truths, conveyed with the strength of God's emotions. God's relationship with this prophet is portrayed in greater detail than with any other prophet. The call is famously portrayed in Jeremiah 1:1–10 in a scene that is both tender and startling. Candid two-way conversation ensues. Jeremiah feels too young, too powerless, and lacking in capacity to speak, so he would expect to fail all primary requirements for the job. Yet God affirms his appointment and promises to give Jeremiah the very things he lacks: divine authority and divine words.

Subsequent conversations between God and Jeremiah continue to be very candid and invite two-way honest, robust engagement. Jeremiah often asks questions, and God often answers him directly. God is clearly the leader in his initiatives, commands, enactments and judgments, yet he is a leader who listens. The relationship includes vigorous argument, and yet their words imply mutual trust. God's directions and responses demonstrate intimate knowledge and understanding of this particular man, his strengths, weaknesses, culture and context, and show no sign of being generic or mechanical. The overall impression is that God is far from being a distant leader; he is very close to Jeremiah and Jeremiah is very close to him. That is unlike the true position of the people around him.

The closeness between God and Jeremiah models the closeness which God as Leader offers, once again, to the people. The repeated calls, through this prophet, to *turn* or *return* to God give opportunities to remember and to be moved by the affections of the past relationship. God, through his prophet, chooses to plead with his people, in the hope of a warm response. Time may be short, and hope may be minimal, yet the rekindling of relationship must be attempted.

God's passions are displayed through Jeremiah's passions. The language is at times emotive and intimate, at times threatening and frightening. Yet God as Leader avoids manipulation. He speaks and is true to his word. God will never be satisfied by displays of mock loyalty intended to win favors. He is not interested in hypocrisy or pretense, nor in setting up an impersonal, remote bureaucracy. He wants to know his people, and to be known by his people.

This situation arises after many repeated warnings through previous messengers of God, but now God's patience is running out. If the people adamantly refuse to follow their rightful Leader, he will not force them to follow him. He will, however, lay their options before them, and communicate his heart. He will make known the consequences of their decisions. The covenant is at stake. The future of the people is at stake. Reality must be faced. And time is severely limited.

God, through his prophet Jeremiah, gives King Zedekiah two options (Jer 38). If he wants to live, he should surrender to the Babylonians who come to take over. Yet he chooses the option that will lead to destruction: he stubbornly resists the Babylonians. He pays the price. Even after Zedekiah has been taken, the remaining leaders seek advice from God through Jeremiah. They ask whether they should stay in the land or go to Egypt. In response, God tells them that they will thrive if they stay but suffer if they go. They, too, pay the price for rejecting this good advice.

God sees woundedness in the lives of his people, a deep and severe level of woundedness that can only be honestly described as incurable (Jer 30:12). Some, who falsely claim to speak for God, ignore the signs of terminal illness and treat them lightly. These wounds cannot be healed by a kiss and a band-aid. Surgery is needed. Hearts need to be circumcised, metaphorically speaking. God's purpose is to heal and save. However, if the people cannot respond to appeals and instructions, then, as a last resort, a crisis is needed. God lays out his plan to discipline his people in order to heal them. Judgment must come in order to effect a change, but this judgment must be carefully measured by justice.

Early in the book (Jer 1:10) Jeremiah is appointed to uproot, tear down, destroy, overthrow, build and plant. Later (Jer 31:28), God himself claims that all six of these functions are part of his own leadership strategy. His long-term desire is to build and to plant, yet with a highly resistant people it is first necessary to dismantle and evict false ideas, false trust, false comfort, and false self-image. In this case, false illusions need to be shattered in a way that causes shock. God loves his people enough to speak words of truth and to risk being misunderstood as he stands behind judgment. He wants a renewed covenant, renewed hearts, and renewed people, who will walk in harmony with each other and with their Leader.

Along the way, Jeremiah feels confident enough to question God about his justice while also acknowledging that God is always righteous (Jer 12:1). Jeremiah is not dismissed for his emotional outbursts in times when he is under duress as a direct result of his difficult and often unwelcome role on behalf of God. Sometimes God speaks a word of reassurance (Jer 15:11, 19-21), sometimes he shows Jeremiah that both God and prophet are treated similarly (Jer 18), sometimes he silently allows Jeremiah to let off steam (Jer 20:7-18), and occasionally he gives a word of rebuke (Jer 12:5; 15:19).

It is much more exciting and impressive to be the leader of a church or organization in a growth phase. Most books about human leadership focus on this aspect of leadership. But systems run down, people can become disappointed, disgruntled and difficult. They can go off track and become distracted by unhelpful and even destructive ideas. A whole group can become hardened into complacency or even rebellion. What might a leader do if they are appointed to a severely run-down organization?

I think of a demoralized church who needed a short-term minister to fill a gap. The leaders approached Peter who was aware of the condition of this church. He knew that he had a choice: to just keep the dysfunctional system going or to bring a serious challenge for change. The first option would inevitably cement their decline and lead them towards imminent closure. The second was risky, very risky. It had been a very long time since anyone had dared to challenge these people. It's not that the people were outwardly unpleasant. Far from it. However, their complacency locked them into a lethargic position where any relationship with the God they said they served was marginal at best. Their "niceness" covered many aspects of dysfunctionality in their community. When interviewed for this position, Peter warned the leaders not to hire him if they wanted to maintain their present situation. If they did hire him they should expect change. He challenged them to decide which way they wanted to go. Fortunately for the church, the leaders chose change and Peter's time with them became very productive, not yet in growth, but in helping the people to make some necessary changes before growth could become possible. God as Leader still calls some people to be his agents in dismantling and pulling down unhelpful personal and organizational edifices in order that more healthy life and growth can appear.

EZEKIEL

Ezekiel is a younger contemporary of Jeremiah and writes after Jeremiah's dire warnings have come to pass: their land has been taken over by the Babylonians, their precious temple has been destroyed and the leaders, together with most of the people, have been taken into exile in Babylonia. Ezekiel is taken too and feels the griefs along with his people.

In the book of Ezekiel, God as Leader appears more distant and even more aloof than in any other prophetic book. The separateness of God, rather than his closeness, is emphasized. There is a reason for this: the people have presumed the right to be close to him without keeping loyalty and without respecting his person or his leadership role. They have unconsciously regarded him more like a paternalistic but spineless friend, whom they could ignore or manipulate at will—rather like a Santa Claus who can be counted on to bring presents, irrespective of whether one has been naughty or nice.

The exile itself, followed by the fall of the city and its treasured temple, deeply challenges this thinking. There is widespread shock that these people could be subject to judgment from their own divine Leader. What happened to the promises of help and protection? How can God, who has rescued them on numerous previous occasions, now abandon them, send many far from his presence, represented by his temple, and allow enemies to overtake the physical space reserved for intimacy between God and his own people?

In the ensuing chaos and grief, the separate roles of God as Leader and people as responders need to be made clear. Even though the relationship between them has often been likened to marriage, God and the people still have separate identities, separate needs and separate responsibilities. Boundaries have become blurred, not only between Leader and people, but between the needs, rights and responsibilities of each citizen. God as Leader needs to bring clarity, boundaries and order.

This divine Leader also has his own considerations. While we see much more of God's concern for the needs of humans in the Scriptures overall, and as is exemplified in the image of God as Shepherd in this book (Ezek 34), we also see here rare glimpses of God giving careful consideration to matters from his own perspective. In Ezekiel 20 God makes the decision three times (vv. 9, 14 and 22) not to punish people who deserve his punishment. The reason given is somewhat surprising. It is not on account of his compassion for the people (not that this is denied), but for the sake of his own name, his own reputation. He decides, on these occasions, that he is not willing to be misunderstood and mocked by the people of surrounding nations. This is reminiscent of the times when Moses persuaded God not to wipe out his people for the sake of his own reputation (e.g., Exod 32:11–12). Yet we also see God take many other decisions where his name is put at risk—for example, in allowing Jerusalem to fall. He makes decisions that balance his own integrity and his people's needs and prioritizes according to his own criteria.

God's independence is clear. He is not a puppet of the people, even though he is very aware of their situation and needs. He disapproves of prophets who merely speak what the people want to hear. He is not in need of, or interested in, having his ego stroked. He will not give out words of blessing to elders who seek them at will like a child seeking a lucky dip prize. He moves around in total freedom and refuses to be bound by the people's expectations of where he "should" be located.

The visionary entrance of this divine Leader is on a very grand scale, such as would rival the splendor of any earthly ruler (Ezek 1). Anticipation builds as a brilliant and compelling light show announces the commencement of a grand procession. From the heart of a fiery core, four highly mobile living beings, with many faces, hands and wings, dance around. Each is accompanied by whirring wheels whose rims sparkle with iridescent eyes. Gradually the awareness of another more majestic being emerges. First, we see an expanse of sparkling ice, then we hear awe-inspiring sounds and then witness the reverence of the living beings for this greater being, as they fold their wings and give way to him. Then the visage of the divine Ruler is glimpsed but never fully grasped. Fire and light interplay around the Leader who has some characteristics like his subjects, but who is clearly far superior to them.

Perhaps there is a memory stirred of the glory of God as Leader of the Exodus journey. The pillar of cloud by day, and the fire by night, instilled confidence in their Leader in a strange land. Now, God has come to them in another strange land, where the people feel lost and depressed (Ezek 37:11). They need to have their confidence renewed in the Leader who is able to do what they cannot do, and who has the capacity and boldness to lead.

God as Leader is not pompously claiming a higher position than is inherently his. There is no arrogant boasting here, rather a revelation of that which exists but has been obscured by ignorance. God simply is above and beyond any human leader: that is reality. Ezekiel recognizes this and falls down before him (Ezek 1:28). Yet the purpose of this magnificent display is not to leave humans groveling in the dirt. He speaks specifically to this one man, Ezekiel, and calls him to stand up and participate in a conversation with him. God refuses to engage with him while he is lying helplessly on the ground. God's Spirit surges into Ezekiel and raises him to his feet. This Leader who is worthy of utmost respect pays respect to his subject. He uses his power to lift him up to a place where the conversation will now occur in mutual respect between two free parties.

I am not a fan of pomposity or attempts to impress. I grew up as a very shy child who tended to be repelled by those who put themselves in the limelight. While I am still very aware of my own areas of shyness, most people today do not immediately describe me as shy. When I was first asked to lead a group, I was a very reluctant leader. My own fears, self-image and rigid ideas about pride and humility got in the way. I remember the moment when, as the conductor of a choir and orchestra, I needed to step out into the spotlight, again and again, for curtain calls. Being the leader, in that context, meant that I needed to express my humility and gratitude, not my arrogance, by stepping out into the limelight. Some of my false ideas about shows of pomposity and pride were turned on their head. There are many times when a leader must accept the spotlight and the responsibilities that go with that, but it is the human craving for attention that is a snare. God as Leader has every right to be center stage and he shoulders the responsibilities that go with that. But his decisions about when to display his presence and power are not for reasons of showmanship.

God as Leader refuses to judge people by their families. A proverb is quoted, "The fathers eat sour grapes, and the children's teeth are set on edge." But this proverb is also repudiated (Ezek 18:2–3). This Leader is not partisan and will take time and care to get to know each individual and judge each one on their own merits, rather than the merits of their tribes. The emphasis on separation between Leader and people is extended to a careful separation between people, in order to prevent prejudice and unfairness. The people bring a false charge that God is unfair (Ezek 18:25). In fact, their blurring of boundaries has led to their acting unfairly. Each person must be respected for their own needs, rights and responsibilities. No citizen may transgress the boundary of another, in their person or in their possessions.

Leadership must be conducted above the level of emotional pressures in order to bring order out of chaos. An objective approach, implying careful measurement of rights and boundaries, brings clear thinking to people who are caught in the emotional chaos of grief.[1] There will be no room for blame-shifting, but everyone will be personally accountable.

Yet the relationship between this Leader and these people began with a covenant (Exod 24). It began with the free initiative of God the Leader and required the free participation of the people. Relationship is not the same as control, yet the people have unconsciously tried to control God and viewed him as less free, as less mobile and less able than he is. God's originally stated intention was that he would serve as their God (their Leader, not their follower) who would dwell among them and they would be his people (Exod 29:45–46). This intention is restated many times in Ezekiel. Leader and people will remain distinct, with separate identities and roles, yet will live, work, and relate together to build a healthy community.

There are times for a leader to step back. There can be an over-entanglement with some people, especially those who are emotionally very needy. That is certainly not to say that people with needs should be ignored or, worse, mistreated. But a leader has other considerations and needs too, and he or she cannot lead a whole group well if a few people have a controlling hold that drains their time and energy away from caring also for the needs of others. In fact, the emotionally needy are not led well if there are no boundaries on emotions.

I remember an emotionally needy woman called Peggy who was in a group where I was the leader. She consistently chose to come to my front door in precisely the time periods when I said I could not be available because I was teaching piano. It was not because she was unable to come in the periods when I would be available, nor was it because there was a genuine emergency. But it was because she wanted to test whether I would give my attention to her above anyone else. Eventually, after polite explanations of my unavailability at that time and requests to come at different times, I resorted to locking her out. Unfortunately, she spread slander that I was uncaring and refused to help in times of need. But when I saw her some years later, after being away, she thanked me for helping her to understand that genuine friendship requires respect for boundaries, respect for each other.

Unfortunately, some try to squash the leader's capacity to lead, through jealousy or envy. In Australia, we have a lot of sad experience of the "Tall Poppy Syndrome." The picture is of one poppy being taller than the rest, and the instinct is to cut it down so that no poppy sticks up higher than the

---

1. Rochester, "Grief in Exile and the City of God."

rest. Anyone who stands above the rest in talents, achievements, beauty, or money can be subject to some aggressive, even if often subtle, knocking down. We pride ourselves on being egalitarian, and that is, in many ways, beneficial for society. However, the flipside is that gifted people and leaders can be ruthlessly dragged through the metaphorical mud. Ezekiel's wisdom on keeping clarity in boundaries, and not being beholden to those who might drag good leaders down, is apt.

God the Leader encourages the people by giving Ezekiel visions for the future to pass on to the people. There is a vision of a final battle where God will win over all of his enemies (Ezek 38–39). Then there is a grand, yet intricately detailed vision of a new temple (Ezek 40–48). For a people in grief over the loss of the only temple they have known, this gives them hope. This vision has measurements of walls and sections, divisions of land, and tightened regulations for sacrifices. Everything is done in an orderly way, where there are clear separations between right and wrong, and even sacred and secular. For a people who have experienced chaos, this right ordering gives security and peace. And into the midst returns the glory of God the Leader himself (Ezek 43:1–7). The order is good, but life itself comes from the presence of God, back in the midst of his people. A mysterious river flows out from under the temple, giving fresh life to fish and watering trees that will produce fruit for food and leaves for healing (Ezek 47). Life will be good. God and people are back in right relationship.

QUESTIONS FOR REFLECTION OR DISCUSSION

1. How do you relate to the idea of the covenant relationship between God and his people, involving mutual knowing and mutual responsibilities?
2. Does your relationship with God feel more like that of Jeremiah, or that of Ezekiel? Or neither?
3. What are the relative advantages of direct and indirect communication styles?
4. How do the prophetic roles of vision, review, and correction fit into your concept of leadership?
5. Why might it be wise for a leader to avoid entanglement with emotionally needy people?
6. How do Jeremiah and Ezekiel help you to understand more about God as Leader?

PART 6

God the Hidden Leader

Chapter 21

Keeping Order

It is easy to focus on the expressions of God's leadership that are obvious, up front and dramatic. But leadership tasks must include such considerations as vision, planning, resources, balancing, team management, aesthetics, order, creativity, needs, impact, enemies, and more. These require thinking, observing and listening. These are all behind-the-scenes leadership functions. Even if the leader works with a team and delegates certain responsibilities to others, a lot happens behind the scenes as far as the rest of the people are concerned.

We have noticed hints of planning as God's Spirit hovered over the waters prior to the more spectacular decisive acts of Creation. As we look through the rest of the Old Testament and observe, with the ancients, the cycles of nature, we recognize that the Leader who set up the system must also oversee the functioning of the system. In the book of Esther, God's name is not mentioned, yet a careful reading of the narrative points to God's very active movements in key moments behind the scenes.

Any leader who is at the top of a vast empire is shrouded in a certain degree of mystery. God is no exception. However, in our media-dominated age, there is a drive to shatter that mystery, except in countries like Thailand, where any negative message about the king or members of the royal family is a serious offence with grave consequences. In some countries, private conversations and actions are secretly filmed and publicly exposed. The purpose is usually to embarrass leaders or shame them at their weakest points and then to relentlessly pull them down. While there is a legitimate need to name and penalize corrupt leaders, in accordance with the laws to which they are subject, there is no legitimate right to intrude into private space simply to feed the insatiable curiosity of the masses. If a leader has no space in which to do his or her behind-the-scenes work, the leader wastes times and energy on unnecessary distractions and the work suffers. God sets up and protects space, as is pictured in the tabernacle and then in the temple. He also sets up and protects time, as is celebrated in the weekly sabbath day of rest. His holiness is to be respected. He listens well but insists on his legitimate right as Leader to plan and work on his responses behind the scenes.

There are also times when God seems to be absent. Sometimes people, then and now, are perplexed, troubled, angry, even desperate to have God's presence. They can't work out any wrong that they have done and there seems to be no obvious explanation. Why doesn't he appear now, as he did in previous times? Their need is urgent. In the Psalms, specific answers on God's part are not usually given. Yet the ones praying are often moved to find rest and trust in God's goodness, and that, for them, seems to be enough. In the story of Job, the wait is long and grueling. The reasons are shrouded in mystery, yet God's intervention to change the situation and the relationships does become clear at the end.

There are other occasions when God's absence signifies a breach in the relationship. He is the one who is angry. Where people have already received instructions from God as the highest leader, they are expected to put them into practice. There are consequences built into God's system. If smaller signals are ignored, worse consequences may occur. God as Leader will give time and warnings for people to return to his good order, but if the bad behavior threatens the wellbeing of the group, he will need to act.

In this chapter we will explore God's hidden leadership in his maintenance of order in the world as it is presented in Psalms and Proverbs and then, from a quite different perspective, in Ecclesiastes.

THE CREATION ORDER IN PSALMS

Several psalms call us to wonder at the work of Creation achieved and maintained by God our Leader. Whether we look from a child's perspective at the moon changing its phases, or the stars twinkling at night, or whether we look from an astronomer's perspective, pondering with amazement the systems far beyond our everyday experience, we are called to say, "O Lord, our Lord, how majestic is your name in all the earth" (Ps 8:1, 9).

The Psalms assert that God not only formed the mountains and stilled the roaring of the seas, but that his work is ongoing. God's provision did not end at Creation. The psalmist writes, "You care for the land and water ... to provide the people with grain" (Ps 65:9). Through God's continuing provision of rain grain grows, flocks thrive and people are fed. Even clouds and winds are under his command; he cares for birds and donkeys, wild goats and wild lions. They all need food and he leads them to it. Even the sea creatures, from the minutest fish that swim at the surface, to the mysterious creatures in the depths, are all under his care. God's ongoing work is vibrant, as he delights in the exuberance of life (Ps 104).

When we become parents and marvel at each finger and toe of our newborn child, we know that we are but instruments of God's miraculous creation in our day. Even in the hidden place of a mother's womb God works, artistically and meticulously moving some threads together and gently separating other delicately held molecules to make a child, a child with a future in which God will still work. God's knowing of our thoughts, even before we speak, resonates with his deep, core knowing of us when we were being formed in the womb, and his knowing us right through into our futures, even if we try to run away. As Leader, God continues to show informed concern for each individual human being, in full knowledge of their unique idiosyncrasies (Ps 139).

THE CREATION ORDER IN PROVERBS

The book of Proverbs assumes that the created world contains order and declares that this order is brought about through God's wisdom. We are called to observe creation, particularly the ways of animals, to be amazed by them and even to learn from them. The ant illustrates diligence and good order to the lazy person (Prov 6:6-8). The ways of eagles and snakes elicit amazement (Prov 30:19). Ants, rock badgers, locusts, lizards, lions, roosters and billy goats all show qualities that humans can respect and also relate to (Prov 30:26-31).

There are instructions for herdsmen and farmers. It is important to observe carefully the condition of the flocks and the state of the grass in order to know the animals being cared for, and to know the plants that they need (Prov 27:23-27). It is also important to pay attention to the soil, to prepare the ground before sowing seed and to remove the weeds (Prov 24:27, 30-34). We are encouraged to care for the needs of the animals (Prov 12:10) in contrast to the cruel treatment shown by the wicked. Surely, God's invitation for us to pay sympathetic attention to his creatures reflects his ongoing interest, attention and care for both them and us.

God's wisdom in ordering creation is the same wisdom that calls us to live well. If we want to be wise, we need to search for God's order for living. This includes instruction, integrity and even common sense (Prov 9; 13:15). If we refuse to follow the path of wisdom, by acting foolishly, being lazy, or showing contempt for God's ways, our paths will lead to chaos.

God is at work behind the scenes to maintain and reinforce this order, whether it is for the cycles of nature, creatures of field or forest, or for the lives of people. Although the word "God" or "the Lord" does not appear as frequently in Proverbs as in some other books, there are about 100 proverbs which specifically mention God. In others there is are passive verbs which *imply* that the one doing the action is God. For example, Proverbs 16:5 says that the proud will not go unpunished. The idea of God winding up creation like a giant clock, and then leaving it unattended, does not fit the picture we find here. He remains attentive and engaged in hidden leadership work.

We find that the Lord takes pity on the poor (Prov 19:17) and provides for the righteous (Prov 10:3). He takes destructive action against the proud (Prov 15:25). These are all generalized statements that do not take exceptional circumstances into consideration, and do not give specific examples of how this might happen. They do, however, provide a general framework that points to God's often unlabeled actions to correct dysfunctions that interfere with good order.

Although humans make plans, they are subject to God the Leader's Yes and No (Prov 19:21). It is the Lord who smooths the paths of those who heed his words (Prov 3:5–10) and it is the Lord who gives blessing and curses (Prov 3:32–24). Human conduct is weighed by the Lord (sometimes made explicit, sometimes implied, e.g., Prov 5:21–23). God hates cheating in any form (e.g., Prov 11:1; 12:22), prejudice in legal cases (Prov 17:15) and acts of sacrifice without true respect for God (Prov 15:8).

While Proverbs does not use dramatic language about judgment, as the prophets often do, by careful observation of God's order and his ways, both through nature and through the instructive passages about living, we discover that God's words and warnings about consequences ring true. But, as we see in other biblical books, there are exceptions to these generalizations, and God himself can intervene to change expected outcomes.

God is engaged in renewal and maintenance. Good order is regarded as a thing to be desired, even something of beauty. Order provides a framework and a rhythm, to enable all of the elements of the system to flourish. God's ongoing leadership over his created order is exercised behind the scenes. We rely on the sun going down in the evening and coming up in the morning. There is a deep fundamental trustworthiness that all people recognize in the rhythms of nature, so that when a deviation from it occurs, we are shocked.

The system, however, is not mechanical and does contain within it a degree of elasticity, but even when patterns change there are also boundaries to those changes. A season of more extreme heat or more extreme cold does not last forever. Even in the midst of extremities, day and night, summer and winter keep on keeping on. We can so easily become angry with God about an earthquake or volcano or other natural catastrophe, that we forget to thank our Leader for the general patterns of reliability that we have enjoyed for most of our lives and can count on for the future. If we fail to recognize God's creation and leadership over these systems we miss the opportunity to communicate with him.

Australia is prone to droughts, floods, fires and cyclones. It felt like our recent severe bushfire season would never end. But it did, and earlier than expected, with drenching rain. I have seen several photos of homes and churches of praying people where the recent bushfires went right up to their fences but did not touch their properties. Many have publicly reported the inexplicable and dramatic wind from the sea that turned the life-threatening bushfire in the small town of Mallacoota back on itself, away from the community. What is also known is that the desperate situation led at least one man, trapped with others by the edge of the sea, to pray aloud. I cannot answer questions about why some people died and others were saved, some houses burnt to the ground and others escaped. They are questions for God the Leader. But we can and should observe what is observable: not only the climate patterns, but the patterns involving communications between humans and God. And we can be grateful for each rescue, each human act of sacrifice, courage and kindness, each divine intervention.

Today, a key word in leadership talk is "vision." It is exciting to participate in something new. It is definitely energizing to think that we can start something fresh, without the encumbrances of the past. New vision and creative energy are needed. However, there is another word that has become a bad word in leadership circles: "maintenance." This is usually understood as simply keeping things ticking over. However, maintenance needs to be respected, appreciated and revitalized with richer understanding and renewed vision.

A vision very quickly requires dogged maintenance for it to work. Otherwise, initial enthusiasm can quickly degenerate or be lost. Some leaders mistakenly think that leadership is all about being in the limelight. They are lazy when it comes to paying attention, in the quiet places, to the functioning of the whole system—to checking that even repetitive patterns are still imbued with refreshing life, that people's gifts are appropriately utilized, that feedback is used productively for corrections and modifications, that teams are well oiled and that God's Spirit has cleared channels in which to work productively.

We need leaders with the capacity and motivation, not only to be creative visionaries but to oversee, maintain and renew systems well. People who merely enthuse about new ideas, before their last great idea has had an opportunity to take root, can become wearing.

WHERE IS GOD IN ECCLESIASTES?

Some people think that Ecclesiastes is a depressing book because God's presence is not always evident. "Meaningless, meaningless, everything is meaningless" sighs the writer. The same things recur, over again, "under the sun." Nothing is really new, nothing really seems to be going anywhere. In fact, life seems like one giant treadmill.

The man at the center of the book is the teacher, a wise sage who sets up different scenes to enable his university-age students to see the consequences of different lifestyle choices. Does life lived in pursuit of wine, women and song ultimately satisfy? No. Does workaholism or intellectual attainment do it? No. Yet, working and enjoying daily food is a gift from God. With all the oppression, injustice and loneliness in the world, is there much point to life? Yet, there is a time for everything, and a place to be quiet—before God. In the end, the treadmill stops. In the end God will be the ultimate judge. In the end, it is wise to fear God.

We do need to see the consequences, the final results of our choices. Once we begin to fear God, we can then discover the hidden places in this book—and in this life—where God and his wisdom can be found. There are gems of hope packed tightly between boulders of hopelessness. There are threads of wisdom woven through the warp of foolishness. There are signs of life in the midst of the decay of death.

God the Leader speaks at the micro level as well as the macro level. He does not merely keep creation rolling on a treadmill but pays attention to the intricacies of a new shoot, to the fresh glory of a new sunrise. The fear of God is, indeed, the beginning of wisdom, and in that we discover, much more than we dared think possible, that life is the focus of God's concern and that he gives it meaning.

QUESTIONS FOR REFLECTION OR DISCUSSION

1. God the Leader's ways often seem mysterious. What do you feel about this?
2. How much of a leader's time is spent in activities behind the scenes?
3. How do you understand what Psalm 139 says about God's prenatal knowledge of his children?
4. How can we integrate our experience of natural disasters with God's care of his creation?
5. What value should leaders place on the tasks of "maintenance"?
6. To what extent can we expect God to be involved in the details of our lives?

Chapter 22

Behind the Scenes Leadership

There are some books where God is not named as a prime mover, and a couple where he is not mentioned at all. In the Book of Ruth, God is referred to several times in conversations, indicating that the main characters, Naomi, Ruth and Boaz, identify with Israelite beliefs. However, there is no clear description of God's actions in the story, in contrast to many other books of the Old Testament. In the books of Esther and Song of Songs God is not mentioned. However, the inclusion of these books in the canon of the Bible indicates that people long ago understood that God was involved, even if his work was not made obvious.

When we are children, our parents and other parent-like figures are close, visible and usually within calling distance. As we grow up, we are put into many situations where we are, for varying lengths of time, on our own. Initially, we may panic and be unsure of whether we can do what is asked of us, find where we should be going, speak to people we don't know, etc. Yet those who lead us know that these times are important and necessary for our own development. Our leaders might appear to be invisible, yet the tests we are put through are, unbeknown to us, carefully calculated and limited. These times of hidden leadership turn out to be of crucial importance.

I am grateful for the opportunity to have been in Girl Guides. Our Guide Captain was a woman of reliable justice. Her aim was to give us the skills to become independent in certain areas, and then to let us go out and put those skills to the test, without her presence. There were many times when we, a small group of girls between the ages of 11 and 15, got lost in the bush. It would have been unthinkable to cry. After all, we were equipped with compasses and a rough map, and we were taught how to use them. We could light a fire and cook our food. The older girls had to lead. We were greatly relieved when we came to a railway line and could follow it to a station to catch a train home. Our leader knew roughly where we were and trusted us. Our skills had been assessed, but now they needed to be tested in real life. There are times when good leaders intentionally step back. They trust us to put into practice what they have taught us. They do take a risk, but without taking risks they are not leading but controlling. We may catch glimpses of them occasionally, when they affirm or rebuke, but they may not be as far away as we imagine. Often, they are quietly smiling with pride, knowing that we are now free to do more than we could do before. And we gain a sense of achievement in passing that test.

RUTH

The Book of Ruth is a delightful story of God at work, behind the scenes, in the lives of very ordinary people. No one in this story expects to be in the limelight, yet we learn at the very end that these seemingly unimportant people become close ancestors of David, the most important King of Israel. Later, in New Testament times, Jesus would come from this same family line. This lineage suggests that God is intensely interested in ordinary, unassuming people who take steps to try to live uprightly before God and in their relationships with other ordinary people in their own society.

The book opens by setting the scene: "In the days when the judges ruled. . ." We know more about this period from the Book of Judges. The times were marked by more disorder than order. The end of the Book of Judges sums up the era by saying, "In those days Israel had no king; everyone did as he saw fit." Yet in the midst of this human disorder some order is created through a few ordinary people, like Naomi, Ruth and Boaz, who acknowledge God's behind-the-scenes work through their everyday conversations.

The first scene depicts family chaos: a famine in Bethlehem (the name ironically means the "house of bread") drives one man to take his wife and two sons to live in the neighboring but foreign land of Moab, where people worship different gods. The man dies. Then the two sons marry Moabite women, but both of these sons die without children. In her grief, the widow, Naomi, hears that God is now providing food once again in Bethlehem, and makes the momentous decision to go back alone. Perhaps the story hints, without explicitly saying, that Naomi's decision is not just to return to her own people, but also to return to her own God.

It is a risky journey for a woman in her situation. What about safety along the way? How will her relatives in Bethlehem receive her, after she appeared to desert her own people? She will take the risk. She gives words of blessing in the name of her God to her daughters-in-law and bids them farewell. But one of the girls, Ruth, pleads to go with her. She says her famous words of commitment: "Wherever you go I will go, and where you stay I will stay. Your people will be my people and your God my God. Where you die I will die, and there I will be buried" (Ruth 1:16, 17). Although Naomi was expecting to go alone, she now has her foreign daughter-in-law as her companion. And Ruth's declaration of allegiance to Naomi's God places her under the protection and guidance of that God.

We are introduced to a farmer, Boaz, a relative of Naomi's late husband. He is an upright man who exercises a gracious authority over his workers. He hears of Ruth's kindness to her mother-in-law and quietly provides for her a protected place to glean the grain for herself and Naomi, just as the law instructs landowners to do for the poor. He goes further, by instructing his men not to harass or embarrass her, but rather to help her. In this, he keeps the law of helping foreigners and widows, because of their vulnerable positions. His speech makes ready reference to God as he converses with Ruth, who fully expects to be treated as a second-class citizen. He says, "May the Lord repay you for what you have done. May you be richly rewarded by the Lord, the God of Israel, under whose wings you have come to take refuge."

Where is God in this part of the story? We see that Naomi was prepared to take the journey back to Bethlehem alone and is unexpectedly given a committed companion. Ruth was expecting to be treated as an outsider and to live the rest of her life without certain social privileges, and now unexpectedly finds herself working in a field belonging to a man who honors, protects and accepts her. Since both Naomi and Ruth are taking steps towards God, the narrative is leading us to discern the movements that God the Leader is making, behind the scenes, to meet their needs.

The next issue to exercise Naomi and Ruth concerns the possibility of Ruth marrying again. In a society where parents and male relatives play an important part in seeking to arrange a suitable marriage, Ruth's situation is difficult. Naomi is her only functioning parent and there is no male relative. In addition, Ruth is a foreigner. Even though she has put her trust in Israel's God, many may still be suspicious of her.

I have spoken to many people of marriageable age, both men and women, in India where marriages are still arranged. I have heard the deep concerns of those without male relatives to arrange their marriages, and I have prayed with them. Some were orphaned in childhood, others have only a mother and no father, uncle or brother. If there is any hope of bringing a proposal to another family, it cannot be done in a conventional manner. I have also seen many surprising answers, where usual obstacles were circumvented.

Naomi and Ruth, two widows, have no one to help them. They cannot engage in the normal negotiations for marriage. Naomi considers Boaz; he is a good man and has shown consistent kindness to Ruth. In addition, he may be in the correct family relationship to marry her as a kinsman-redeemer. But how can she ask him? There is no normal social setting in which Naomi or Ruth could approach a man to have that kind of discussion. Because Naomi gives evidence of being a sincere follower of God, it is likely that she prays.[1] Naomi then devises a test which must be performed secretly. It requires Ruth's absolute obedience, in a way that could put her reputation at risk.

In obedience to her mother-in-law's plan, Ruth visits Boaz in the threshing floor at night. A woman among men in such a place after dark and after eating and drinking would normally raise questions about her morality. Then Ruth says, "Spread the corner of your garment over me, since you are a kinsman-redeemer" (Ruth 3:9). The first part could be interpreted as seduction in another context. However, there are several indicators within this part of the story that Ruth is not acting like a prostitute, and that they do not engage in the sexual act. First, Boaz acknowledges that everyone knows her to be a woman of noble character (v.12). Since he has shown himself to be of honorable character, we are dealing with two people who are not likely to take advantage of the situation. Second, Boaz understands the role of the kinsman-redeemer to mean marriage, and he says he will wait to see if another relative, who could have a closer claim, would want to marry Ruth. He will protect her during the night hours and give her food to take back to Naomi in the morning. This gift for Naomi supports his understanding that Ruth is bringing a marriage proposal from Naomi.

Those from traditional Western cultures may be perturbed by a marriage proposal arising from the woman's family and assume that this was wrong in patriarchal Israel. Yet, in current arranged marriages in India a proposal can come from either family. In fact, Boaz supports this when he says to Ruth, "You have not run after the younger men, whether rich or poor" (Ruth 3:10). We see no hint in this story that Boaz considers the proposal wrong. He understands the difficulties for this family of two widows and realizes that an unusual approach is necessary.

---

1. In Genesis 24:13-14 we read that Abraham's servant prays in order to find a suitable wife for Isaac and we see there a different satisfying outcome.

So Boaz, Naomi and Ruth wait for the kinsman-redeemer situation to be clarified at the town gate, the place functioning as the public law court, and for things to be done properly. The other relative declines, Boaz declares his intentions publicly, and Ruth becomes his wife. The marriage is publicly blessed, God is invoked, and the son that is born is a blessing to Naomi, as well as to the parents, and, in time, to all Israel.

These honorable but ordinary people are supported by God behind the scenes. As they honor God in ways that deal with the basics of life—food, travel, companionship, marriage, giving birth—God honors them. Do they need God to be more obvious? Do they need him to shout out loud and give them instructions? No, for Naomi and Boaz have clearly been taught many important principles from God's instructions, and they seek to follow them. Ruth is learning fast through what Naomi has taught her. Is God still actually leading in this situation? Yes, because at each point of risk for any of the characters in the story, something happens to help them—to meet their needs, to give them guidance, to resolve the tension. God is the behind-the-scenes leader who is quietly at work.

Can we as leaders bear to put other people center stage instead of ourselves? God can. Do we need to be applauded for every piece of help, organization, or provision in which we have led? God doesn't. Are we motivated to see others finally able to thrive more than we are motivated to gain glory for ourselves? God is.

ESTHER

The setting for this story is much later than the Book of Ruth, in the days when the Israelites, who are by now referred to as Jews, are in exile in Babylon, by now under the Persian king Xerxes (also known as Ahasuerus). This is before Ezra and Nehemiah have returned to Jerusalem. The location is in the important capital city of Susa, where the Persian king has his palace. God is not mentioned by name in this book at all. Yet there are some striking ironic reversals in the narrative that are highly suggestive of God being at work.

In the opening scene the powerful Xerxes, the ruler of territories from India to Cush, puts on a lavish display of his opulence for six months. Then, to conclude the celebrations, he invites all and sundry to a week-long sumptuous banquet. At the finale, when he is inebriated, he makes a foolish command for Queen Vashti to appear and display her beauty. The implication is that she should appear disrobed. She refuses to come. The king agrees to ban her from ever entering his presence again, and to appoint a replacement queen who is better than her.

Some time later, Esther, a Jewish orphan girl raised by her male cousin Mordecai, is taken into the king's harem, and is eventually chosen by the king as the replacement queen. However, she, like Vashti, is a woman of principles, and instead of becoming a model of unthinking subordination to a foolish but wealthy king, she becomes a powerful and successful advisor to the king, for the salvation of her people.

Just as we see a comparison between these two queens, we also discover a comparison between two key men in the narrative. The first man, Haman, is from an Agagite family, suggested by several Jewish commentators to be the Amalekites, historic enemies of the Israelite people. Their most notorious crime was to attack the weak, the elderly, the children, and the disabled. The king decides to honor Haman above all the other nobles. Haman's position and future could not be better. However, he is irritated with the Jew Mordecai, the second key man in this story, who sits at the king's gate. It is because Mordecai refuses to kneel down before him; he won't worship a mere man, especially one as untrustworthy as Haman. Haman devises a plot to kill not only Mordecai but all Jewish people and is successful in persuading the king to set the thirteenth day of the month of Adar as the date for this destruction of Jews throughout the king's jurisdiction. In addition, he accepts his wife's advice to build gallows 75 feet (23 meters) high on which to hang Mordecai.

However, just before Haman's evil plan to murder Mordecai can be enacted, the king cannot sleep. He asks for the historical records to be read to him, and he is reminded that Mordecai is the man who saved his life by reporting a planned assassination. In the morning, as Haman rushes in to persuade the king to have Mordecai put to death, the king is ready to ask Haman what could be done to give a man the highest honor in the kingdom. Instead of being executed, Mordecai is the one honored, not Haman. Instead of Mordecai being put to death on the gallows, Haman is put to death on the very gallows he built for Mordecai. And the decree to bring widespread destruction of the Jews is countered by a new decree, under Mordecai's instructions, to allow Jews to protect themselves and to kill any armies that come against them on the thirteenth of Adar.

What causes these reversals? How is it that injustice is overcome by justice, right in the nick of time? The king, although powerful, is not a leader who can be counted on for his wisdom or for any actions against injustice. He is too preoccupied with his own image, his own wealth, his own power. Throughout the whole story he does not initiate any decisions, but is easily influenced by others around him, whether for good or ill. Although he expects people to obey his every command, even if foolish, he is portrayed as spineless. He is not a likely candidate for anyone to rely on to rescue a minority who are threatened with undeserved mass extinction.

In the center of the story, Mordecai sends an urgent message to Esther, telling her of the king's decree, under Haman's hand, to commit mass murder of her people. She just could be in a crucial position to help, and Mordecai urges her to do whatever she can. But Mordecai's message implies that his faith is not based on Esther or King Xerxes. He writes, "For if you remain silent at this time, relief and deliverance for the Jews will arise from another place" (Esth 4:14). God is the implied focus of his faith. Esther, in turn, requests that Mordecai gather all the Jews in Susa and ask them to fast for three days. She declares that she and her maids will also fast. While living as exiles under foreign, pagan rule, Mordecai and Esther need to be discreet regarding references to their God in messages passing through other hands. Neither of them uses the word "pray" but it is implied that they do both pray and consider fasting prayer as important. It is only after the three days of fasting that Esther is ready to risk her life to speak to the king. This has made a very significant difference.

In contrast to the two banquets hosted by the king as luxurious celebrations in the early part of the book, Esther approaches the king to ask if he and Haman will attend first one banquet, and then a second, before she will place her petition before the king. Esther uses great wisdom in hosting her banquets. She carefully works with royal culture to create a conducive environment. Her success is a triumph of wisdom over foolishness.

Where does Esther's wisdom come from? It flows out of the three-day fast. And it is a product of the sound Jewish teaching passed on from Mordecai. It is again implied that God is working behind the scenes, to guide her in wisdom to apply, in this specific dangerous situation, the biblical principles that she has absorbed.

God is still the active Leader of his people, even under a foreign government, even where communications are likely to be watched, even when lives are at risk. He is at work in the reversals of fortunes. He is at work through prayer. He is at work in guiding Esther in wisdom. He is at work in her compassion for her people, just as he himself has compassion for his people. His leadership may be behind the scenes but the outcome is every bit as dramatic as the rescue from the Egyptians at the Red Sea.

THE SONG OF SONGS

We should not attempt to read this artistically arranged collection of love poems in the same way as we approach a story, with its beginning, middle and end. We need to read it slowly, putting ourselves into Middle Eastern rural society, enjoying the artistic beauty, savoring the sensual but never pornographic poetic imagery, delighting in this picture of a fully committed, mutually loving, unique marriage relationship.

God is not mentioned in this book either. But as the Creator who is vitally interested in bringing forth life, whether it is at the beginning of creation or whether it is in the ongoing creation of each new person, God the Leader's original role in bringing a man and a woman together in marriage to reproduce cannot be forgotten (Gen 2:21–23). God designed the attraction between the sexes. Could God also have an ongoing leadership role behind the scenes in fostering other similar man-woman relationships?

The relationship depicted here stands in dramatic contrast to polygamous affairs (SS 6:8, 9) and is congruent with the original picture of one man and one woman becoming one flesh in a relationship of complete openness (Gen 2:24, 25). Perhaps King Solomon wrote this text in his early days of wise innocence, about an ideal marriage, before he gave up on the ideal in his own marriages. Or perhaps someone else wrote it, picturing the bridegroom as King Solomon and the bride as Queen Shulamite (the female version of the name Solomon). When we lived in Ethiopia we discovered that it is common practice for couples to emerge from the marriage ceremony, each wearing a crown. Just for the day of their wedding, they are King Solomon and Queen Shulamite.

A wedding procession is suggested in 3:6–11, in a scene that again brings back memories of Ethiopia. We know, from the rest of the Old Testament, that sex outside marriage is always condemned, so the fact that the wedding is pictured in the middle of the book does not mean that the couple were not yet married in the first part of the book. These poems are about love in marriage and are not in a fixed chronological sequence.

What we see in this book is initiative taken by both the man and the woman. Unusually, more space is given to the woman's words. We see voluntary, exclusive commitment by the man to the woman and the woman to the man. Both delight in each other's physical features, but the emotional content in the two mini-narrative scenes of searching, longing, missing and eventually finding (Chapters 2 and 5) demonstrate that the bond is deeper than physical attraction. Although a recurring refrain warns against stirring up love prematurely (e.g., 2:7b), the time is right for this couple. The man invites the woman to "come away" (2:13b) and in the middle and at the end of the book, the woman invites the man to "come away" (7:11; 8:14). The relationship is fully reciprocal. We see no signs of repression or force or politics or fear. This is Israel's ideal, as God the Leader designed it to be.

God's ideals in marriage, as well as in his own relationship with his people, are not dictatorial but reciprocal. This book suggests that God as leader is active behind the scenes, inviting and fostering relationships that are intimate, tender, reciprocal, loving and mutually satisfying.

QUESTIONS FOR REFLECTION OR DISCUSSION

1. How do these stories relate to your experience of God the Leader?
2. Do you recognize and acknowledge God's quiet work behind the scenes in your life?
3. In what circumstances might it be appropriate to imitate God's hiddenness as a leader?
4. How strong is your need for others' approval of what you do?
5. Do you ever ask for others to pray for you or your community in a time of need?
6. Might God play a part in arranging marriages and other important relationships?

Chapter 23

When God Hides His Face

In some of the poetic descriptions of God in the Psalms we find that he is pictured as being somewhat inaccessible. For example, he makes darkness his covering (Ps 18:11), or he wraps himself in light (Ps 104:1). These images convey the fact that God and his leadership can never be fully seen or fully understood by humans.

Moses desires an encounter with God, but God declares that he will allow Moses to see only his back, not his face (Exod 33:20). However, despite this partial hiddenness, God is said to speak with Moses "face to face" (Exod 33:11). God the Leader is not like a sideshow artist who might be expected to put on a spectacle for a price or to satisfy someone's whim. He will not flaunt everything that he has. But he will interact very personally with those who engage in a reciprocal relationship with him.

However, there are other times when God's hiding of his face has particular significance. There are two very different and important kinds of writing where this is said to occur. The first is in the so-called Lament Psalms and in some similar prayers in other books, and the second is in the Prophets.[1] The reasons for God's real or apparent hiding of his face can be quite different.

---

1. Balentine's study, *The Hidden God*, has contributed to my thinking in this section.

LAMENT PSALMS

The Lament Psalms are the psalms in which people, as individuals or as a community, urgently cry out to God in some kind of suffering or difficulty, when the situation they are in doesn't make sense, when God seems to be absent, or when no solution is in sight. These psalms demonstrate valid emotional outbursts which God invites, hears and often acts upon, but they do not make theological pronouncements about who or what is the real cause of their problems.

In fact, some form of lament is expressed in most of the psalms. In some of these God is accused of hiding his face, or of hiding himself (e.g., Psalms 10:1; 13:1; 89:46). The questions "Why?" and "How long?" are put to God, not to begin an intellectual discussion, but to express frustration and anger to God as the highest power, and even against God who seems to somehow be the ultimate cause of their predicament or the One who fails to intervene.

Most often, the problem is about bad things happening to good people. Their sense of justice is outraged. Sometimes their suffering is precisely *because* they serve God faithfully (e.g., in Psalms 44 and 69). There is no suggestion in these psalms that the person praying has sinned. If they had sinned, then the consequences might be understandable. It is only extremely rarely in the Psalms that the person's own sin seems to have played a part. In Psalm 51:11 God is implored to hide his face from the person's sin, but not from the person who is turning to him in sincere repentance. When people don't feel his presence, their sense of abandonment by God can lead to despair. "My God, my God, why have you forsaken me? Why are you so far from saving me, so far from the words of my groaning?" (Ps 22:1). The need is overwhelming and immediate. The emotions are desperate, raw and confused.

Where is God, the great and powerful Leader whose famous works of old stand in stark contrast to my present experience where I can't see him doing anything? Why did God show his presence and help to others and now, when I need him, he has disappeared? How long will I have to wait for an end to this terrible suffering?

Some of these questions may seem shocking to our ears because of their impoliteness, their direct accusations of God, their demands. Yet, they they are expressions of people seeking to face God, to find God, to present their great need in the face of injustice, whether the suffering is caused by human enemies (most often), or sickness, or even perhaps, for some mysterious other reason, by God himself (Ps 27:8–9). But those of us who have spoken this candidly to God have often found that the most obvious answers come after this kind of prayer.

Samuel Balentine writes perceptively, "Because it is directed toward God, the lament provides a means of coping with the problem of God's hiddenness which acts as a buffer against total skepticism."[2] The exhortation to "seek God" or to "seek God's face" (e.g., 2 Chr 7:14; Jer 29:13; Ps 27:8) is, in fact, precisely what these people are doing as they pray. While their language might be strong, they speak directly to God, in raw honesty, not as a complaint about God to a third party. In fact, they are seeking not only a solution to their problems, but a response from God, acknowledging his presence and ongoing relationship.

In some Lament Psalms an answer to the cry of lament is recorded (e.g., Ps 18:6, 16–19; Ps 30). This is particularly frequent in psalms that are dominated by thanks and praise, where the actual lament prayer is not recorded or only briefly alluded to, but thanksgiving is the dominant expression after the answer has come. However, in many Lament Psalms no answer and no change is recorded, but that does not mean that the psalmist did not, historically, receive an answer.

In some Lament Psalms a surge of boldness suddenly changes the prayer from a focus on questions and problems to a direct charge to God to act (e.g., Ps 10, with a change at v.10 followed by a statement of confidence in God's kingship at v.16). In many other Lament Psalms there is simply a mysterious shift in mood, or a sudden change to a place of calm trust (e.g., Ps 13, in which the change comes at v.13) without any reason being given for it, even though it seems that their prayer has not yet been answered. Scholars have made numerous suggestions regarding these changes, usually involving hypothetical liturgical words of comfort spoken during worship, but none of these can be proven, given that there is a lot of historical distance and no records to substantiate their theories.

Considering that these prayers find continuing resonance today, might we not also consider the experience of more modern people who pray of this kind of prayer? Many have found that by crying out in similar raw honesty they find themselves moving or, as many would say, being moved, to a place of greater faith. The change is not one that they can simply bring about themselves. We cannot simply change our own mood, especially so extremely and so dramatically, without a word, an act of encouragement, or some other help from outside. The change might be expressed in a prayer of specific boldness, like that in Psalm 10, or it may come to rest in a calm, confident prayer of trust, like that in Psalm 13. The answer that they have been looking for has not yet appeared, but a reassurance of God's presence

---

2. Balentine, *The Hidden God*, 167.

and power to respond and act in this situation of need has occurred. And that is enough to hold them.

Where is God the Leader in these difficult human experiences? We are not given explicit answers. Nor are we given answers as to why many good people, who conscientiously remain faithful to God, are in such terrible situations. The inclusion of so many Lament Prayers serves to encourage us that God is not a leader who requires polite, superficial speech, but one who encourages absolute honesty, even if it is aggressive. He may not, in fact, be the cause of the problem, but he is willing to take the brunt of our anger when the true perpetrators are not.

We must not forget that some psalms declare that God has heard and answered prayers, and these suggest that the lament is not the end of the crisis; in fact, it is likely to be met with some kind of saving response from God. The laments demonstrate the emotions of the person in the middle of the crisis from the human side, but their role is not to present the situation from God's side. God may feel very distant, or totally absent, from the person praying, but he may be nearer than they think. In fact, God the Leader may be actively at work planning a solution. But his preference is to do things in relationship, so he may also be waiting—waiting for an open and honest engagement that indicates readiness for collaboration in the solution.

What brought about the transitions to boldness or to confident, quiet trust? Again, there is no explicit evidence given. From my personal experience of similar transitions, and from hearing the stories of many others who pray, there is widespread testimony that God is the one who has moved in the person's heart to affirm his presence, in a quiet but powerful way that may be difficult to describe. This subtle perception of his presence gives an assurance that has power to quieten the heart—a confidence that God will, in fact, lead.

Perhaps the closest analogy is of a child crying because he or she has just been hurt by someone else. Then the mother or someone who is trusted and loved comes and holds the child. The hurt has not yet gone, but the presence and comforting arms of the mother figure enable the child to stop crying. If there is need of further action it is taken, and the hurt is on the road to healing. Or the child whose problem was fear is emboldened to go out again, to ignore the intimidation, and to speak or act. In the Psalms, the boldness often issues in direct or implied commands to God (e.g., Ps 3:7; 68:1). If God is indeed the one who has moved the petitioner and given assurance, this internal change may be evidence of his collaborative work. If God receives a command that is exactly in line with his thinking, his plans, his purposes, his justice, his truth and his compassion, he will move. God and human agree. A change is about to be brought.

LAMENT-TYPE PRAYERS AND OTHER EXPERIENCES OF GOD'S ABSENCE IN THE NARRATIVES

Samuel Balentine has observed that these prayers are frequently followed by a divine response of some kind.[3] Outside of the Psalms, these prayers are mostly shorter, and are not necessarily in a poetic or even complete form. But the advantage of looking at them is that we can see how each prayer relates to its context and whether there is evidence of God responding to their prayers.

I once did a study of the lament-type prayers throughout the rest of the Old Testament, outside the Psalms, and found that in many cases the person who had prayed in this way found greater discernment of some revelation of God, often in addition to a more tangible answer to the prayer.[4] This was particularly marked in crises where one person brought his or her lament prayer directly to God, in contrast to others in the same crisis who did not. The latter group did not gain any new insight or expand their understanding of God's character or of the path to take. Such comparisons can be seen below in the situations of Moses, Jeremiah and Job.

Moses

Moses' lament prayers on the wilderness journey led to many candid and emotional conversations with God. In these cases God responded, sometimes changing an action he had said he would take, and Moses gained insight. They are well worth reading (e.g., Exod 32:9-14; Ex 33:12-23; Num 14:1-20). On the other hand, there is no evidence that the people who grumbled to each other, without facing God, were able to gain anything from their crises, apart from enjoying the provisions that were supplied by God in answer to Moses' prayers.

Had God the Leader actually abandoned his people on this journey? The evidence of continuing leadership and provision of safety, food, water, and clothing that did not wear out demonstrates that he had not left them. But the people who merely turned to each other in grumbling, instead of facing God directly with their prayers, missed out on the richness of mutual communication with God that Moses enjoyed.

---

3. Balentine, *The Hidden God*, 124.
4. Rochester, *Israel's Lament and the Discernment of Divine Revelation*.

Jeremiah

In the face of harsh, unjust criticism, God's prophet Jeremiah utters many pained prayers of complaint to God (e.g., Jer 11:18—12:6; 15:10-21; 17:14-18; 18:18-23). His acute suffering has come because people don't like the messages God has given him to speak (see his call in Jer 1). These brutally honest two-way interactions with God are not just gap-fillers in the story, but the places where the movement in the story is rooted. Most of these passages contain God's revelatory responses to Jeremiah's complaints. Moreover, we see evidence of God continuing to speak to and through Jeremiah elsewhere in the book. Jeremiah discovers, again and again, God's presence and insight, even during times of catastrophe.

In contrast, many of the other so-called prophets, who prove to be false prophets, fail to recognize the seriousness of the evil that has penetrated their society. Perhaps they don't want to recognize it because they are part of it. They fail to understand Jeremiah's concerns, and so fail to question or address God about the times. They fail to learn, fail to see what they need to see, and succumb to the disaster that they could have averted. They call themselves prophets but only hear from their own imaginations and receive no insight from God (Jer 23:9-32).

Job

The story of Job (see Job 1:1—2:10) is tragic from the human perspective and, for Job, very perplexing. Yet his friends view the situation simplistically, as if the cause must be Job's sin and the tragedies must be judgment on him. Job responds to his friends' cruel and repeated false accusations in many rounds of long and difficult argument (Job 3-37). In the process, he also faces God in some lament prayers. One of his complaints to God is that he is hiding his face from Job (Job 13:24; 34:29). There is, however, no mention that these friends, who pride themselves on their knowledge of theology, ever pray. Not for Job, not with questions about such a tragedy happening to such a good man, not even for wisdom in what to say to Job. They assume they are right and continue to berate Job, learning nothing.

Then, after seemingly endless rounds of debate, God comes to speak to Job (Job 38-41), not to the friends whom God says have spoken falsely. That, in itself, makes clear who God recognizes as being in a continuing relationship with him. God's questioning of Job, whether he was there at creation, reaffirms God's authority and mystery, an authority that is above that of the friends and above Job's limited knowledge.

God never explains his reasons for allowing the tragedies, but he does give some directions: for the friends to bring sacrifice, and for Job to intercede for these friends (Job 42). God acts to create reconciliation. Then gives many gifts to Job, in fact double what he had at the beginning, as some kind of compensation for what was lost.

Yet we are still left perplexed about the mysterious opening scene, the scene which is kept hidden from Job, the scene between God and Satan. Perhaps it is given much less for clarification than as an indication that God the Leader is at work behind the scenes in mysterious conversations and directions with beings that are other-worldly. Are we really meant to understand it, or to create a theology from it? I suspect that we are rather meant to see how easy it is for us to become ignorantly judgmental like the so-called friends, precisely because we don't understand all of God's hidden and other-worldly doings. As Job is instructed, maybe we too should trust the one who brought forth creation in mystery. He always was and always will be the Leader who acts behind the scenes in ways that are beyond our understanding, even if he seems to be hiding his face for a time.

GOD'S HIDDEN FACE IN THE PROPHETS

An experience of God's absence may also indicate God's response to human sin, according to the prophets. We have seen that this is not always the case. Sometimes a person may feel abandoned by God when they are sinned against (as Joseph may have felt) rather than because of their own sin. At other times God's presence may simply not be obvious; it may seem hidden, but God is not actively hiding himself. However, there *are* times, especially in the life of the nation Israel, when the prophets say that God turns his face away from his people on account of their repeated and intractable sin.

This idea stands in contrast to the picture, given in Aaron's prayer, of God's face shining upon someone for blessing (Num 6:24–26). In the context of human rebellion, it indicates that God is withholding his presence, his favor, and his protection because of the sin that stands between the people and God (Isa 59:2). When God actively hides his face in this kind of context, it is a sign that he is angry (e.g., Isa 54:8). The hiding of God's face because of sin can result in the people being handed over to their enemies (Ezek 39:23), or God not hearing their prayers (Mic 3:4).

No doubt all of us can remember times when a parent or teacher or boss or other significant leader has shown their disapproval or anger by going quiet, or by a particular look which indicated that they would not engage in any further discussion on a certain matter. God the Leader says No to stupid ideas, to rebellion against what is wise and right, and to hot-headed arrogant schemes. There comes a time when he withdraws his protection so that people can experience the consequences of their own insistence. The exile is an example of that. Yet, we have seen from the prophets that God's hiddenness is not the last word. After appropriate discipline, the possibility of seeing his face and his favor again always exists.

QUESTIONS FOR REFLECTION OR DISCUSSION

1. In your experience, when has God seemed to be absent?
2. Have you ever spoken to God as candidly as these people in the Old Testament spoke?
3. Do you have any experience of God answering your most shocking prayers?
4. Have you ever experienced God's silence when you were in the wrong?
5. As a leader, have you lamented to God?
6. Are there times when a leader should keep temporary silence?

PART 7

New Hope

Chapter 24

Rebuilding

The people's experience of exile in Babylon demonstrated that God's prophets had been speaking truth from God the Leader when they gave those shocking warnings of exile. Instead of ridiculing these warnings, the people could have taken them seriously and acted on them. The exile could have been averted. But many of these same prophets also spoke surprising messages of hope, of a future that would not end with the exile, and of God who would once again be recognized as the Leader caring for his people and living in their midst.

After the exiles have been separated from their land for roughly seventy years, the period under Babylonian rule predicted by Jeremiah (Jer 25:11), a new Persian ruler Cyrus takes a radically different approach from his Babylonian predecessors. He not only gives permission for exiles to return to Israel but also promotes and provides for the rebuilding of the Jerusalem temple (Ezra 1). Those who wish to return to Jerusalem and help with the process of rebuilding are invited to do so. However, we are told that this change is actually orchestrated by God, the Leader over them all, who anoints Cyrus and takes hold of him for the purpose of enabling God's people to go back to their own land (Isa 44:28; 45:1–13). We know very little about Cyrus's understanding of Israel's God, and how that might have related to his knowledge of his Persian deities. We only have his general acknowledgement that his rulership is given to him by the Lord, the God of heaven, together with the commission to build a temple for him in Jerusalem (Ezra 1:2). We also know that he followed similar policies with other people groups. Irrespective of his personal limits of understanding and awareness, the narrative presents God as the ultimate Leader in the return of his people to the land of Israel.

God's leadership in this phase can be followed through four books: Ezra, Haggai, Zechariah and Nehemiah. Ezra and Nehemiah chronicle the story as a narrative, while Haggai and Zechariah continue the prophetic line. However, it is easiest to follow the story if we move between these four books in roughly chronological order.

EZRA 1-6

In response to Cyrus's decree, heads of families lead the movement towards Israel, armed with gifts from neighbors of items made of silver and gold, and they resettle in various towns in their old land. In Jerusalem Zerubbabel the governor and Joshua the high priest call for the people to build an altar, to celebrate the Feast of Tabernacles, and subsequently to lay the foundation of the new temple. In their celebration of this new step of hope, they jubilantly give thanks to God (Ezra 3). However, their rejoicing is short-lived. There is serious opposition from non-Jews who are now living in the land. The story, as it is continued here and in Nehemiah, includes repeated tensions with these neighbors who claim to want to help, but the returning exiles refuse their help. We are puzzled. These neighbors initially claim to have the same goals, to seek the same God, and to honor the same King Cyrus. However, after their help is refused, they engage in serious, active sabotage against the Jews, including sending slanderous letters to the authorities. They are believed, so they succeed in stopping the building of the temple for around fifteen years. It now seems that these people had a hidden agenda whose oppositional intent was discerned by the returnees but was not obvious to the reader.

The hope of rebuilding the temple and re-establishing their public relationship with God is dashed. An invisible net of despondency grasps the new settlers. They reduce their focus to their own family property: their houses and fields, and hope that they can find some success in more limited, domestic endeavors. God sees the discouragement and at an opportune moment intervenes. By now Darius is on the throne and, because of his support for the original decree made by Cyrus, opposition is quenched. However, after such a long period of obstruction, the people now need help before they will engage in rebuilding. God the Leader engages the prophets Haggai and Zechariah to direct the governor Zerubbabel and the high priest Joshua to return to the task of building the temple.

We see today that leadership is much easier when the people are enthusiastic and successful. Not many put their hands up to lead a group whose enthusiasm has been repeatedly ridiculed, sneakily slandered and forcibly obstructed. Those who do volunteer might be under a delusion that their winning smile or attractive personality will turn the group around. Or that their academic studies of another parallel social group will give them the analysis and strategies they need. Or that a formula learnt at a leadership conference will provide the winning key. I have seen many of these would-be "saviors" fail. Cemented discouragement requires in-depth and often sacrificial leadership that is prepared to take a multi-pronged approach.

HAGGAI

Haggai is a practical man of few words who comes straight to the point. Their procrastination in building the temple is not just because of their opponents. They have become distracted by the lure of materialism. They are totally absorbed in making their homes fancy and their fields more lucrative—while God has been quietly relegated to the "too hard" basket.

I wonder whether this familiar human process might be related to the problem that Jeremiah had tried to address: trust in the material temple while quietly sliding away from the God whom the temple represented. It's easier to focus on an object that can be seen, and easier to put effort into a project that promises financial gain or the admiration of influential people.

There are signs that something is wrong. Haggai is called to draw people's attention to those signs, and he doesn't mince words. Plenty of crop seeds have been planted, but harvests have clearly not lived up to expectations. Food never seems to be filling. Clothes never seem to be warm enough. Money seems to disappear without having bought much of value. Life is continually frustrating—these people are always longing for more, and never understanding why nothing is really satisfying, why nothing works as it should, why the formulas of life seem to be failing (Hag 1:5–6).

A repeated cycle of disappointed expectations should lead people to ask questions and seek wisdom from beyond and above those cycles—questions that need to be referred to the one who set up the systems of nature and life. In fact, God has been managing the systems in the hope of catching people's attention so that they will discover that there is something more to life. They have lost their vision and their purpose, and they are sinking in the daily grind.

Haggai knows that people are interested in knowing what benefit there will be in prioritizing the building of the temple over their other concerns.

In practical terms, the implied benefit will be that systems will work properly and frustrations will decrease (Hag 1:7). Order is important for smooth functioning, and the right priority helps to set up good order. The relationship between Leader and people must be reset. And the Leader's vision has the capacity to reinvigorate them. Haggai speaks, the people restate their allegiance, and God declares, "I am with you." The result is a widespread divine stirring of the people to work together on building the temple (Hag 1:14).

Haggai is charged with speaking two more significant messages from the Leader God. The first (Hag 2:1–9) is about comparison. There are some who inevitably compare the new project with the glory of the past and find the new project wanting. A few can remember the old days, when they, as children, were impressed by the gleam of shiny metals, the spectacle of fire and ritual, the elaborate priestly costumes and the awe-inspiring grandeur of a divinely inhabited edifice. The present hack work with ordinary-looking soil and materials does not compare. Could God ever bring something amazing out of mere dirt and rocks? They need to listen to the Leader's vision and to believe that the answer is "Yes!" In fact, there is a new promise of a future glory that exceeds the old, resources that at present seem beyond their reach, and an impact that will go far wider than the families who participate in this project. God as Leader is not stuck in emotional attachment to the past but leads them forward, giving them a new vision for a new day.

The second message (Hag 2:10–19) marks a very definite change, a point that future generations will be able to look back to. As they act in obedience to God the Leader's request by laying the foundation of the temple, his promised help will be made evident. The governor, Zerubbabel, will be given God's special favor as he leads under God's directions. A leader cannot give effective leadership without the people following. Now there is teamwork, and much more will be accomplished than would have been possible by a leaderless people or a people-less leader.

Haggai is a man who deals with what works and can himself be trusted to be honest and hard-working, without blowing his own trumpet. He will not simply say what others want him to say. When he "calls a spade a spade" people take notice because they know there is no malice, no pretense, no manipulation. Rather, his underlying kindness is what provokes his honesty. And he has earned respect through his life of integrity.

Many who resemble Haggai may not even call themselves leaders but may be widely known as the kind of people who are the "salt of the earth." They may have no paper qualifications or official positions of leadership. Yet people follow them, so they are, indeed, leaders. I know many good unofficial leaders who are like Haggai, several of them being farmers and tradespeople. I have watched others wait for their views in meetings before they will vote, because they want to hear truth on the matter from someone who has their interests at heart and will not be easily fooled. Although the truth may sting, it will be heard. If such people are attuned to God as Leader, they can serve their people very effectively for a long time.

ZECHARIAH 1-8

Whereas Haggai speaks in this-worldly, straightforward, practical terms, another prophet of very different temperament, Zechariah, is also chosen to speak in the same period. Zechariah is a visionary whose priestly background has trained him to understand symbolic and other-worldly language. His writing is far from straightforward for us to understand but bears thoughtful pondering because it is very rich in meaning, not only in relation to that generation but also looking ahead to future generations. His many visions include a large number of references to the coming Messiah and reveal many of the functions of that Messiah. Yet Zechariah, like Haggai, also brings strong encouragement to the people and to their leaders, Zerubbabel and Joshua, to get on with the practical work of rebuilding the temple. Here is another example of God sending more than one messenger to communicate in different styles, and to emphasize different aspects of his message.

Something beyond outward obedience is called for, something that is more personal and more relational. God the Leader says, "Return to me" (Zech 1:3). The true connection between this Leader God and his people is through the heart. Other prophets have said so before, particularly Jeremiah. The fall of Jerusalem occurred because the people's hearts turned away; now this group of people recognize that they, too, need to re-orientate their hearts, not just their hands, back toward God. Through the retelling of eight visions received in one night, while he was awake, Zechariah brings encouragement from God to his people to keep going (Zech 1:7—5:11).

In the first night vision (Zech 1:7-17) God addresses the justifiable anger of the Jews against their unjust and harsh treatment from neighboring nations, who appear to have got away with it. He comforts his people by telling them that he, too, is angry, and that he pledges his support for Jerusalem. The aggressive powers that have scattered the Jews will be terrified and torn down by a highly unlikely new power: the power of the craftsmen who are working on the new temple (Zech 1:18-21). By following God's instructions, even in apparently mundane matters like working with tools, divine, victorious power is mysteriously released.

A man with a measuring line appears to measure the building site of Jerusalem (Zech 2:2). Contrary to the normal practice of building walls and gates first, to ensure the safety of the buildings within, God's strategy will be to establish first a home at the center for his glory, and to leave the walls and gates to a later date. He will take care of security himself and enlarge the city. This implies the need for trust in their Leader, and directly challenges their fears in the light of known animosities in the region.

However, there is still a lingering question about the worth of this city; after all, a long line of God's prophets have pointed out its faults and pronounced that its fall has been deserved. Will it be safe to rebuild, or will it once again be discarded as worthless? God understands the question and gives the assurance that it will now be regarded as clean, as free of guilt, and be given a completely new start.

God the Leader inspires through imagery. A vision of a golden lampstand aglow with seven lights (Zech 4), evocative of the former tabernacle and temple, immediately stirs longings for a rebuilt temple. Continuous light shining out to disperse the darkness of enmity, ignorance, and even their own discouragement gives hope. The oil to keep the lamps alight is supplied by olives from two trees, representing the two appointed leaders for this work, Zerubbabel and Joshua. This temple-building will be successful through a power that is not military—the power of God's Spirit. And Zerubbabel is assured of the strength to complete the task he has begun.

However, God the Leader will not ignore secret violations of his law by his own people. A massive flying scroll with writing on both sides, reminiscent of the Ten Commandments, sends out a curse on those who have broken the law but have not been held accountable (Zech 5:1–4). Sometimes a crime is hidden, and evidence cannot be found. If so, the only thing that can be done is to turn the person over to God to bring a curse if he or she is guilty (e.g., Num 5:11–22). There are two specific sins mentioned: stealing and swearing falsely in God's name (Zech 5:3). Perhaps these problems are particularly prevalent, or perhaps they represent the whole of the Ten Commandments.[1] In any case, God has means that he will use to pursue the secretly guilty, right into their private homes. God will uphold justice.

In fact, in the next vision, God shows his desire to take away all wickedness from this land, together with people who perpetuate evil (Zech 5:5–11). It will be as if a basket filled with all the wickedness of the land will be carried off, through the air, back to Babylon, the city which symbolized wickedness. God will purge the people from evil so that right living and

---

1. These relate to Commandments 3 and 8, the middle of each group of five commandments.

right relationships can be restored. Finally, God the Leader sends out spirit chariots to bring judgment on all enemies of God and his people, enabling peace to return.

God's leadership envisages and enables harmony between religion and state. There will be mutual respect between those in the roles of governance and those in the roles of priesthood, each role being given for its own purpose. And there is a mysterious hint that God the Leader will even unite both roles in a future man who is pictured as a Branch and suggestive of the Messiah (Zech 3:8; 6:12).

God the Leader has a grand purpose. His restoration plan will be good for people of all ages. He encourages the healthy, playful chatter of children, and the retirement needs of the elderly. He is concerned about safety and peace. His desire is to lead a people who will relate to each other honestly, justly and wisely (Zech 8).

Neither Haggai nor Zechariah would fit into the stereotypical images of leaders promoted today. Where Haggai speaks with too much brutal honesty for the comfortability of many, Zechariah speaks with too much obscurity. Neither is a nicely balanced, great team player, middle-of-the-road, Mr Nice Guy kind of leader. Yet God the higher Leader creates a balance for his people by calling these two very different men, at the same time, to clothe his messages with different expressions that fit their personalities, education and experiences. He uses diverse means to communicate to diverse people. While the essential meaning of both prophets is congruent, some people will resonate with one style, others will resonate better with the other. Some might initially grasp what Haggai is saying, and then later become curious enough to grapple with Zechariah's more symbolic messages.

Zechariah might be called a daydreamer by some and be accused of not having his mind sufficiently occupied with the here and now, the nuts and bolts of making a decent income.

Although Zechariah no doubt has daily work to do, his greatest gifts to his people lie in his learning and the openness of his mind and imagination to God's inner workings and visually symbolic communications. There are no signs of his mind being unbalanced or of a susceptibility to crazy ideas. His thorough soaking in his Scriptures gives him an informed understanding and healthy boundaries. He is not "taken over" by some unknown spirit but retains his own identity and ability to ask questions. Deuteronomy 13 and 18 give sensible warnings to test the veracity and character of a prophet. Zechariah the prophetic dreamer turns out to be reliable, not only in what he says for his own time, but in predictions for times after him. And God as ultimate Leader values him as a wise conveyor of truth to his people.

Under the leadership of Zerubbabel and Joshua, Haggai and Zechariah, the temple is finally completed and celebrated (Ezra 6:13–18). It is worth noting that God as Leader does not limit the leaders under him to one personality or leadership type. Zerubbabel the governor, a man of royal lineage and trained to lead, might be a popular choice. Joshua the high priest, a good man born into the right family for this role, might also be expected. But God has very important leadership roles, whether official or not, for others whose gifts or personalities might today fall outside any expected profile for a leadership role. A good leader, following this divine model, is able to assess people well and open the door for others to be able to lead in their strong areas.

EZRA 7-10

God appoints a man of impeccable priestly pedigree, a devout and learned teacher of the law, to lead another contingent of exiles back into the land of Israel with the backing of another Persian king, Artaxerxes. Ezra is to teach the law and to use the wisdom his God has given him to set up a suitable legal system to administer justice. However, as Ezra and his group pause along the way, they discover that one group that is important to the smooth functioning of the temple, the Levites, is missing. Ezra takes action to remedy this deficiency. Distribution of tasks in an orderly way is important, so some competent men of required background and competency are found and are willing to come (Ezra 8:15–20). On reaching Jerusalem, materials that have been brought for use in the temple are carefully weighed out and given to responsible people. Ezra ensures that there is full accountability.

However, he is greatly distressed to hear that the people have intermarried with women of neighboring peoples (Ezra 9), against the instructions given to their ancestors when they first settled in this land (Deut 7:1). Ezra turns his lament to God the Leader, acknowledging the wrongdoing of the people and both the kindness and righteousness of God (Ezra 9:5–15). Others are moved to repentance and propose a separation between the men involved and their foreign wives and children. It is implied that God the Leader supports this move. In our age of cross-cultural marriages and familiarity with people from many races and religions, this kind of leadership seems harsh or racist. We have seen that God is not prejudiced against people of different ethnicities, or even inter-ethnic marriages *per se*, so the driving force is not racism. However, leadership that refuses to set any boundaries for the safeguarding of its people is naive. This required separation was primarily to protect a vulnerable group physically, morally and religiously against groups known to be aggressive.

God intended that priests should teach and set boundaries between right and wrong, in order to protect the people. Although there was an official lineage of priests, all of the people were to share in these tasks (Exod 19:6) and to teach their children (Deut 6:7).

Once I was the leader of a large musical group. A man who was part of the group had some mannerisms that were a little unusual. Some prejudice arose within me, but I was assured by someone who I thought knew him well enough that he was odd but harmless. So, I accepted the assurance and we were well into our rehearsals for a major production when I was alerted by a combination of comments and behaviors that rang alarm bells in my mind, especially in regard to some of the young girls in our group. No one else noticed. During a night when I couldn't sleep, I rang the police and mentioned his name. I was told very strongly that we must not allow him to attend rehearsals or even performances, especially where children were present. He was a known pedophile who was only out of prison under the strict condition that he not go anywhere near children. The next morning the police told him he had violated this condition and was not to attend again. After this man heard that, he used many elaborate and deceptive means to try to trick me and arouse my sympathies for him, demanding that he be allowed back. However, I felt that God, the ultimate Leader not only of myself but of the group, was leading us to keep this boundary in place. For the safety of our group, and also for himself, the separation needed to stay firm.

NEHEMIAH

Some time later, a man called Nehemiah, a senior administrator in the court of the Persian king in Susa (and given the quaint title of cupbearer) is concerned about the security of Jerusalem. He hears the distressing news that the walls around Jerusalem are broken down and the gates have been burnt. He is overwhelmed by this news, and weeps, fasts and prays earnestly for some days (Neh 1). We remember that God had directed the first group of returnees not to begin with rebuilding the walls and gates, but to first set a place for God at the center. That has been done. Now God stirs in the heart of Nehemiah to turn his attention to the state of the walls and gates. He takes the risk, despite his fears, of asking the king if he might be released to rebuild. Amazingly, King Artaxerxes agrees and offers support.

Nehemiah is an experienced and trusted facilitator who is used to managing people, materials, finances and time, in order to achieve a clearly envisaged goal. When Nehemiah arrives in Jerusalem he carefully examines the condition of the walls, makes a realistic plan, calls the people to rebuild, and then faces several rounds of tough opposition. It is God who has called and enabled Nehemiah to lead this work. It is implied that it is God who gives Nehemiah discernment when enemies try to trick him into being deflected from the work, when repeated messages are sent requesting fruitless meetings, or when a man deceitfully lays a trap for him (Neh 6). Because his life is lived in the fear of the Lord, and because he does not give in to common leadership temptations, like receiving special privileges, and because he hears the legitimate cries of the poor and takes action to help them, God is able to protect him from gullibility, and the work is completed, with good community participation, in good time.

In this situation, where the people feel that they, their city, and their God are ridiculed and disgraced, God leads the people to see success in the building of the physical walls as their priority. When that is finished, Ezra the priest and scribe is called to lead the people to listen to readings from Moses, to celebrate a religious festival (the Feast of Tabernacles) and then to consider and confess their sins. Nehemiah is moved to reorder the community according to God's laws (Neh 13).

It is delight to see the type of leadership that good facilitators can give. We can learn much from Nehemiah's personal frugality and integrity, his detailed assessment of the situation and strategic planning for rebuilding, his mobilization of family groups to participate in the project, his discernment and rejections of baseless attacks and distractions, and his ability to estimate and keep good time. Within this narrative we are also reminded that God the greater Leader is the orchestrater of this whole project and the one who is the instigator of Nehemiah's involvement. Nehemiah's compassion, motivation and successful leadership, in all its aspects, are God-given and reflect characteristics of the God he serves. When his mission is completed, he is content to step away and return to his previous work. He does not hold on to power beyond the time or limits of his mandate. That requires humility and obedience to the Leader who is over all.

ZECHARIAH 9-14: VISIONS FOR THE FUTURE

God the Leader encourages the returning exiles not only to rebuild the physical temple and the walls of Jerusalem but to imagine the future under his direction. God tells his prophet Zechariah to assure the people that God will defend them, and that surrounding nations which appear strong right now will be pulled down (Zech 9:1-8).

At a time when the kingship in Israel has long ceased, the people are given an image of a king coming to them (Zech 9:9-10). There is something unusual about this king: his gentle humility, shown in his riding a mere donkey instead of a war horse. In fact, the war horses and other military symbols will be broken down. He will bring salvation and peace, obviously without shedding blood.

There are other mysterious visions, concerning a worthy shepherd and a worthless shepherd (Zech 11) and God giving his people a spirit of grace and supplication, so that they grieve bitterly for one whom they have pierced (Zech 12:10-14). Then there is an image of God's shepherd being struck and the sheep being scattered (Zech 13:7-9).

The book finishes with a vision of God's triumphant conquest over Jerusalem's enemies (Zech 14) and many people from other nations going to Jerusalem to worship God the Leader, God the King. And even the most ordinary objects, like the bells on the horses and the cooking pots in the temple will be made special—holy to God the Leader!

Even if the people of Zechariah's day could not comprehend the meaning of these visions, the main implications are clear. God thinks ahead, God has a plan, God is confident in achieving that plan, God's plan will be very good for those who follow his leadership. People always do better in fulfilling immediate goals if they can catch a vision of a good future plan, into which the immediate goals fit.

QUESTIONS FOR REFLECTION OR DISCUSSION

1. What have you noticed about God the Leader in this rebuilding phase?
2. People take notice of Haggai because he "calls a spade a spade" and there is no malice, no pretense, no manipulation. Have you known people like this?
3. What can we learn about the dangers of stereotyping people?
4. What is valuable in Zechariah's message from God?
5. Why did the prophets often use poetic imagery in their messages?
6. "People always do better in fulfilling immediate goals if they can catch a vision of a good future plan." Do all leaders have to be visionary?

Chapter 25

Expansion: God's Mission Beyond Israel

God's leadership goals have always been expansionist, well beyond Israel. In fact, his goals have always had the people of the whole earth in sight. We have all known examples of rapacious expansionism that benefits no one except the greedy empire-builders. We know the travesty of war and the injustice of crushing peoples into cruel subjection. We also know the more subtle, manipulative forms of expanding influence that don't mind treading on or dispensing with others and are at home with distortions of the truth. God's expansionism bears none of these marks.

What is the basis for God's expansionist goals? First, he is the creator of every person on the face of the earth so he cannot contain his interest to one small people group. Second, the gods worshipped by others are impotent,[1] and people who follow them are deceived.[2] Third, God wants good, in fact the best, for all peoples, and knows that, if they follow his leadership, they can experience it. There is no hint anywhere that God's expansionism is motivated by his own self-interest.

In assessing our own expansionist leadership goals, we need to determine our motivation and the consequences for all people affected. Even if we are born to be an heir or heiress of an empire, our rights are limited.

---

1. See 1 Kings 18:16–45 for the competition set up between God and the foreign Baals worshipped by the majority of prophets in that day. Even though the Baal-worshippers put on an impressive religious display, their god proved to be incapable of exercising any power. In contrast, God answered Elijah's straightforward, simple prayer with a dramatic show of power.

2. See Isaiah 44:9–20 for one passage where the deception of idolatry is exposed.

Most of us are not born with any inherent leadership rights, and none of us has a personal claim over multiple nations, let alone the whole earth. We may legitimately observe that people under certain other leaders are deceived, oppressed, abused, neglected or mistreated, and we may consider whether we might be able to help. We can rightly be motivated to bring good, and to lead at a personal or a corporate level to improve people's quality of life. But we must be very aware of the limits we must impose on our personal self-serving ambitions.

God's expansionism is legitimate and has no limits over the world he has created. Our expansionism is limited. There are legitimate boundaries to our areas of leadership, whether in politics, our workplace, family, or church. Even if God calls us to a particular task or to speak particular messages, we are still limited. Sometimes our leadership does need to be extended beyond its present boundaries for the greater good of other people. But let us beware of grandiosity that deceives us into thinking that we do not have the in-built limitations of frail humans, and that confuses the needs of others with our own selfish goals.

God's expansionist ideas, plans and activities are his mission. Some have mistakenly imagined that the idea of God having a mission beyond one people group is only found in the New Testament, but it is rooted in the Old Testament. Walter Kaiser has written a helpful introduction to this topic.[3] At the beginning of the Old Testament story God calls one man, Abram (later called Abraham), to go to the land God would show him. In doing so, God promises to make him into a great nation and that all peoples on earth would be blessed through him (Gen 12:1–3). God's call to this man is not simply for individual or even family or national benefit. God is already thinking far beyond what a 75-year-old childless man can envisage.

We know that word about God the Leader does reach beyond Israel, often through people telling others what they have seen of God's miraculous works. Moses and Aaron are sent by God to speak to the Egyptian Pharaoh, not only to ask for the liberation of the Israelites, but also to demonstrate God's power and superiority over the Egyptian gods through the Ten Plagues. As the Israelites flee, and as the Pharaoh and his forces pursue the Israelites (Exod 14), God says to Moses, "The Egyptians will know that I am the Lord." In fact, some of the Egyptians try to persuade Pharaoh not to continue, as they recognize that God is fighting for the Israelites. Perhaps it is not surprising that some even choose to join the Israelites (Exod 12:38).

Jethro, the Midianite father-in-law of Moses, has no doubt heard much about Israel's God from Moses. When he visits his son-in-law in the

---

3. Kaiser, *Mission in the Old Testament*.

desert after the famous parting of the sea, he listens attentively as Moses recounts everything that God has done and is genuinely delighted. He praises God, makes sacrificial offerings to God and eats a celebratory meal with the elders "in the presence of God." Using the symbolism of the day, Jethro has chosen to join himself to the God of Israel. In the course of time, other outsiders are told about God by ordinary Israelites just speaking what they know. For example, an unnamed person speaks to Rahab the Canaanite prostitute, and Naomi speaks to Ruth, the Moabitess; both find their faith in the God of Israel.

At another time, a young Israelite girl is captured by raiding Syrians and serves in the home of the commander Naaman. As we read the story in the context of many other references to God's mission, we wonder if God the Leader has, in fact, sent this girl without her conscious awareness of it (2 Kings 5). Although she is a slave, removed from her family, she surprisingly shows no bitterness towards her captor. Instead, when he has a skin disease she shows spontaneous compassion, and says to her mistress, "If only my master would see the prophet who is in Samaria! He would cure him of his leprosy" (v. 4). Eventually this great man does find the healing that the slave girl has spoken of, and, in the process, is humbled and declares, "Now I know that there is no God in all the world except in Israel."

In addition to these and other examples, we find many encouragements for God's people in Israel to look beyond their borders. Psalm 67 begins with the people praying a blessing for themselves, for their own people. Yet they are inexplicably moved, most likely by the quiet inner promptings of God their Leader, to pray for all the nations. By verse 5 they take up the cry themselves, and enthusiastically pray again these words, "May the peoples praise you, O God; may all the peoples praise you" (repeated from verse 3). By the conclusion of the psalm their perspective has changed. Yes, God will bless them (their original prayer), but they now realize that God's desire is to do more, so they add, "and all the ends of the earth will fear him." They know that fearing God brings benefits from God.

In many other places the exhortation to tell of God's works or God's glory is given more directly (e.g., Ps 96:3; 105:1) and some people respond by declaring that this is what they will do (e.g., Ps 57:9). Assuming that some will be sent to tell people of other nations about God, other psalms even call on these outsiders to praise God (e.g., Ps 117:1).

The four Servant Songs in Isaiah (Isa 42:1–7; 49:1–6; 50:4–9; 52:13—53:12) speak about a role for an unnamed but specially called and sent person whose impact is to extend beyond Israel, bringing light to the Gentiles.[4]

---

4. The Servant of the Lord often refers to the people of Israel in Isa 40–55. However,

Isaiah 66:18–21 speaks of God sending some people to the nations to speak to them, then God selecting some of these other people to be priests and Levites. Many prophets envisage a time of drawing numbers of people from other nations to Jerusalem to seek God.

God's leadership goals are certainly expansionist and missional through the Old Testament. However, it is important to note that God never expands his leadership through militant means. The only warfare permitted in the Old Testament was restricted to the purpose of giving his people a homeland, a place to settle. That was bounded by very strict limits of location and of which tribes could be fought. There were also more stringent rules than those of neighboring nations about how wars could be conducted. Offers of peace were to be given before a battle could be joined, and deaths were to be limited. God never condones warfare or violence for the purpose of bringing people to follow his leadership. God's methods are invitational, not coercive. God's messengers put themselves at risk in order to alleviate risk to others.

This leads us to consider human desires for expansionist leadership, and, even if the aim is to help other people, to ask *how* such expansion is to be conducted. Will it be done in the most conciliatory way possible? Will the new structures and systems work to support people or to crush people?

I was horrified to learn that some of my very remote ancestors centuries ago murdered Jews in Germany and Spain and no doubt in many other places. When I was a child one of my close friends was a Jewish girl. In fact, she is still one of my close friends, and is a delightful person. She learnt from her parents about the waves of mass murder of Jews in Europe, long before Hitler's atrocities. Some very misguided so-called Christian leaders attempted to convert Jews by force. If the Jews didn't convert, they were killed. When we were children my friend asserted that my ancestors killed her ancestors. It was certainly true that some of her ancestors had been unjustly murdered by European royalty and their henchmen. I protested that I had no such ancestry and that I was not related to Hitler. However, I discovered, many decades later, that her childish assertion was more accurate than either of us realized. When I discovered that her words were in fact true, I felt great pain. Of course, she is now wise enough to distinguish between that disgraceful behavior and true Christian behavior, but many others are not. I have other remote ancestors who led the Crusades, but while their goals *may* have had some good elements, their method does not fit with any

---

in these four passages the Servant becomes more individual, a person certainly representative of the people Israel in some senses, yet moving beyond Israel in other senses, e.g., the famous verses in Isa 53. I, with many others, take these to be Messianic, fitting the descriptions of Jesus' ministry as described in the New Testament.

method of expanding God's kingdom that we see in the Old Testament or the New Testament. They may have claimed to act in God's name, but they did not act in accordance with God's character.

We will look now at the very familiar story of Jonah, focusing not on the nature of the big fish, but on God's sending of this man to speak of him beyond Israel, even in what appeared to be hostile territory.

JONAH

Probably the Jonah, son of Amittai, who is mentioned in 2 Kings 14:25, is the character in this story. If so, he lives in the time of King Jeroboam II of the Northern Kingdom. God the Leader calls this prophet Jonah to go to a totally unexpected place: Nineveh, the capital of Assyria, the territory of the arch-enemy. Nineveh was probably the largest city in the known world at that time and was notorious for its wickedness. God is not naive; he knows the character of the place and the people and asks his prophet to preach against it. This would require unusual courage and faith. Prophets are known for being stretched beyond their comfort zones, but this assignment is too daunting for Jonah, so he finds a ship that is sailing in the opposite direction and gets on board.

However, God does not give up that easily on his mission or on his prophet. First, he sends a violent storm that threatens the safety of those on board the ship. Ironically, it is the pagan captain and sailors who call out to their gods, while Jonah needs to be prodded to call out to his God. Lots are cast, seeking divine guidance, to find out who on board is responsible for this unusual storm, and the lot falls on Jonah. Jonah acknowledges that he is running away from God and is therefore the cause of this storm. After the sailors very reluctantly do as Jonah asks and throw him overboard, an immediate calm causes the sailors to fear God and make vows and sacrifices to him. Despite Jonah's running away, God is still leading. Through this life-threatening crisis, outsiders to Israel discover God and revere him.

Jonah is rescued by the famous big fish and stays there three days.[5] He prays.[6] While his life is under threat he inwardly turns back to God, cries out for help, acknowledges that salvation is from God, and, like the sailors, now makes his own vow to God. He finds himself on solid ground

---

5. The expression "three days" is taken to cover parts of three days, not three periods of 24 hours each. This is according to Hebrew idiomatic usage, as when referring to Jesus' three days in the tomb (Friday afternoon to Sunday morning).

6. Even if this prayer is considered to be inserted later, it represents Jonah's inward journey while in his utterly desperate condition.

with a second chance to obey his original commission. This time he heads towards Nineveh, and, when he gets there, he preaches his message. Instead of mocking him, as he might have expected with good reason, these people, including the king, listen attentively. The result is astounding! There is a genuine humility and there is a widespread turning away from violence and evil. God sees this, has compassion on these very people who had previously been the chief perpetrators of evil in the area, and does not bring on them the destruction that was threatened. God has achieved his purpose: to give opportunity for the violence to be averted.

Jonah, however, finds it difficult to accept that such long-standing enemies can find a place in God's mercy. Would it not have been better to send calamity on them? And would he not be better dead than to be seen providing a way for despised enemies to escape disaster? Being a prophet to his own people is acceptable but being a prophet to unworthy outsiders is not. However, since God is the true Leader, he has the right to challenge Jonah about his attitude. And he does.

Jonah is curious enough to sit outside the city of Nineveh to watch what will happen. So he makes a comfortable place under the shade of a vine, and is glad about the shade. But God is the giver of the vine and decides to take it away through a worm that eats through it. Now Jonah suffers the raw, blazing heat and once again thinks he would be better dead. Again, God challenges him about his attitude. We are left wondering whether Jonah will cooperate with God in the next phase of his life. Perhaps we are also left wondering how we might have reacted if placed in a similar position.

The hero of this story is not Jonah but God, who is the Leader from beginning to end. Jonah still finds it difficult to think beyond his own comfort—whether it is preferable to stay with his own people, or to stay out of controversy, or to require ideal working conditions. God *is* concerned for people in places like Nineveh, even if they are acting badly. And he will also provide for the needs of any messenger he sends.

I was once involved with a traditional church where, over a period of three weeks, one couple and two singles independently and very unexpectedly contacted me from outside the church. All were involved in some activity that they sensed was seriously wrong and wanted to change. In separate conversations, I discovered that all were quite troubled by their sense of wrongdoing. I was surprised that these non-religious people seemed far more willing to hear the truth about their behavior than many of the people inside that church. These four wanted to turn their lives around, and they did turn to Jesus Christ for saving power to do that. They wanted to meet with Christians and learn more.

However, when I told the church leaders about these outsiders wanting to become Christians, they were horrified. How could such people, considering some of the things they had done, come into *their* church? Did these outsiders think they could be accepted as Christians when they had not been brought to the church as babies, had not grown up in the Sunday School, and had not served on the various committees? Did I dare to think that these outsiders would ever be equal to *them*? Sadly, many in this church had, without realizing it, quietly moved away from biblical teachings and examples. Perhaps the story of Jonah had been ridiculed, without paying attention to its real message. Perhaps they didn't realize that they had become like Jonah—not by actively running away and inviting a storm, but by digging their heels in and not going anywhere or doing anything that could possibly open the door to anyone who was just a little different, or from a different social class, or who could, in any way, make them feel a little less than comfortable.

We see many other hints that God the Leader is interested in and involved with the people of other nations. He acts justly with all peoples (e.g., Jer 18:7–10). Many Israelites will be sent to other nations to tell of their God (Isa 66:19–21), and God's Spirit will be poured out on all people (Joel 2:28). God the Leader has a vision that includes people of every ethnic group. But we can understand his heart, his wisdom, his multi-faceted ways of leadership through his relationship with his people, Israel.

QUESTIONS FOR REFLECTION OR DISCUSSION

1. Is it surprising that God, as Leader of the Israelites, has also expressed a desire to reach people of other nations throughout the Old Testament?
2. What methods does God use to reach people beyond Israel? What methods are not condoned?
3. What criteria should govern our expansionist goals?
4. What can be learnt from the story of Jonah?
5. How would you formulate God's "vision statement" or "mission statement"?
6. What has been most helpful in the reading of this book?

Chapter 26

God the Leader

Is it possible to create a simple list of attributes of God as Leader? Perhaps, but only with limited success. For God's leadership has a flexibility about it that adjusts to each new situation and the needs of his human group in each context. That very flexibility is, in fact, a hallmark of his leadership.

We might be drawn to his mighty power, but then we also need to consider his tenderness. He is said to roar like a lion, yet he stills a troubled soul with an inaudible movement. He communicates with clarity and candor to those who are in relationship with him. Yet he withholds his answer for a time from others who outwardly seem desperate to make contact. He is a master planner, yet he allows a degree of chaos before intervening.

We, too, need flexibility in our leadership. We need discernment as to whether to speak strongly or softly, whether to push forward or pull back. One of the hallmarks of God's flexibility is his wisdom. In the West, wisdom is currently undervalued. Those who have accumulated rich wisdom through experience tend to be ignored or cast aside, in favor of the young who are rich in energy but not necessarily in wisdom. We can learn wisdom, not only through making observations in life, but particularly by watching the workings of God's wisdom more closely.

Sometimes God's position as the Leader is obvious. The clearest example is when he goes before the Israelites through the wilderness as a pillar of cloud by day, and a pillar of fire by night. The people here are in crisis, and a crisis requires clear, unequivocal leadership to take the people to safety and to prevent them from returning to danger. Sometimes his position is hidden, behind the scenes. Yet there are enough clues, for those who know his ways, to see his leadership, and to follow it, even then.

In times of crisis, giving clear commands is the kindest leadership for the safety or success of the people. But when time can be used more leisurely, commands should give way to discussion, and ordering should give way to listening. Teaching can be given and chewed over. The immature can fall and be picked up and allowed to make mistakes again. Others will never develop without sufficient opportunity to spread their wings a bit. A leader may give people training and then watch them attentively, ready to carry them, as God carried Israel, when they need it. Sometimes a leader may need to be almost invisible for a season, trusting that the people are equipped to do what he or she has led them to do.

Some leaders always want to be shouting from the front. Others seem reluctant to give a clear lead. Yet we need to recognize when we need to lead from the front, and when we need to encourage from behind, and be willing to do both. Sometimes, whether as parents or teachers or trainers of less experienced members of staff, we need to walk away for a time. Having done the teaching, we need to allow the young to think for themselves, to make their choices, to work out the applications of our teaching, and to take some risks.

There are many demonstrations of God's passionate love. Yet that love desires to protect his people, not from the kinds of risks and challenges that can build character, but from outright harm. So boundaries are set for behavior within Israelite society, and boundaries are set against harmful behavior from outside enemies. Boundaries require active discrimination between good and evil, between what is helpful and what is harmful. Where a threat is assessed to be destructive, God's love is expressed in cutting off the threat.

Good parenting is under threat. Boundaries in families and in societies are under threat. While many aspects of modern life are different from Old Testament days, the principles laid down by God the Leader are timeless. Screens of all sorts—computers, phones, TVs, video games—can stir up hidden dangers, whether they be violence or callous indifference, pornography or escapism. The detrimental effects may not be immediately obvious. Our very individualistic societies can cause isolation, without the safeguards and benefits of responsible community living. We need to look again at God the Leader's boundaries and the good purposes that lie behind them.

For all the flexibility in the expressions of God's leadership, his character remains the same. In fact, it is important to be able to rely on the character of a leader. What changes is God's *style* of leadership, in order to lead in the best way in different contexts. This reflects his concern for people. God is not a robot or a bureaucrat. Our leadership should never be merely mechanical.

We will benefit much in our own leadership if we continue to get to know God as Leader. Better than knowing a mere set of characteristics, as helpful as that may be, is to continue the journey with this Leader—to continue reading and reflecting, to continue conversation with him, to continue observing his ways in our lives.

Bibliography

Balentine, Samuel E. *The Hidden God: The Hiding of the Face of God in the Old Testament.* Oxford: Oxford University Press, 1983.
Banks, Robert. *God the Worker: Journeys into The Mind, Heart, and Imagination of God.* Eugene, OR: Wipf & Stock, 2008.
Barclay, Oliver R., ed. *Pacifism and War.* Leicester: InterVarsity, 1984.
Berkhof, Louis. *Systematic Theology.* Grand Rapids: Eerdmans, 1953.
Block, Daniel. "Leader, Leadership, OT." In *The New Interpreter's Dictionary of the Bible: I–Ma*, edited by Katharine Doob Sakenfeld, 3:620–26. Nashville: Abingdon, 2008.
Duguid, Iain M. *The Song of Songs.* Tyndale Old Testament Commentaries 19. Downers Grove: IVP Academic, 2015.
Heschel, Abraham. *The Prophets.* New York: Harper & Row, 1962.
Kaiser, Walter C. *Mission in the Old Testament: Israel as a Light to the Nations.* Grand Rapids: Baker, 2000.
Keller, Phillip. *A Shepherd Looks at Psalm 23.* London: Pickering & Inglis, 1970.
Laniak, Timothy. *Shepherds after My Own Heart: Pastoral Traditions and Leadership in the Bible.* Downers Grove: Apollos, 2006.
Pitkänen, Pekka. "Ethnicity, Assimilation and the Israelite Settlement." *Tyndale Bulletin* 55 (2004) 161–82.
Robinson, James W. *Captain Robinson: the Reminiscences of a Tasmanian Master Mariner.* Edited by Michael Nash. Sandy Bay, Tasmania: Blubber Head, 2009.
Rochester, Kathleen M. "Grief in Exile and the City of God: Reading Ezekiel with Augustine." *Stellenbosch Theological Journal* 5 (2019) 347–60.
———. *Israel's Lament and the Discernment of Divine Revelation.* Saarbrücken: Lambert Academic, 2012.
Sohn, Seock-Tae. *YHWH, the Husband of Israel: The Metaphor of Marriage between YHWH and Israel.* Eugene, OR: Wipf & Stock, 2002.
Stevens, Marty E. *Leadership Roles of the Old Testament: King, Prophet, Priest, Sage.* Eugene, OR: Cascade, 2012.

www.ingramcontent.com/pod-product-compliance
Lightning Source LLC
Chambersburg PA
CBHW062020220426
43662CB00010B/1412